1,000,000 Books

are available to read at

Forgotten Books

www.ForgottenBooks.com

Read online
Download PDF
Purchase in print

ISBN 978-1-334-02945-5
PIBN 10553352

This book is a reproduction of an important historical work. Forgotten Books uses state-of-the-art technology to digitally reconstruct the work, preserving the original format whilst repairing imperfections present in the aged copy. In rare cases, an imperfection in the original, such as a blemish or missing page, may be replicated in our edition. We do, however, repair the vast majority of imperfections successfully; any imperfections that remain are intentionally left to preserve the state of such historical works.

Forgotten Books is a registered trademark of FB &c Ltd.
Copyright © 2018 FB &c Ltd.
FB &c Ltd, Dalton House, 60 Windsor Avenue, London, SW19 2RR.
Company number 08720141. Registered in England and Wales.

For support please visit www.forgottenbooks.com

1 MONTH OF FREE READING

at

www.ForgottenBooks.com

By purchasing this book you are eligible for one month membership to ForgottenBooks.com, giving you unlimited access to our entire collection of over 1,000,000 titles via our web site and mobile apps.

To claim your free month visit:

www.forgottenbooks.com/free553352

* Offer is valid for 45 days from date of purchase. Terms and conditions apply.

English
Français
Deutsche
Italiano
Español
Português

www.forgottenbooks.com

Mythology Photography **Fiction** Fishing Christianity **Art** Cooking Essays Buddhism Freemasonry Medicine **Biology** Music **Ancient Egypt** Evolution Carpentry Physics Dance Geology **Mathematics** Fitness Shakespeare **Folklore** Yoga Marketing **Confidence** Immortality Biographies Poetry **Psychology** Witchcraft Electronics Chemistry History **Law** Accounting **Philosophy** Anthropology Alchemy Drama Quantum Mechanics Atheism Sexual Health **Ancient History** **Entrepreneurship** Languages Sport Paleontology Needlework Islam **Metaphysics** Investment Archaeology Parenting Statistics Criminology **Motivational**

REV. JAMES BRUTON GAMBRELL, D. D.

PUBLISHED
BY
THE BAPTIST STANDARD
May, 1909
DALLAS, TEXAS

[*All rights reserved*]

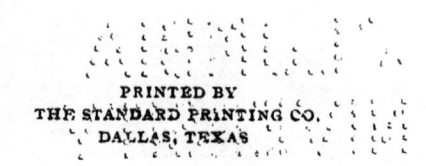

PRINTED BY
THE STANDARD PRINTING CO.
DALLAS, TEXAS

CONTENTS

Concerning a Long-Drawn-Out Campaign for Progress 9
Up Fool Hill 29
The Te-Hee Girl 34
Who Owns the Wool 41
The Working Value of Free Government in Religion 45
The Army in the Ditch 52
Country Mothers 58
Concerning Mules 61
Concerning Criticism and Limitations 66
Further Concerning Criticism 72
Plain Lessons From a Loving Writer 78
Concerning Church Government 83
Decisive Battles in Human Life 93
Grasshoppers and Giants 98
Saints and Angels 104
Bill Morgan's Economy 109
Purposeless Preachers 116
The Pains of Progress. The Unrest of Faith 121
The Last Struggle! 125
Questions in Baptist Rights 128
Concerning Being Nearly Right 131
Concerning Doing Exactly Right 135
The Greatest Question 139
Which Way, This or That? 145
The Law of the Harvest 149
Evangelizing the Far West 154
Church Sovereignty and Denominational Comity 159
"Squire Sinkhorn's" Mistake 161
Principles Underlying Co-operation Among Baptists 167
Stackpole Unification 173
The Battle Ground for Missions 178
Great Meeting, and Some Remarks 181

CONTENTS—Continued

Blessed Be Books for They Are a Blessing ... 185
Lopsidedness in Missions ... 189
Two Large Examples, With Lessons ... 193
The Passing of the Bully ... 197
A Letter to Young Preachers ... 201
Beautiful Fighting ... 204
Dreading the Process ... 208
A Fine Example of Organized Efficiency ... 211
The Problem of Denominational Progress ... 214
Lizard Killing ... 218
Two Chapters on Money and Methods ... 223
Conservatism and Corns ... 227
A Case of Apostolic Succession, With Notes ... 231
The Evil of the Fighting Spirit ... 235
Paul, The Tent Maker ... 241
Two Points of View—Self and Sacrifice ... 245
Trumpeting Hardshellism ... 252
The Workings of Hardshellism ... 257
A Plea for Simplicity ... 261
Concerning College Degrees ... 265
Nationalization of the Southern Spirit ... 268
The Work of Preachers ... 273
Concerning Religious Notions ... 277
The Case of the Missionaries ... 281
"Poor, Yet Making Many Rich" ... 285
The Safety of the Baptist Methods of Work ... 292
The Form and the Power ... 297
A Sling and a King ... 301
The Nature and Uses of Conventions ... 307

THE BAPTIST STANDARD'S NEW VENTURE

BY

DR. B. H. CARROLL

All hail to the Baptist Standard:
"Long may it wave
O'er the land of the free and the home of the brave!"

Like an eagle it minds to soar to greater heights that it may see wider horizons. It has already a wide field of usefulness and feels a mission to regions beyond.

Religious journalism, on right lines, deserves higher honors than it has ever received and may through the wisdom of its policy, the variety and spice of its contents, and the power of its spirit, yet startle the world with achievements.

The Standard's new honor is the promise of a book embodying the articles of Dr. J. B. Gambrell, culled from its columns. It will be a unique and most readable book.

Dr. Gambrell's fame rests largely on three excellencies: (1) His charm and power as a platform speaker. Any audience will hear this great "Commoner" when he rises to speak. (2) His administrative leadership in getting churches, associations and conventions to do right things. (3) His ready pen in timely articles. The character of the man backs up these excellencies.

Now the proposed book, as I understand it, will group the articles which in their day, each fitted to its exigency, reached and influenced the hearts of thousands. "Uncle Gideon" is as famous in his line as "Uncle Remus" on another line. Such books constitute a charming, racy, helpful literature. The French never excelled as historians, but they lead the world in memoirs. These memoirs give more

CONTENTS—Continued

Blessed Be Books for They Are a Blessing ... 185
Lopsidedness in Missions ... 189
Two Large Examples, With Lessons ... 193
The Passing of the Bully ... 197
A Letter to Young Preachers ... 201
Beautiful Fighting ... 204
Dreading the Process ... 208
A Fine Example of Organized Efficiency ... 211
The Problem of Denominational Progress ... 214
Lizard Killing ... 218
Two Chapters on Money and Methods ... 223
Conservatism and Corns ... 227
A Case of Apostolic Succession, With Notes ... 231
The Evil of the Fighting Spirit ... 235
Paul, The Tent Maker ... 241
Two Points of View—Self and Sacrifice ... 245
Trumpeting Hardshellism ... 252
The Workings of Hardshellism ... 257
A Plea for Simplicity ... 261
Concerning College Degrees ... 265
Nationalization of the Southern Spirit ... 268
The Work of Preachers ... 273
Concerning Religious Notions ... 277
The Case of the Missionaries ... 281
"Poor, Yet Making Many Rich" ... 285
The Safety of the Baptist Methods of Work ... 292
The Form and the Power ... 297
A Sling and a King ... 301
The Nature and Uses of Conventions ... 307

THE BAPTIST STANDARD'S NEW VENTURE

BY

DR. B. H. CARROLL

All hail to the Baptist Standard:
"Long may it wave
O'er the land of the free and the home of the brave!"

Like an eagle it minds to soar to greater heights that it may see wider horizons. It has already a wide field of usefulness and feels a mission to regions beyond.

Religious journalism, on right lines, deserves higher honors than it has ever received and may through the wisdom of its policy, the variety and spice of its contents, and the power of its spirit, yet startle the world with achievements.

The Standard's new honor is the promise of a book embodying the articles of Dr. J. B. Gambrell, culled from its columns. It will be a unique and most readable book.

Dr. Gambrell's fame rests largely on three excellencies: (1) His charm and power as a platform speaker. Any audience will hear this great "Commoner" when he rises to speak. (2) His administrative leadership in getting churches, associations and conventions to do right things. (3) His ready pen in timely articles. The character of the man backs up these excellencies.

Now the proposed book, as I understand it, will group the articles which in their day, each fitted to its exigency, reached and influenced the hearts of thousands. "Uncle Gideon" is as famous in his line as "Uncle Remus" on another line. Such books constitute a charming, racy, helpful literature. The French never excelled as historians, but they lead the world in memoirs. These memoirs give more life-like pictures of the times, its customs, spirit and genius than any history could do. We learn of a reign, a generation, by a single character.

God has not given all to the one, but each gifted one is peerless in some good. The Lord be praised for the diversity of gifts and let all rejoice in each one's excellence. Dr. Gambrell's inimitable way of putting things—his easy, lucid, off-hand style, his quaint humor and power of apt illustration in homely things the people can understand, and withal his lofty purpose to do and say right things will make his book widely popular. For one I have long wanted to see his current greatness crystalize that posterity may know somewhat of the great good man whom his contemporaries delighted to honor, and so warmly appreciated.

He has a standing offer from me for another book. A series of lectures to preachers on pastoral theologies and duties. Our Seminary stands ready to pay him for the lectures

As I commenced with "all hail to The Standard" I close with, "Let The Standard circulate and circulate and keep on circulating."

B. H. CARROLL,

July 9, at Louisiana B. Y. P. U., at Mandeville, on Lake Ponchartrain.

Concerning a Long Drawn out Campaign for Progress

THIS article is written as a preliminary dissertation on a long drawn-out struggle in Texas for Baptist progress. The articles, which succeed this, in "Ten Years in Texas" may be read in the light of the statements found in this dissertation. They were written, from time to time, to meet the situation, as it appeared, and to fill a place in a general scheme of education designed to lead Texas Baptists to higher ground. Not one of the articles was written with any thought of its ever appearing in a book, and no attempt was made to give to any article literary finish. In fact, they were designed to trim the situation into shape. It is the roughness of the file, that gives it its value in the particular kind of work for which it is designed.

In this article, there will be no attempt to follow any chronological order of events, but only to touch the main features of a great situation, out of which is evolving a magnificent missionary force. If the succeeding articles have value, they take their value largely from the fact that they touch practical questions in denominational life. No particular order will be found in the discussions of principles and policies. Any soldier, who ever tried it, knows there is a large difference between an orderly review of a great army, and the movements of that army when it is really in a fight.

My first real touch with Texas Baptist life, was in the Houston Convention in 1896. I was there as a visitor from Georgia. The Houston Convention was, in all respects, a

BY J. B. GAMBRELL, D. D.

lively affair, though one would not wish to say much more about it. This writer had seen war before, real war—four years in the Confederate army—and then he had seen denominational wars and been in them some, but a near view of the Houston Convention gave a new and lively impression of what could really be done in a fight for order. I recall that a brother asked me toward the conclusion of the Convention, whether I would not like to come to Texas, and, with sincerity, I said, "No, I want to go to Heaven, and I don't see any good road through Texas." That was the way it really looked to me.

But the issues raised before the Houston Convention, and, which had been settled two or three times before, seemed to be finally settled in that Convention, when, after a long and painful struggle, the two parties voted on the report covering the ground of contention, and voted with absolute unanimity. That gave the idea that a little tenderness might heal old wounds, and that the Baptists of Texas might really be brought together, if only tact were used.

Being elected Superintendent of Missions by the Board not long after that Convention and earnestly solicited by leaders on both sides of the differences to accept the work, I finally did accept, and did it with the idea that there would not be much trouble in ending all contentions, and launching out for a great campaign of progress. Some of the brethren did not think so, and it took the writer some months to learn as much as some of the other brethren knew when he came. We were really in for a great struggle to be carried on by stages, which, in its outcome, was to fuse and unify Texas Baptists. We were to come to higher ground and come through tribulation. The very situation called for it.

Texas is large on the map and large every way. Here people are gathered from the four quarters of the earth, representing all kind of notions, principles and prejudices. There had been from the early days in Texas a militant spirit among Baptists. The fact is, the Baptists are a militant people. They were so in the beginning, when John the Baptist laid the ax to the roots of the trees and shook all the regions around Jordan; and, when we cease to be, we will not be very much account. From time to time, in the past, efforts had been made to unify Texas Baptists, and finally the several general bodies in the state merged into one and the two leading papers in the state merged also.

Many brethren felt then that there was real unification, but it must be rememebered that there is a difference between contact and unity. Apples, in a barrel, are in contact and are together, in a sense, but they are not united. Jonah and the whale were together, Jonah inside, but Jonah and the whale were not united, and they did not stay together when a commotion came. We will have learned a great lesson in our churches, associations and other working bodies, when we clearly see the difference between contact and unity. Paul's idea of a church was one standing fast "in one spirit, with one mind, striving together for the faith of the gospel." That is the true ideal for a general body. When the unification movement came in Texas, and all the general bodies merged, all the people were not merged in spirit or mind, and there were among those, committed to the unification movement, diverse sentiments and feelings. It had to be so when there had been no unification of the highest and best sort, and unification can never be accomplished by simply writing things on paper. The spirit will always be greater than the letter.

Let it be remembered that people are in Texas from everywhere. This writer was in a frontier village, in a rough, frontier hotel in Texas where there were eleven people. He took a census of the company. Two were born in South Carolina, two in New York state, one in London, one in Canada, the others one to a state in America. The twelfth man was a servant and a Mexican. That is a picture of the make-up of the population in Texas. And as people came from everywhere, they brought with them such ideas as they had. Baptists from Georgia had Georgia ideas. Those from Kentucky had the Kentucky spirit and ideas. Those from Kansas had Kansas notions. In getting people together, it is not so bad if they are bent, as to ways and methods, provided they are all bent the same way. There is not much difficulty in stacking up spoons, made in the same mold, though they are not straight. It is altogether a different matter, however, to undertake to stack up wheel barrows, because they were not made to fit.

Then the situation was further endangered by sectional feelings. Texas is large, and the people live far apart. Distance is much in the thinking of the average human being. The different sections developed their leaders, and these leaders did not always agree. Moreover, the situation had been greatly aggrevated by numerous papers, those instruments of wrath or blessing, according as they are used. All along, papers had developed feuds; and, when the papers were merged into one, the feuds were not all dead, though they slumbered for a season. Then, a little later, after a state-wide attempt at unification, another paper was started, made necessary by the unwise conduct of the first paper. With such a broad, unformed situation and two papers, with contrary alignments, there was abundant opportunity for what happened, a great, newspaper war, brought on by "newspaper competition." The Baptists have not been happy in their management of newspapers. If the Philistines had known how to run newspapers, Samson could not have played them a worse trick than to have started them in the newspaper business in opposition to each other. Then he would not have needed foxes and fire brands at all. A newspaper can be, and a good one is, the greatest instrument of good wielded by any man. It has more eyes to see, more hands to work, more feet to go, more tongues to talk than anything else known to civilization. But, if in the hands of an unwise man, it may, and likely will sow discord and strife wider and more disastrously than anything else in the world.

And there were other conditions in Texas, not good, all to be worked out in God's way. Great numbers of preachers had come to Texas with the idea, that if they were once here in this new country, they would count for a great deal. Some of them had failed on other fields. They came here to find further disappointment. It really takes a well balanced man and strong, to hold his own in a rapidly growing, unformed situation, such as Texas has been and is now in a large measure. It is not every preacher, who can be quiescent and sweet, under disappointment. Most men, when they fail, look outside of themselves for the cause of their failures; whereas the cause is commonly within, and it is human nature to blame the failure on somebody else.

In the very condition of things in Texas, there had grown up a kind of feudalism in the denomination, the thing that Paul condemned in the church at Corinth. One was for Paul (that was not his name in Texas) another for Cephas and so on. If the leaders could agree, there was a measure of peace. If they did not, then the masses would gather around their favorite leaders and there was no peace. It was a kind of stack-pole unification, a personal leadership, which went finally to newspaper leadership.

Another thing might be mentioned, which intensified the situation. Some men, of a fighting disposition, felt that they counted for more in a fight than they did in plain work, and, if things got quiet, and every thing smoothed down to steady work, they would not amount to much. We have yet a contingent of this sort of people in Texas and elsewhere, but more of them in the Southwest than anywhere else. In the older and more settled parts of the country, the denomination has outgrown them. Texas was really a paradise for such men, and hither they flocked.

Then, of course, we had what is always with us in our denominational life: the foolish prejudices of country people against town people and town people against country people. When people come to think about it, they know there is no sense in it. But, when there is a lively fight going, people feel a great deal and think very little, and that helps to keep up the fight.

Let us take still another look. On this broad field were exploited different denominational interests. Besides the Baptist General Convention of Texas, there was a Sunday School Convention. Then the several schools had their interests, and there were independent Sunday School workers and evangelists; all of them doing more or less good, all of them trying to push forward, and often very much in each other's way. Sometimes at a single association, or a Fifth Sunday meeting, there would be half a dozen general men present to represent separate interests, each one pulling for the best hour. Was there ever a situation in the world made more to the hand of a man, with his pocket full of wedges, and his mind made up to split things? Dr. Burleson is credited with saying that there are three classes of Baptists in Texas: "the sitters, the splitters and the builders." We will be getting on toward the millenium when the two first tribes diminish and the third increases to cover the land.

When this writer came to Texas as a "tender-foot," he found a condition about as described, with a great battle on. The conflict raged around the Board of Directors and the Baptist General Convention of Texas, which had already begun a forward movement of great significance. One of the general papers in the state stood unflinchingly by the Board and its policies, which was the same as standing by the Baptist General Convention, which appointed the Board and outlined the policies. The other paper was in sharp conflict, and was waging war with great zeal and no little ability. The woods were afire all over the state, and it was a question of saving what could be saved and holding things together for a better day. The plan of attack was by ceaseless assaults on the Board, its workers and on the Convention itself. The accusations were as ceaseless as the tides of the seas. They ran on the general lines made historic by the Hardshells in their fight, also, the early Campbellites. The sovereignty of the churches, the people were told, with insistence and continuously was being ruthlessly disregarded and trampled on by a set of bosses. The people's money was being wasted. The management of the Board, and of the Convention itself, was full of trickery. The most unthought of accusations were made against the workers of the Convention. No man escaped. Men grown gray in honorable service, were held up as totally unworthy, and some of them as grossly criminal. It was all in the spirit of the early Hardshells, and by the same methods, though the contentions were different. All this was urged in the name of missions; and all of it to break down public confidence in the Convention and its agencies, to the end that failure might result, which would be charged on the chosen leaders of the denomination.

The denomination, and those chosen to lead a forward movement faced a grave situation. We were to make a great experiment with the democratic principles of the Baptist people. Would the consecration, intelligence and fidelity of the denomination be able to withstand these attacks? That thousands of good people believed the false and malicious charges made, could not be questioned, and they were openly and honestly allied with the opposition to the Convention and its work.

For one, I did not entertain a doubt that the principles of democracy in the denomination would be vindicated. I never doubted, that while we were riding rough seas and

BY J. B. GAMBRELL, D. D.

traveling rough roads, in the end, neither the work, nor the workers could be ridden down by newspapers, however blatant they might be. I felt sure that, in the end, people would turn to the right side. I never had any more doubt of it, than I had that the Heavenly bodies will keep their places under the unseen, but powerful law of attraction. The demonstration, wrought out in Texas, ought to be worth a great deal to the denomination at large. It stands for a free press, even though the press may be misdirected, and it ought to give assurance to the public everywhere that in the ongoing of things, ordained by the Lord of Glory, truth, in an open field, will win. Under the constant enfilading, the question was often asked, if these things be not so, why do you not sue for your character? In the body of this volume, will be found an answer to that particular question. But it is worth emphasizing here that the great principle of freedom of speech and a free press, will work always for the right side, if only people have patience, with perseverance, to give time to the working out of those forces among men that finally determine human conduct.

The situations are so analagous, that I quote here from the second inaugural address of Thomas Jefferson, President of the United States. It may be remembered that, during his first administration, the vast Louisiana territory was acquired, and but few public men were ever set upon as furiously as was Thomas Jefferson. He had passed through a four years' ordeal of this sort, when he came to his second inauguration, and from the address then made, the following is quoted:

"During this course of administration, and in order to disturb it, the artillery of the press has been leveled against us, charged with whatsoever its licentiousness could devise or dare. These abuses of an institution so important to freedom and science are deeply to be regretted, inasmuch as they tend to lessen its usefulness and to sap its safety.

They might, indeed, have been corrected by the wholesome punishment reserved to and provided by the laws of the several states against falsehood and defamation, but public duties, more urgent, press on the time of public servants, and the offenders have, therefore, been left to find their punishment in the public indignation. Nor was it uninteresting to the world that an experiment should be fairly and fully made, whether freedom of discussion, unaided by power, is not sufficient for the propagation and protection of truth, whether a government conducting itself in the true spirit of its Constitution, with zeal and purity, and doing no act which it would be unwilling the whole world should witness, can be written down by falsehood and defamation. The experiment has been tried; you have witnessed the scene; our fellow citizens looked on, cool and collected; they saw the latent source from which these outrages proceeded; they gathered around their public functionaries, and when the Constitution called them to the decision by suffrage, they pronounced their verdict, honorable to those who had served them and consolatory to the friend of man, who believed that he may be trusted with the control of his own affairs."

"No inference is here intended that the laws provided by the states against false and defamatory publications should not be enforced; he, who has time, renders a service to public morals and public tranquility in reforming these abuses by the salutory coercions of the law; but the experiment is noted to prove that, since truth and reason have maintained their ground against false opinions in league with false facts, the press, confined to truth, needs no other legal restraint; the public judgment will correct false reasonings and opinions on a full hearing of all parties; and no other definite line can be drawn between the inestimable liberties of the press and its demoralizing licentiousness. If there be still improprieties which this rule would not restrain, its supplement must be sought in the censorship of public opinion."

This is exactly what happened in Texas. Though it was claimed persistently that the Superintendent of Missions and others were usurping authority, and were unworthy of confidence, year after year, the people responded, vindicating their servants and upholding the work, into which they were putting yearly increasing thousands of dollars. It is easy now to see a providence in all this. It takes churning to get butter, and Texas was having a general churning up, and a better alignment of forces for the broad, strong, comprehensive methods adopted by the Convention in the interest of denominational unity and progress has resulted.

During these strenuous years, every principle and practice of the denomination, touching co-operative work, has been put to the severest test: and we have had in Texas something like the Acts of the Apostles all over again. There has been developed every phase of church life revealed to us in the Acts, and we can duplicate on Texas soil every kind of character brought to light in those early records of the planting and training of churches. We have had men after the Pauline order, mighty in word and deed, strong in doctrine, forceful in action, wise in cousel, tactful in execution—leaders of the people along the highways of progress. And then we have had some after the order of Peter, hot and cold, slipping and sliding, up and down, but up the most and up finally and up to stay. We have had some after the order of John Mark, a "tender-foot," who started on a journey with Paul and Barnabas and thought of his mother, or somebody else, and turned back.

We have had divisions after the order of Paul and Barnabas; when their contentions waxed so warm over John Mark, they parted asunder, each going his own way with his message. We have had John, the evangelist, loving, fervent in spirit, yet plain spoken on occasions. And Barnabas, glorious Barnabas, with a weak spot for his kindred, and a soft hand to cover the sore places among his brethren, healing wounds and smoothing the way for men to come into usefulness. We have seen Diotrophes, as large as life, loving the pre-eminence, refusing to receive brethren and casting these out of the churches, who would receive them. And Demus, who loved this present world, and went out of the great fight for progress to enjoy the pleasures of the world for a season. Alexander the coppersmith has a numerous progeny in Texas, still in the copper business, when they go to church. And the Nicolaitans are here still as unsavory as in the days of the long past. And Ananias and Sapphira still make a vain show and lie to the Holy Ghost touching money.

We have glorious women here, the Marys and Marthas, undaunted, and Lydia, and all of them; a great company out of which to form a missionary movement to conquer the imperial state of Texas, and join with others to conquer the world. Best of all, we have God the Father, God the Son, and God, the Holy Spirit working miracles of grace in the salvation of thousands of souls and leading on from victory to victory.

With this vast complexus of forces, good and bad, it was a question of supreme importance how to so conduct a campaign, in which battles followed battles, like the rolling waves of the ocean, as to finally gather the constructive forces together for construction work, and to eliminate the destructive forces. One simple plan has been unvaried for a decade and more. It is not original. Nobody in Texas deserves the least credit for inventing it. It was revealed in the Holy Scriptures, emphasized and put inpractice by the Apostle Paul, the world's greatest missionary leader. What was the plan? To magnify, on the one hand, the work itself, and to minify, on the other hand, all of those incidental ques-

BY J. B. GAMBRELL, D. D.

tions which were constantly thrust in the way and held before the people as worthy of their first attention. One conversant with the New Testament, and especially with the Acts of the Apostles, will see at once that this plan is identical, in principle, with Paul's plan. You could not get Paul to talk any length of time about mere objections. His was affirmative preaching. No matter where he was, nor what his surroundings, he answered every objection by preaching the truth. If he was called on to answer as to his conduct, the best answer was the gospel. Paul was not much on taking care of himself, a kind of small business engaged in by little preachers. He was out taking care of the Kingdom, and he covered all the ground of pesky little objections by affirmative declarations of the truth in a great conquering spirit.

The general plan in Texas has been to treat all the objections thrown in the way as mere incidents to a great movement. Some of them have been quite uncomfortable, and sometimes expensive, but they have never been allowed to take first place. The policy has been to work on, planting, cultivating, gathering a crop, giving just so much attention to the fences as might be found necessary to save the crop from destruction by outside forces. Not a single leader in the Convention has ever given to the attacks on himself the first place. In pursuing this plan, it has been the policy of the Convention to keep before the Baptists large things. "It is easier to do large things than little things," has been the slogan of our people. A great people cannot be rallied to little things. More people, a hundred to one, will join in a bear hunt than will turn out to kill a mouse. Year after year, great missionary and educational enterprises have been projected, and great schemes of benevolence. If a Convention is not going to undertake great things, why should there be a Convention? Why call on tens of thousands of Baptists to do things, that a few might do if they would. There is no justification for the time, or the expense of a Convention, unless it undertakes great things. Year after year Texas Baptists have rallied to the ever enlarging enterprises of the Convention, until they have themselves become large. This policy has had the happy effect to enlist our great laymen in large, worthy enterprises in which to invest their money, and they have been enlisted to take care of these large enterprises. It generally happens that men, who have sense enough to make money, have sense enough to give it to the best advantage; and having given their money, they will give their influence and time to seeing that their money is not lost. The philosophy of this plan is as simple as human nature. But it has a strength in it far above humanity. God never helps triflers. The scheme of bringing enterprises down to the prejudices of the least informed, and to the ideas of the covetous has in it the seeds of death. God is with the people, who are trying to do His will to the limit. Let any people anywhere lay themselves out for the Kingdom, and all the powers of Heaven will fight for them.

In the ongoing of things, it was found by the Convention that it was every way bad to have the meetings of a great body disturbed by ceaseless wrangles over things, which had been settled over and over. If there was to be strife and confusion, it must be on the outside and not on the inside. A bomb exploded in the open may do some harm; but exploded in a house will wreck things. After severe pains and struggles, the Convention reached the conclusion and solemnly determined not to recognize within the limits of the Convention the right of any man to use his privileges there to disturb the body. It was the great principle of civilization, a principle inherent in every church, in every voluntary body in the world, invoked by the Convention in self defense. Baptist principles are put to a severe strain. Over and over, it was said by people of other denominations, "You people have no way to take care of your-

BY J. B. GAMBRELL, D. D.

selves." It was finally demonstrated, we had the best way, the simplest and easiest way. But in carrying out this simple principle, which inheres in every self-governing body, it befell a good many of the brethren to be haled before judges. This was an added obstruction. This writer spent seven months. all put together, in a Texas court house. It was not very edifying, nor was it half as pleasant as a camp-meeting with the cow boys in the west, but it became necessary that the principles of the Convention should be tested. I have no desire to go into any of the particulars. After numerous trials, verdicts, reversals and such like, the case went to the Supreme Court of the State, and the Supreme Court, following all the Courts of the country, from the United States Supreme Court down, decided that the Convention stood on its rights. The backbone of the litigation was broken by the Supreme Court. It was sent back and finally settled by the plaintiff and one of the defendants. The settlement was an "agreed" judgment. It was stipulated by the plaintiff that all charges made and passed on by the Convention might stand, and that is of record in the court house today. It was a pretty rough experience, but we got off better than Paul did, for he was in jail a good many times, and we all escaped. Notwithstanding all, the cause grew exceedingly, and even in the court house one soul was converted by the conduct of some of the brethren under fire of attorneys, and that, I take it, is remuneration for all that anybody suffered.

During all these years of intense opposition, Paul's experience was duplicated. There were adversaries and open doors. Difficulties abounded on every side, but difficulties are opportunities spelled another way. And every Christian ought to learn to spell. The very conflicts through which our people passed, with a heroic pressing of the work, with an intense, ever widening sweep of evangelism, were fusing the spirits of our people, enlightening their minds through ceaseless discussions and welding them into a great army of conquest, so that it happened as it did when Paul was a prisoner in Rome. The things that happened have fallen out rather to the furtherance of the gospel.

Through all the conflicts, there never was but one real danger, and that was, that those who were pressing the work, would, in an evil hour, turn aside from the work and enter into vain janglings over inconsequential things. If this had been done, the cause in Texas might have been prostrated for an indefinite period.

If this writer might, with modesty, say a word, as to his own feelings and his part in the long drawn out battle for progress, he would say that never, for one moment, did he doubt the conclusion. There is no defeat for a cause, well pushed, if it is right. Nor has he for one hour, nor even one moment, taken a disquieting view of what has been said. Democracy in religion, as in state, carries its own antitoxin.

If people did not know better, they were to be pitied. If they did know better, judgment belonged to God. If one can commit his soul to the Savior, in well doing, surely he might commit his life and his reputation. Nor has this writer ever had a doubt of the honesty and sincerity of the great mass of Baptists who have not agreed with him, nor has he had at any time a doubt, that, in the long run, the policies of the Convention would be thoroughly vindicated, and that there would be such a real unification among Texas Baptists as never could have been but for the thorough shaking up we have had. I believe in the Baptists, that is, taken as a body, and I believe in the great democratic principles, which govern Baptists. Baptists have never failed except when they have failed to apply their own simple principles with fidelity.

Among Baptists, everything rests on the voluntary principle. It follows, therefore, that, if we enlist the people for any purpose, it must be by enlightenment. They must understand what is wanted. It has been in the program for all these years in Texas to pour a constant stream of light on the whole situation, making plain every part and showing the path of progress. And, as the work of enlightenment has gone forward, the people have joyfully walked in it, and gathered around the things making for progress. Baptists have failed more in the teaching part of the Commission than in other parts. People have been saved from sin, to waste their lives, because they did not understand the right ways of the Lord. We are in process of rectifying this mistake.

Evangelism has held the first place with us, even amid the conflicts, which have been so marked a feature of a decade of progress. Not for a day, has that primal work been side tracked or ignored. We have kept to the divine order laid out in the great Commission. Woe to a people, who give a second place to that for which Christ came into the world—to seek and to save the lost. It is not pretended that sufficient emphasis has been placed on the main thing, or on anything belonging to the Kingdom: but soul winning has had the first place, and is taking the lead with Texas Baptists more and more. It is winning the day gloriously, winning all over the field, winning over all difficulties, winning for everything good. A revival from Heaven, is the most irresistible force among the sons of men. Every evil passion is shamed and conquered by it. Every good thing is drawn to it, and is helped by it. Suspicion, evil—surmising, malice, strife, covetousness, backbiting, all things bad give way before it. The world compaign for spiritual conquest, after the ascension of Jesus, began at Pentecost, in an all conquering revival, which swept difficulties out of the way, while it swept thousands into the Kingdom. It was never intended that the Kingdom should grow in a cold atmosphere. The revival spirit will insure progress, and without it decay, disintegration and ruin will overtake any church or working body.

Out of the fervent, soul seeking spirit, characterizing our people, everything good is coming to bless us. It is fusing our people into one spirit, and bringing us to have one mind. It is bringing a new day. No, it is bringing back the old days of heroism of which we read in the Acts. It is opening fountains of liberality, so that our people are more and more giving of their money after the fashion of the early disciples. It is winning non-co-operating Baptists to genuine co-operation. In a camp meeting, in which this writer did most of the preaching, there was a brother preacher, who came to spy out our liberties. He had heard much that was bad and believed it. One day the spirit of the Lord was on us in great power. Souls came into the Kingdom with shouts of praise. The brother preacher, plain, honest man as he was, came up and with a straight look in the face said: "I don't believe you are as mean a man as I heard you were. I don't believe you are mean at all. You love Jesus, and I love you." We had the atmosphere in which to understand each other, and from that time on, we have walked together in the fellowship of the Spirit, and in helpful co-operation.

The soul seeking spirit is the cure-all in the Kingdom. Far above everything else, it has won the day in Texas. Our preachers came from the protracted meetings to the court house, when summoned there by Caesar, and from thence returned to press the same enobling work. It has given us the noblest comradeship and been the greatest strength to the movement for unification and progress. It has been after the order of the Acts. No matter what difficulties befell the laborers of that period, they kept to the main thing. After that fashion have things gone in Texas.

The passion for souls has eaten up, or killed out unnumbered small questions, which infested the camps of Israel

BY J. B. GAMBRELL, D. D.

like the frogs of Egypt, filling the whole land with their croaking. The walls of Jericho fell down when Israel shouted, and the walls of opposition have dissolved into nothing as the shouts of redeemed souls have been heard from the Sabine to the Rio Grande, and from the gulf to the borders of Kansas.

This spirit of spiritual conquest has permeated and lifted up the churches which have put themselves into the war for progress. It has enlarged their numbers and greatened their spirit. It has enlarged their benevolence also, and, as they have received, they have given to press the work out and up and on. We owe the large gain in Texas to the spirit of evangelism.

It is worth saying that the strength of our Convention work has been greatly increased by a right handling of evanlistic forces. All evangelism ought to go out from the churches, and lead back into the churches for their strengthening. It is not enough that a person be saved. He should be instructed, baptized, properly related and trained for future service. This is the New Testament plan, adopted, and worked out in Texas. To what extent it succeeds may be judged from the fact that, in one year, the missionaries of the State Board baptized 7,712 converts. These now belong to the regular army of conquest, whereas, if they had been converted in nondescript, unrelated meetings, their lives would have been largely lost to the churches.

In the early days of the hard struggle for unity and progress, every effort was put forth to play one interest against another, one class against another, the country against the town, one school against another school, the Sunday School Board against the Mission Board, one group of men against another group of men, one paper against another paper. The whole land was dry and thirsty and full of dry weather cracks. Never did the "splitter" have a better day for his business. One of the most important things possible was to make every one see, that, in the Kingdom, there can be no divided interests, and, if disaster comes to one part of the work, all must suffer. Sometimes an apt story is better than an argument. Before one of our gatherings, where every element in the state was represented, the writer related the following war experience: During the Civil War he and his brother made an excursion into the Federal lines and captured a prisoner. To escape, we must needs cross the Nansemond River, something like a mile and a half wide. We were hard pressed by a force of Federals. Our only chance to escape was by a leaky boat. When well out in the stream, it was discovered that the boat was filling with water. This fact had the effect to unify us on the spot. We had our differences, but they were inconsequential, compared to the main thing. The blue and the gray, the flags, union or secession, state's rights or a federal union, were all of little consequence to us. We co-operated heartily and beautifully to keep that boat afloat.

The application was not difficult. If we did not sink small differences for the general good, all would be lost. And that was the view many took; and that spirit largely saved our constructive work in Texas. Personal preferences and personal interests have had large play in denominational affairs, and have wrought immeasurable mischief. The very exigencies of affairs forced Texas Baptists to get on high ground, where they are likely to remain for time to come. To eliminate the personal elements in a complex situation and sink a thousand small differences in the large and commanding interests of the Kingdom is to get on conquering ground.

In ten years, the work fostered by the Convention, increased more than 500 per cent and the effective force of the denomination has grown even more than that. We are now making progress toward the complete unification of the denomination, with ever increasing rapidity. And it is a unifi-

BY J. B. GAMBRELL, D. D.

cation not around men, but on the principles and practices of Baptists, as held by the denomination throughout the country.

At the opening of this good year, 1909, old line Baptists in Texas stand, a great army, strong and purposeful, constantly reinforced by tens of thousands fresh brought into the Kingdom, and ever increasing numbers of our brothers, who are coming to understand the old ways and have delight in walking in the paths the fathers trod. In the next ten years, if we increase as in the last decade, we should number in Texas more than 600,000 white Baptists alone and fulfill Paul's ideal of efficiency: "standing fast in one spirit, with one mind, striving together for the faith of the gospel." In another decade, Texas Baptists may count for more in the furtherance of the truth than all the Baptists of the South stood for ten years ago. Texas will some day have 50,000,000 people, and then, when the continent is crowded all over, there will be 100,000,000 people in Texas. Then its population will be about as dense as that of Massachusetts.

We are now mobilizing and training an army to lay this imperial state at the feet of Jesus for his use in the conquest of the whole world. Enlargement fills every mind and heart. Baptists in the country and in the towns, in every section of the state, of all classes, the rich and the poor, the cultured and the unlettered stand fast for truth and progress in one spirit, with one mind, and all for the furtherance of the gospel. Unification on sound principles is assured. The lines of progress are all laid. If any 20 men in the state were to die in a night, the gerat movement for progress would go on. The past is safe. The present is big with hope, and future will inherit all the past and the present.

UP FOOL HILL

FOOL HILL lies just where the undulating lowlands of boyhood rise sharply up to the highlands of manhood. It is climbed only by big boys, and the big boy is an institution in this world. He is, indeed, a series of personalities in one extraordinary combination. The only certain thing about him is his uncertainty. Like a spit-devil, he is loaded, and will go off with a spark, but just which way he will go is an unknown and an unknowable thing. But the chances are that he will go zigzag, and whichever way he does go you can trace him by the sparks.

When you notice the boy feeling of his upper lip, and a suspicion of something slightly darker than the skin appears, you may begin then to look sharp. The boy has come to the foot of fool hill, and he will begin very soon to climb. The great problem is to get him up the hill in good repair. That done, you have blessed the world with a man.

Big boys are nearly certain to have the big-head. This is no bad sign. It is an awkward sense of power, without the wisdom of discipline. Our boy entering the fool age is a caution. His voice is now fine and splitting, now coarse and grating. He begins a sentence coarse and ends fine, or fine and ends coarse. He is rank and sets digging to the world. All his judgments are pronounced and final. There is nothing he cannot decide instanter. He knows instantly and by intuition who is the greatest lawyer in the whole country, if he is a reading boy, or the best doctor. He can tell you who will be the next governor or anything else politicians are so anxious to know. He is authority on prize

BY J. B. GAMBRELL, D. D.

fights, or cards, or anything else he knows nothing about. And when he pronounces anything he has spoken. The governor is "Dick" somebody, and the supreme judge is "Tom." And, by the way, he often differs with these and other dignitaries. He sings in unearthly strains, with tendencies to the pathetic and the savage all in a breath.

"He is Nearly Certain to Have the Bighead."

With the big boy there is nothing medium. He uses adjectives freely and always in the superlative. He sees things in strong colors, for he is in the flood of passion. Fight! Yes, fight anything and on the shortest notice. He ought to fight to prove himself, so he feels. About this time his mind undergoes some radical changes. He wonders at the dullness and contrariness of his parents. It is a constant worry to him that he can't manage his father without a world of trouble, and he wonders what is the matter with "the old man" any how. Churches and Sunday-schools are too dull for him, and the preacher is just nowhere. He can give him any number of pointers on theology and preaching.

Rushing on and into everything like mad, he stops short and bewails the coldness of this unfriendly world. Now he has more "dear friends" than he can shake a stick at; now he feels that he has not a friend in the world. He wants sympathy, while he tries the patience of everybody who has anything to do with him.

Chip on Both Shoulders All the Time. "Fight Anything!"

Such is the boy in the fool age. The great question is what to do with him. He is climbing "fool hill" now, and the road is bad. Father, mother and friends are all anxious and sometimes vexed. Homes are deprived of all their peace by this great double-action marplot. But the question will not down. What shall we do with him? If he is turned loose now, he will be like a wild engine on the track smashing things. If he is not handled wisely there will be a catastrophe. The ever-recurring question is: What shall be done with the big boy climbing fool hill? Often the impulse is to let the fool go. But that will not do. He is now like a green apple—sour, puckerish and unwholesome; but, like the apple, if we can save him, he will ripen into something good. We must save him. Saints and angels, help us to save this human ship in the storm, freighted with father's, mother's, sister's, brother's love, and with the infinite wealth of an immortal nature! We must save him for himself, his loved ones and his country.

The chances for saving him will depend mainly on what has been done for him before he struck fool hill. If, from infancy, he has been taught to revere sacred things, if he has been taught subjection to authority, if his mind has been stored with scripture texts, with noble poems, and recollections of the pure, the sweet, the good, you have in him the saving elements. We must never forget that in the final analysis every person saves or loses himself, no matter what influences help or hinder. A well-taught boy may climb this dubious hill without a bobble, but if the new life

BY J. B. GAMBRELL, D. D.

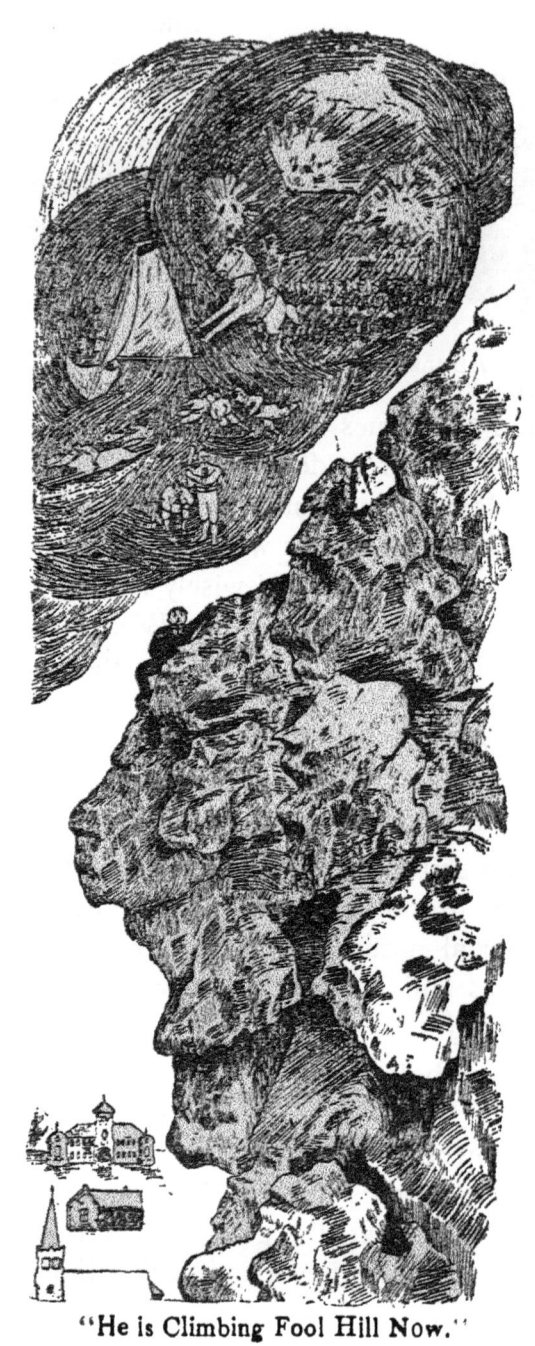

gains the temporary lead the chances are that the enduring good elements will reassert themselves and become paramount. Hence the transcendent importance of ballasting this ship betimes, before the storm sets in. Noble ambitions early planted and carefully nurtured are of great importance. During this period of trial, great wisdom and tact are needed. There must be a gradual lengthening of the ropes. If you tie this mustang up too tight he will break the rope, and maybe break his neck. It often happens that more can be done by indirection than otherwise. Some good woman, other than the boy's mother, may be a savior to him.

He feels his great importance, and you must recognize him. It is just here that the churches have failed and the

"He is Climbing Fool Hill Now."

"It is Just Here That the Churches Have Failed and the Saloons Have Succeeded."

saloons have succeeded. Show this embryonic governor that you recognize his parts and call on him for service. The harder the service the better he will like it. Get in with him, and do not be too critical, but pass his imperfections by. He will be nearly everything, but never mind; he only sees things large and sees them double and mixed, being now partly boy and partly man, and seeing with two sets of eyes.

You are fighting the devil for a soul, and you can't afford to be impatient, or give way to anger, when your fool boy takes an extra flounce. When he gets on a bad bent, give line, as the fisherman does when there is a hundred-pound tarpon at the other end of the line. In the quiet times pull on the line, but not too hard. And remember all the while that time and heaven are on your side. With age comes discretion. Once up fool hill the road stretches away ever smoother and better to the pearly gates.

Our big boy is among us. His folly breaks into dudishness. He is an unturned cake, but likely there is good substance in him. He is worth cooking. If you see him on the street, take him by the hand and say a good word to him. His mother will be glad of it. Look him up and ask him to your house. Reach after his heart, for he has one. Two worlds are interested in that young fool, and underneath his folly there lies sleeping, maybe, a great preacher, teacher or other dignitary of the commonwealth.

This article is affectionately dedicated to the big-headed boys by one who loves them.

BY J. B. GAMBRELL, D. D.

THE TE-HEE GIRL.

THIS interesting specimen of the human race makes her first appearance in the sphere of woman's activity just when, by a mysterious management and dexterity, ever too deep and intricate for masculine comprehension, short dresses grow long and turn themselves around the other way. There are preliminary symptoms of the metamorphosis which certify to the observant that something is about to happen. The girl of the play house and the dolls; of the wild romp and the free air; of the innocent freedom and sunny smiles, begins to move with a halt in her gait. The boys she played and romped with find her more reserved and distant. She no more invites their free manners. She is distinctly more difficult. She is harder to interest in their childish fun. There are signs of reserve and embryonic dignity.

There are flashes of prophetic fire in her eyes as now and then she looks away into the depths, becomes abstracted, waking up when spoken to with a strange, unaccountable start, and with a flush on her cheeks. About now, inadvertently, she lets slip remarks about how she used to love dolls. She has put the dolls all away as things to remember childhood days by; but now and then she goes quietly into the old play-house, all unseen, and gets out all her playthings and has a good time once more ere she quits the realm of child-life for good and all.

She becomes experimental. Standing before the glass, she combs her hair out smooth, turns to see how far down the back she can make it reach, gathers it up and tries her hand doing it in a knot a la the fashion. She bends her knees to make her yet undeveloped dress strike the floor, and studies the effect with a smile of satisfaction. There come into her voice new tones, now sharp and unsympathetic, now low and tender. She oscillates quickly between the extremes of feeling. Now it is a flood of tears, and now fun alive. Distinctly her laugh changes from the rippling, musical laugh of the free and easy girl, to a nervous, half suppressed, indefinable "te-hee," "te-hee," which, on slight provocation or no provocation, runs at kind of trotting rate "te-hee-hee-hee-hee," on till the spell is off.

Our dear girl is now oscillating between the two great estates of childhood and womanhood. As she swings backward and forward out of one kingdom into the other, her feelings are in a tumult trying to adjust themselves to the kaleidoscope of rapidly shifting views. Nature, the mother of all mothers, is kind and wise. She is cautious with her child. As the eagle trains her eaglets by short flights, catching them now and then and bearing them back to the nest for rest and further growth, so nature carries her daughters out a little into the woman world and brings them back

BY J. B. GAMBRELL, D. D.

into the childhood world for a little season of development and wise counsel before they finally depart to live under the weighty cares and burdens of perfected womanhood. She plays with them, reasons with them, encourages them, warns them, helps them, as the spray dashes on them, thrown up by the confluence of the bright brooklet of childhood with the ever-broadening river of womanhood, stretch-

ing away toward the ocean of eternity. If, all untrained, and all at once, the girl were cast into the swift current of womanhood, with its swells of passion, there would be a catastrophe, and the highest, sweetest hopes of the race would go down amid wails or despair.

This transition period is of infinite value and must not be despised. Nature, the good mother and wise teacher, is perfecting her finest handiwork—a woman. Heaven help, and all good people pray and wait! Nature must have time. Turning the dress around and adding to the skirt won't make a woman. Nature must round out her work by degrees. The physical, spiritual and mental must be worked down into harmony before there is much easy going where our te-hee girl lives, moves and has her being.

If you know one of them you may look out for lively times. She has spells. What sort of spells, do you ask? All sorts. She is a living kaleidoscope, different at every turn, but always pictureque. She gets into a social fever and goes on a rampage of calls and social functions. She suddenly has a chill and speaks of the "neauseating social drivel." She glows, dilates and sparkles at some gathering of the gay, and forthwith retires to some quiet spot, looks long and sadly into the face of the moon and weeps. Great feelings and great thoughts of opposite character chase each other through her heart and mind. Just what she will be or do is not settled with her, but it will be something out of the ordinary. Whether she will be an actress or missionary is not fixed, but either would be "just lovely." Thaddeus of Warsaw is her ideal. Napoleon dazzles her. She dotes on soldiers. She is now in the militant age, ready for all comers. The unpardonable sin is cowardice. Prudishness, as she regards her mother's anxious care of her, is the abomination of desolation, standing where it ought not, in the midst of her garden of pleasures. As she runs the whole gamut of feeling in an hour, you must learn her moods and chime in if you would help her. Far be it from this writer to speak of managing this unspeakable creation of God. It is not so much a matter of management as it is of hedging round about till she quits having spells. At this effervescing period, room is a consideration, but room may have limitations, and wisdom concerns herself with limitations. Suppression is against nature, and nature has the last word on every question. On this question nature speaks the oracular word by the mouth of the te-hee girl herself.

The te-hee girl is an aggregation of uncertainties, but amid the ebbs and flows of her feelings you may be sure that with the wisdom of a prophetess she steers her life boat for the port of matrimony. With love-light in her eyes and a splendid vision brightening her soul, she stands alert for the main chance. She may be dull on mathematics or languages, but in that finest of all the earthly sciences, the knowledge of loving and lifting the world higher by love and home, she will stand at the head of her class. Even more; from

BY J. B. GAMBRELL, D. D.

learning she quickly becomes a head-professor in the world's great university of life. She dotes on beaux, green apples and sour pickles.

The boy of corresponding age is awkward, mostly hands and feet, when he first ventures into the delectable realms of love-making. Not so the te-hee girl. With a smile and a "te-hee-hee,' she appears in the parlor, smoothes down her dress with a stroke or two of her hands, and she is ready for business. In her great line, she is far more a born artist than Raphael or Sir Joshua Reynolds. What boys have to learn she already knows, and more. She can make a dozen grown men feel that each is her favorite at one time, in one room, all present at once, and she is just a girl. She can say an endless number of little sweet nothings and set men to hunting for the meanings while she runs on "te-hee-hee-hee-hee-hee-hee." If one becomes too ardent, she congeals a thin wall of ice between her and him. If she wants to hear how he would say it, she thaws the ice and makes it easy. When he has said it, if she is not interested, she is amazed that he had any such thought and what he hoped was love, toughens into a Platonic friendship. With her magician's wand she can instantly transform the sweetheart into the "sister," and the man goes off calling himself a fool, which is not correct, for it was only the trick of a magician.

This te-hee girl could give a Tallyrand odds in diplomacy and leave him in a labyrinth of words wondering what she really meant. Not only in words, but in maneuvering she is captain. If from refined sensibility or for other reasons she does not wish to hear a declaration of love, which her fine intuition tells her is waiting a chance, she will see that the chance does not come. She may go into the parlor and meet the man, knowing he is loaded, but as he begins to lead up to the point she will hear her mother calling her, or will suddenly remember some neglected duty, or, like as not, she will take with a deep sisterly love for her little brother or sister, whom she can't bear to let go out of her sight, or she will hedge herself with words. Squinting in all directions, she can leave a cold track behind her if she wishes. If she is ready she can beat Gen. Lord Roberts clearing the coast. Her little brothers and sisters all find employment elsewhere. Her duties are all attended to at the proper time, and she is smiling in the possession of a good conscience. Her ear is deaf to all sounds but one. She is found in the flower garden or some other nice place for the business in hand. If her mind is clear and her heart right, she will marry at the drop of a hat, and the man who finds her in this state of mind will have to be mighty careful or he will drop his hat before he leaves. If the hat is dropped, and the two pure, loving hearts are united, there will be another home, civilization will be advanced, and a wholesome impulse given toward heaven, the eternal home.

The te-hee girl is a conundrum, a combination of opposites. She is a green persimmon, puckerish, but with luscious possibilities when time and a little frost have done their work. Her supreme want is a judicious mother into whose ear she can pour her troubles, and who will protect the impulsive child from herself. The girl is mistress of all till she falls a victim to her own feelings. Never mind her moods. She is sure to make trouble. In the course of events it is likely to develop that she cannot be induced to go to bed at night or get out of bed in the morning. She will laugh and cry out of season; but never mind any of it. Guard her. Care for her health. It is more to her to a future home than a diamond mine. Teach her, between spells, the plain, womanly duties of life. Impress on her the wealth and worth of a pure, strong woman. Adroitly select for her worthy company of the opposite sex. And, mother, in those sweet hours which are passed between sensible mothers and dutiful daughters, plant deep in the rich, warm soil of this tumultuous heart the great saving truths which shall, as a cable, anchor this heaven-freighted vessel to the throne of God. If it is brought over from childhood's rippling streamlet and started on the broad current of womanhood in good repair every way, two worlds will be blessed.

Dear girl, laugh on, cry on. All good people love you. Such were the strong wives and mothers of today, and such the white-haired grandmothers whose faces bear the impress of another world. Heaven guard you and bless you! Without you there would be a big gap in the world. I believe in you, but often wish you had more sense. Nevertheless, you will have wisdom. Let God's Word and Spirit teach you, that you may never have to learn in the hard, bitter school of folly.

WHO OWNS THE WOOL?

By Rev. J. B. Gambrell, D. D., L.L. D.

IN LAW and in reason the wool on sheep belongs to the owner of the sheep. If a man owned sheep, and sold them, he could not afterwards enforce a claim to the wool they might grow. The right in the wool follows the right in the sheep. The wool is an appurtenance growing out of sheep. God's people are God's sheep. They are His by creation, by preservation, by redemption, by their own consent. There never was a better title to any property. This title holds the sheep and the wool. The sheep can not hold property because they are property themselves. The wool is theirs, only as their skins are theirs, and their hands and feet by way of accommodation. The supreme title is in God, and this title holds against all comers. Our times are in His right to do what He will with His own.

Not only are the sheep the property of the Creator, but the goats are also. "The earth is the Lord's and the fullness thereof; the world and they that dwell therein." That title takes in everything. Rebellion can never overreach the Divine sovereignty over all men and everything. "The commandment is exceedingly broad" because the Divine authority is as limitless as creation. We have made a poor study of the Bible if these simple truths have not lodged themselves in our hearts. Conversion comes simply as a recognition of the Divine ownership in us. It is an acceptance, on our part, of our proper relation to our Creator and Redeemer.

During the great Hardshell struggle, the cry which ran up and down the ranks of the disturbed Baptists was one touching rights in the wool. Hardshells are covetous professors of religion who give little or no money to God. They hate missions and missionaries because of the cost. They would put an end to all Christian missions if they could. They say: "When God wants the heathen converted, He will do it without any help from men." This is a specimen of their random and unscriptural talk. In the great struggle above referred to, the Hardshells declared that the missionaries were out shearing the sheep. I have myself heard the cry, with a peculiar twang or sneer to give it all the opprobrium possible, just as now we hear kindred sneers. In many places the missionaries flinched under the accusation, and thus compromised the deepest and most important principle revealed in religion—God's ownership in the wool which grows on His sheep. In yielding God's rights in the wool, they threw up His rights in the sheep; for there is no conceivable way to separate these rights. If God can hold the sheep, He can hold the wool; if He can hold the wool, the sheep will not go much astray.

The greatest question in the world today is: Who owns the wool? Or, to drop the figure, to whom does the property, the gold, the silver, the cattle, and all belong? If that is settled on the right principle, the whole question of Christian living is far advanced toward a glorious settlement. Until it is settled, nothing is settled right. Or, in other words, if we settle our financial relations to God on the right principle, our lives are bound up with God's in such a way that we can never go far wrong.

The mightiest controversy of the age is over "rights in the wool." It is, or ought to be, a controversy both in the pulpit and among Christians in the pews of every church in

Christendom till God's right is admitted and acted on. To flinch on this fundamental doctrine is to trifle with the greatest practical question the world confronts. Let God's right to the wool of His own sheep, to say nothing of the hair of the goats—I say let God's right be settled, and we are at the opening of a new era in the world's history. The triumphant march of God's army is slowed up, waiting for us to settle the wool question. There can be but one adjudication, and that is, that whoever owns the sheep owns the wool also.

Shear the sheep? Yes, frequently and close. The pastors are the shepherds; and it is their business to feed the sheep, care for them, and shear them. A shepherd who neglects to shear the sheep ought to be turned off. He is an unfaithful servant of the Great Owner. Pastors need to face this question. They must face it, for the time is at hand when pastors will be judged according to their works, not by their dignity or their pretenses, but their work; and one of the works is to shear the sheep.

But the question has two sides: God's side and our side. Is it not hard on the sheep to shear them? Not at all. It is good for them every way. If sheep are not sheared they become unhealthy. How many of God's saints are surfeited with the things of this world? Their spirituality is smothered by a plethora of the things of this life. Many are sick because their lives have no outlet. Their affections are turned after their earthly possessions and not set on things above. One of the best things a pastor can do for his people is to induce them to give liberally to the cause. He is doing the best thing for his people when he brings them to recognize their obligation to God in financial affairs.

So important is this matter in the churches and in the lives of the people, that it demands special and extremely earnest treatment. Some of the sheep must be cornered and

BY J. B. GAMBRELL, D. D.

crowded, before they will submit to the process clearly taught in God's Word; but they must be sheared.

The question takes on another practical turn. Where our treasure is there will our hearts be also. This is Christ's word fulfilled in every life. If sheep are not sheared they drop their wool, or the devil picks them up. Alas! for the waste of God's money in the service of the world, the flesh and the devil—and this to the hurt of God's people. Sin costs more than religion. Bad habits cost far more than the most liberal giving to God's cause, if we count money, and what is more than money. Robbery of God is a horrible and undoing sin. Giving to God has the wonderful power to bind the life to Him.

Two sisters, daughters of a wealthy father, were converted and started out side by side in the divine life. The father died and left each a fortune. One became at once a liberal giver. The other withheld more than was meet. The first has been these many years successful, useful and happy in her simple life, giving more and more constantly, both of herself and her money. The other is withered. She spent her money for the world. In grazing on the Devil's pasture the Devil robbed her of money, of health, of happiness, of usefulness, and now her life is not much but a lament. Each is reaping as she sowed. As sure as we live, Christian giving is a long step towards right living.

One more thought. Money kept back from God becomes a curse to a family, often ruining them, both for time and eternity. This is the testimony of Scripture and human experience. Giving liberally on the right principle is the best possible education and safeguard for a family. And the right principle is the principle of God's ownership of the sheep and the wool. Next to redemption the greatest question in the Christian world today is the question of rights in the wool. If God's sheep were properly sheared, they would abound in health, and countless missionaries could be sent, as torch bearers, to every benighted region of the globe. The tears of widows and orphans could be dried, the sick cared for, pastors supported, homes illuminated by the Word of God, and the world belted with the light of truth. This wool question is a tremendous issue in the hearts and lives of Christians and churches. If we settle God's right to the wool of His sheep, we settle the world's destiny.

THE WORKING VALUE OF FREE GOVERNMENT IN RELIGION.

THIS writer recently felt called on to write at some length on the corrective force of freedom in religion. The remarks in that rather extended article applied largely to a single phase of the question. In this article it is proposed to deal with the working value of free government. Much has been said as to the strength of hierarchal forms of government, and the weakness of the congregational form. One has said of the latter: "It is a rope of sand; it is no government at all." And, very recently, a Baptist minister in a public assembly extolled the strength and working force of Methodism, and depreciated the free government of Baptists from the working standpoint. All of these estimates are wrong. Two or three things will be assumed as a basis of what shall follow in this discussion:

1. It is assumed that all true religion is voluntary, and that all true service is responsive to the claims of Jesus Christ upon the individual heart and conscience. It must follow from this that that is really the strongest religious force which most directly and powerfully appeals to the heart and conscience of the individual. Much of what is called religious force is not religious force at all, but human

force supervening between the individual disciple and his divine Lord and Master, and is, to that extent, weakness and not strength.

It is assumed that the churches are voluntary organizations, and that each church is a complete unit in itself, and invested with all of the rights and privileges possible under the law of Christ, and to each one is committed the entire commission to be carried out according to the will of its Head.

Having assumed these positions, without formal discussion, I proceed to enquire into the real working force and value of the free system practiced among Baptists. No matter what system of government may obtain in any religious community, the real religious strength of that community is no stronger than the intelligent devotion of the separate members aggregated. It follows, therefore, that the strongest religious force is that which appeals most directly to the renewed heart, and tends most to intelligent, voluntary service. It is the obscuration of this vital principle that is the weakness of many a church. The measure of devotion to Jesus Christ is the measure of the strength of Christian service. It is for this reason that the whole system of raising money by methods other than that suggested by Paul, giving "with simplicity," is to be deplored. All the roundabout methods, by way of oyster suppers, the ordinary church fair and the like, do, indeed, bring in an element of worldly, fleshly strength, but, to the same degree, they lessen the real religious force of a church. They proceed, as a rule—perhaps, not all of them—but, as a rule, they proceed on the occult understanding, never expressed, but always felt, that we can harness to the gospel car the world, the flesh and the devil and make them help pull in the right direction. As a fact, that team, the devil always working in the lead, never was hitched to the gospel car that there was not a runaway and a smash-up, and real harm done. Paul's instruction was to "give with simplicity." That means straight out, and the more direct the appeal can be made from the cross to the heart, not only will the contribution be better, but larger, for the whole Christian system moves by the impelling force of love shed abroad in the hearts of God's people. If our free churches have fallen behind hierarchal churches anywhere in giving it is because we have abandoned the legitimate use of the free doctrine and either done nothing or betaken ourselves to unworthy methods to do that which the love of Christ would enable us to do far better if we appealed to it. As a matter of fact, wherever there is a Baptist church that has been shown the truth about giving and been appealed to solely on Scriptural ground, it has led all the churches in the community in its benefactions. It is to shamefully discount the power of divine grace, which has led multitudes to the stake for the love of Christ, to suppose that there is something that will be better in the way of inducing service.

Let us proceed a step further in our co-operative work. The appeal must be made to the intelligent devotion of each church. Always and everywhere, if we would see the best results, let it be understood that no church is compelled to co-operate with any other church, or through any organization whatever. Let the whole question be thrown back where the Scriptures put it in every case, and the conscience of the church itself will determine what it will do. This does not mean that the church may not be visited, and that it is wrong to make written and oral appeals, but let it be understood constantly that the church must itself finally determine what its duty in any case is. The great advantage of this free system is, that it forces, along with every development of the work, a process of education. Love itself may err through lack of knowledge, and many excellent people have been led astray on great questions that came before them because they were not in-

by J. B. Gambrell, D. D.

formed. Whoever invokes the co-operation of free, intelligent churches must carry the responsibility of informing the churches. What does this mean? It means development, quickened interest in everything that pertains to the cause, and, finally, a vastly stronger church, because any church is as strong as the aggregate strength of its membership, and, in estimating a church it must be weighed rather than counted.

When John was dealing with the church of which Diotrephes was a member, he dealt with it in an open, plain manner. His plan comprehended the enlightenment of that church to the point that Diotrephes would be impossible. Does it need any argument to prove that the more enlightened a great communiy of people become, the more strength they will have? Certainly not. So then the free government, by its direct appeals to the churches, and by its collateral educational work, must inevitably greatly add to the strength of the church.

Let's take another view of it. All progress has been attended by pains and commotions. This is true in temporal things. It is true in spiritual things. It accords with the experience of every redeemed soul, from the time it first felt the conviction of sin onward until it entered the gates of the New Jerusalem. Every advance in holiness created a painful impression of imperfection, and necessitated a renunciation of former ideals.

In the onward going of a great denomination in any given territory as, for instance, in Texas, progress everywhere wakes up the sleeping elements of opposition. Progress means, always, the relegating of a non-progressive leadership, and many non-progressive leaders instinctively know this, and array themselves against everything looking to change. Many good, but uninformed people, are naturally against the new order of things, and must be brought over by reasons clearly shown. That is precisely as it ought to be. Changes ought never to be made except for good reasons. But, in the process of discussion, which is open and free, the public mind is educated. There is an open arena for men to show of what sort they are. In these discussions men go on the scales and are weighed in the presence of the whole multitude, and because all the people have more sense than some of the people, in the wind-up, which may come after three, or four, or five years, the majority opinion will be right, and men will take their proper positions. The progress will be a real progress, because this true democracy is right, and human progress is assured. Therefore, the great, free government system is the strongest system in the final test.

But we must deal with what always becomes an incident of progress—an obstructive element. This element, in many localities, will hold the people back for a time, and in some churces it may be strong enough to effectively prevent co-operation. In the great winnowing process a separation will go on. The obstructive elements, such as cannot be assimilated into the denominational life, will be thrown out. While open discussions may raise storms, the storms are certain to separate the chaff from the wheat.

There is, also, a particular advantage to the free government in our churches. A church that cannot, and does not, approve the general policies agreed on by other churches, is free not to co-operate. There can be no compulsion and no tyranny. The church can stand out and by itself. But the voluntary principle in co-operation works both ways. If any given church, or any given man, does not want to co-operate, he or it need not do it, and then, if a great many other churches do not want to affiliate with any church, or any man, they need not do it. The principle works backwards and forwards and forwards and backwards.

A hierarchal government has all the local congregations put into one great church, and whatever trouble there is in one church becomes a trouble with all the churches. Every local church trouble may be carried up to the conference, or assembly, to become the plague of everybody. With the free government our conventions and associations have to deal with a singel thing, i. e., whether they are willing to affiliate with that body, and whether the messengers there present are willing to sit in council with this man. Beyond that they have nothing to do with the local churches. One church can die, and the others go on. It is somewhat on the joint-snake order. I have always thought a joint-snake had a decided advantage over the other sort. If he has his back broken at one joint he can drop that out and couple up and go on. The free church system, therefore, has all the strength of a direct appeal on the merits of every case, putting first every individual on his personal responsibility to God concerning the matter; and second a direct appeal to all the churches, putting the responsibility of action on each. It, therefore, has the great advantage of carrying forward the processes of education which are needful to voluntary, intelligent service.

It has the further advantage of having the shortest method of disconnecting inharmonious elements. It has that great advantage which was so manifest in the free working of the apostolic churches. When Paul and Barnabas could not agree they separated, cooled off and finally got together again. The very organization of our churches is favorable to perpetuating the truth. If a sound element in a church cannot endure the heterodoxy of a majority it can draw out and make another church. If persecution were to scatter all the churches in Christendom, the fragments everywhere could get together in other churches. The free system of the New Testamnt is somewhat like wire grass—the more you dig it up and scatter it the more of it there will be. It was not until this free idea was abandoned that Rome became possible. Nothing has hurt so much in Texas as an effort to half-way invest our general bodies with qualities which they can never have. As councils, they are valuable. They can devise methods and make recommendations, and that is all. The churches cannot invest them with any of their qualities, cannot delegate any of their the commission to conventions. They may, if they wish, employ boards as channels of communication, and conventions power, cannot transfer their responsibilities to carry out can advise and devise; but the churches are the real fountains of power and authority. All we need is to come fully to an appreciation of the great question of the freedom of the New Testament system, and do away with all presbyterial and hierarchal notions.

A closing remark. Baptists are more likely to stand together than other people, and that is because they need not tinker so much with machinery, but keep close back to base lines, and, also, because they have such a ready way of disposing of heretics and othe disorganizers. A friend of mine in Mississippi invented a patent whiffle tree. The trick of it lay in pulling a string, and the runaway horse found himself going at whatever gait suited him, with the buggy left behind. We do not have to take everything to pieces, from top to bottom, to get an obstreperous man out. We just simply pull the string, and off he goes.

BY J. B. GAMBRELL, D. D.

THE ARMY IN THE DITCH.

BONAPARTE stands first among all the military captains in the world for tactical skill. One of the wisest aphorisms ever uttered by him was "The army in the ditch is always whipped in the long run." He meant by this, that defensive tactics are not good active forces. It is a common saying, "It is easy to pull it is, that the army in the ditch is shut up and cannot recoup any lost ground. It has far less liberty of action and its strength lies simply in its endurance. All the higher qualities of military tactics are displayed in open field, where every faculty comes into play.

There is in the aphorism of the great general a profound philosophy which runs along the whole battle-line of life. The mere objector is doomed to defeat in the face of active forces. It is a common saying, "It is easy to pull down and destroy and hard to build up." There is an element of truth in the saying, but it is only one element in a great problem. The man who pulls down is so limited and runs so counter to the strong currents of human progress, that before any great while he himself is swept away without knowing it. The objector is fighting all the healthy currents of human life. The objector is in every church, every association, in every State convention, in all the secret orders, in politics, and notwithstanding his presence and industry and noise, churches are built up, associations and conventions go on, secret orders flourish and great political parties live. This demonstrates the truth of Napoleon's saying.

We have recently had a great demonstration in politics One party was distinctly for things, and the other against, and the constructive policy beat the obstructive policy. We have had a remarkably fine illusration of what I am writing about in Texas affairs during the last few years. Old men have seen the same thing over and over, all their lives. The

Why is it that the army in the ditch is always whipped?

If the Baptists in Texas would have consented to go into the ditch and ward off attacks, we would have come to

nothing; instead of that a wise, conservative policy was diligently pursued, and the attacking element was simply handled in a way to prevent their doing harm. Texas Baptists have won out by what they have done in the work.

Why is it that the army in the ditch is always whipped? There are a good many reasons as deep as humanity. The army in the ditch must bear the shock of attack in every conflict. Any soldier who has tried it, will say it is easier to make a charge than it is to sustain a charge. Nothing tries the metal of an army so completely, as to be compelled to lie down or stand up and take the hammering which an aggressive army is pleased to give. That is the physical reason. There is no momentum working to the advantage of the army in the ditch. There is nothing of that high spirit that goes with a splendid movement. And then, men can not be held to negations. You cannot rally healthy-hearted men strongly to negative propositions. Instinctively, they feel that they are losing by not doing something themselves, and all of the stronger and better element will leave a party which has nothing better to offer than negations. Men of strong, resolute minds with great purposes, with a spirit of conquest in them, will not consent to go into the ditch and stay there.

This brings me to remark that when a people lose for their faith, in politics or religion, the spirit of conquest, when they are willing to simply hold their own, they are then going into decay. A church that is satisfied simply to hold its own is a church that is not going to hold its own. Before it knows it, it will be struck through with dry rot. No body of people can be great without the spirit of conquest. This applies in religion, in politics, in learning, everywhere just as far as humanity goes.

When a people take a mere obstructive attitude, or to fall back on Napoleon's saying, when they go into the ditch, they are making for themselves all the conditions of defeat, as inevitable in the operations of the forces of human life as the law of gravity. God's method of curing evil is to drive out the bad with the good, to dispel darkness with light. The forces that construct and conserve all the forms of civilization are aggressive forces, not negative.

We are now at a good time, with the election over, to lay some truths to heart. I am a Southern man, fought four years in the Southern army, and have never been on the mourner's bench about it, and do not think I ever shall be. But a calm review of the history of politics in the nation for sixty years, makes it clear that about three score years ago, the South made a colossal blunder in going into the ditch. The Southern attitude was defensive. Our leaders took the sectional attitude, and gave the other side the larger portion. The whole case is admirably set out in the memorable speeches of Mr. Hayne, of South Carolina, and Mr. Webster, of Massachusetts. The former discusses the autonomy of the government, the framework of it. Mr. Webster did not answer Mr. Hayne in his argument, but he clothed the frame work with rosy flesh and made it palpitate with warm blood. His was the larger view. The inevitable happened. The army in the ditch was defeated. A most singular and striking illustration of this in history is the case of Spain under Ferdinand and Isabella. The whole nation was thrilled with the spirit of conquest, and when Philip, the Second, came to the throne, he found himself master of the world's greatest empire. The vast colonization scheme of Spain had proceeded from the throne. Philip, seeing himself at the zenith of power, resolved upon a measure to secure permanence of power to the Spanish throne. He committed the astounding blunder of insulating the Spanish intellect by a decree which provided that no Spanish youth should go out of Spain for education, and no teacher from abroad should enter Spain. That was the beginning. Dewey, with his guns, at Manila, emphasized the practical end of the colossal Spanish empire. The Spanish insulated mind ran to enormous conceit and vanity, lost its virility, and under this blight, national strength decayed.

What is the use of all this discussion in a religious paper? Southern Baptists number three-fourths of the Baptists of the world. The gifted Dr. Tucker of Georgia, Southern to the core, speaking of some Baptists, said, "they are many but not much." We are compelled to admit in candor that, for our numbers, we make less impression on the world than any Baptists in the world. Why is this? I give my deliberate judgment that it is largely because, following the trend of politics, Southern Baptists have been insulated. We have been for two generations mostly in the ditch. We have been fighting to keep things out, with the inevitable result, a lack of a robust spirit of conquest necessary to the highest development of any people. We have orthodoxy, for which I am profoundly grateful, for orthodoxy is something that we must all the time exercise great care about, lest we lose it. There has been a large feeling, that we must keep ourselves away from contamination. We will try to take care of the salt and in order that the salt may be pure we want to keep it away from the things that need saving by the salt. Just at this point, the attitude of the Southern mind has been that of the army in the ditch. Our need is an aggressive orthodoxy, an orthodoxy that strikes out for large fields of conquest everywhere, and in that way we will grow. We are all very heroic people, but sometimes we act very much as the Irishman about whom my good friend Dr. Bernard, of Georgia, tells. This son of Erin was wont to speak often and vociferously of the great national spirit of Ireland and of their courage. "There are one hundred thousand Irishmen, ready to fight for Ireland," he vociferated. A by-stander said, "Well, why do they not fight." " 'Fraid of the perlice," was the reply.

I would like to see Southern Baptists get out of the ditch, and take the field. Let us march straight out. If anybody wants to come among us and preach, let him come. If he preaches the truth we will receive it. If he does not, we will refute it, but let us push the conquest in every direction. As we do this, our people will develop. There will grow up among us a consciousness of power. Our institutions will become great. Just at this point let me remark, that our Southern institutions can never become great institutions by refusing to receive and engraft the best thoughts of the world. The same is true of every interest with which we are connected. We need to drop the sectional feeeling and get out of the sectional attitude and expand our enterprises, not as against something else, but for themselves.

All this correlates with a line of Scripture teaching, "Whoever seeks to save his life shall lose it." All religious people, whose plans are broad for the blessing of the world, will save themselves in saving others. The whole New Testament is aggressive. From every angle it looks outward. Certainly we do not find the apostles in the ditch, but everywhere on the high road to the spiritual conquest of the whole world. Less than this is hurtful. It puts us on converging lines, and, in the end, the people facing inward, will play out.

BY J. B. GAMBRELL, D. D.

COUNTRY MOTHERS.

SOME time ago riding on a Georgia railroad, my attention was attracted to three very handsomely dressed ladies sitting near me. Two of them were young ladies and the third evidently their mother. Two seats were turned together and they were intent on having a good time.

Presently the manner of the daughters directed my attention to the rear—they were facing that way, and I saw what to me was a pathetic scene. There came aboard an old woman, plainly clad in garments made after no particular style, but evidently intended for use and comfort. The old soul had a number of bundles, baskets and what not, about which she showed great concern. It appeared at once that she was wholly unaccustomed to traveling on the cars. Her anxious and skeptical questions, her half frightened look, as we pulled out afforded a great deal of merriment to the fine girls just in front, while their high bred mother bedecked with flashing jewels, quietly enjoyed their remarks.

Reversing my seat, I sat and studied the face of the old woman. It was worth studying. A strong face it was, rugged and not very bright, even for age; but over every feature was thrown that inscribable expression, that indefinable grace, which might go under the sweet name of motherliness. And to the practiced eye there was much reading in the face. Work, hard work, had stoutened her figure, bent under burdens long borne. The face told its tale of a long battle fought nearly to a finish. There you could see candor, truth, honesty, discreteness, meekness, simplicity and the charity that never faileth. All these played on a back ground of strong purpose and high courage. And what was pathetic to my eye was the traces of suffering mingling with every expression of her countenance. I knew her—her name! No; but I knew she was a country mother going some where to see a child. The last I knew, by the things she had with her. As I sat there and watched the dear old mother, and noticed the nervous twitching of her hands, the little alarms flashing into her face as the car made some unusual motion, all very amusing to the lighthearted girls near me, the tears came to my eyes, and I found myself transported to the country home where many of the happiest days of my life have been spent. My mind ran on country mothers and what they have been worth to the world. They make no stir in the fashionable world. Their work is not often written up in the papers, and their names never appear in print, except perhaps in the obituary columus of our religious papers. They are for the most part, women of limited education. All their life time they have worked under difficulties. Some of them lived their days out without a single breathing spell from their ceaseless daily task.

But these country mothers are among the world's greatest heroines and benefactors. They have fulfilled the Scriptures in multiplying and replenishing the earth. They have not known many of the finest things to be known, but the noblest and best things they have known well. They do not shine at the theater, or the ball, or at the elegant dinner party; but they are a power in the prayer meeting, the protracted service and wherever duty calls them. They know but little of literature, but they know considerable of the Bible, and believe it to the very hilt. Their children are taught to fear God and obey their parents. They are upright and downright. They know what the trimmings of the peach orchard are good for, among a lot of children. No fancy theories of nature beguile them from the stubborn facts before their eyes. Around the evening fireside, under the spreading trees, out among the cattle, in the garden they have planted in the hearts of their children the rudimental principles of all greatness and goodness. They have toiled, stinted and shifted to give their children some advantages in the world.

And with what result? Well, nearly every great man, whose name graces American history was the son of a country mother. Washington, Lee, Jefferson, Madison, Jackson, Lincoln and all the rest pretty much. Lincoln said, "All I am, my mother made me," and his mother was a poor, hard working Baptist country mother. Nearly all the greatest preachers, lawyers, statesmen, bank and college presidents, railroad men, merchants—indeed the overwhelming majority of the governing men of these States today, were spanked and kissed by country mothers. They can look back and say with Lincoln, what I am, my mother made me. History hardly shows one great and good man who had a weak and sorry mother.

I do not underrate the fathers. They have done nobly; but a father can do but little with his children without the mother. This is said without the least sympathy with the present fashion of throwing the training of the family on the mother while the father goes free. They must work together, the father in the lead; but the mother must bring up the rear.

This is written for the praise of the makers of our country, by one who loves them well, and feels the dignity and grandeur of their work. May they be multiplied in the land. I look with profound sorrow upon the breaking up of our country homes. They are the true nurseries of our country's greatness and the landmarks of our safety.

Let country mother's continue their work in love and faith, and wherever there are true hearts among men and women, let them pay tribute to these makers of greatness.

A little incident brought out a view, a true view of the elegant ladies to my right. The old mother thought she had lost some of her belongings and become distressed. At once the girls were all sympathy and attention till the dear old soul was composed. They were true women, though in all probability they will never do half as much for the world as the rough handed woman whose solicitude they had gently quieted.

CONCERNING MULES.

IT HAS been a great question with many people, why mules are just like they are. The interest in the question of mules is revived just now because some months ago the English government, foreseeing a war in the Transvaal, sent agents over to America, and especially into the Southern country, to buy up mules for service in Africa. They took them over and trained them to artillery service. One of the first real battles of the war, the mules, with that peculiar uncertainty that you are always certain exists, ran off with the artillery and left the English there holding their hands, and the result was the English got badly used up. It is said of a mule, that the only certainty about it is its absolute uncertainty. They never get too old for tricks, but just what sort of a trick it will be next time is the thing that nobody knows.

Profound meditation on the uncertainty of this animal led Josh Billings to moralize and philosophize after this manner: "Young man, never take an unnecessary risk. If I were called on to mourn over a dead mule, I would stand at the head and do my weeping there." It is not certain when a mule has given his last kick.

Now, the question arises, what makes a mule like he is? He is a cross between two species, each of which is docile and reliable. The philosophy of it lies in the want of a definite direction given to the life of the mule. There are two streams of blood in his veins, running cross, and not knowing exactly what he is, whether an ass or a horse, he vacillates and never takes a definite course in life.

BY J. B. GAMBRELL, D. D.

Now the Question Arises, "What Makes a Mule Like He is?"

This same natural law obtains among all mixed people. The Mongrel nations are proverbially uncertain. They have not settled their traditions. They have not settled their habits of thought. Their feelings have not worked out definite grooves or channels along which to flow. They are like flooded districts in time of high water. The currents run and clash, and work out little channels, but, after a while, make for themselves definite channels. The American nation is great, largely because of the infusion of new and alien blood upon a sturdy Anglo-Saxon stock. But, in those portions of America where there is no dominant type, as in certain districts in great cities, which live within themselves, there is trouble. Very much of the wildness of thought in certain sections in the North results from the cross between different nationalities. The hopefulness of the situation there lies in the fact that the old American type is still dominant, and through schools and other means, likely to continue so. To come back now to the mule. The mule is a born kicker. That is his highest gift, and that is an expression of his unregulated and unsatisfactory nature. He is an animal of all whims and humors, and uncertain moods. Every such animal is a kicker, whether he be man or beast.

Pursuing the underlying thought further we come upon the reason why denominational hybrids are so unsatisfactory. A straight Methodist counts for something. He builds up his church. He stands for spiritual religion. He stands, as a rule, for good citizenship. He stands for order. But a hybrid Methodist, one who is half Methodist and half something else, or half nothing; who is with his church at one point and not at another; who gets out as a kind of connecting link between his church and everything else in the world—he is a most unsatisfactory man any way you take him. He does little or nothing for his church, and manages to give the people who are doing something, more trouble by all odds than he is worth. Perhaps he is an evangelist, and has grown entirely too big for his church. Or he is an editor. Or he is a local preacher. You will find him kicking all the time. If he is a Presbyterian, half and half, it is the same sort of thing. If he is a Baptist mule, by as much as there is positiveness in the Baptist theology, you will find him one of the worst kickers in the world. A Baptist, and yet not a Baptist. A Baptist who half believes the Baptist doctrine and three-fourths don't believe it. Right in between, he is, running now with the Baptists, then backing off like a mule, when you come down to real service. The unruliest denominational mule in the world is a cross between a Baptist and a Methodist. There is vim on both sides. He is now very forward in going backwards and now very backwards in going forwards.

Drawing closer within denominational lines, the missionary mule, the man who is half Hardshell and half Missionary is a hard type to get on with. There is something about the genuine Hardshell that is exceedingly winsome to a man of my way of thinking. His candor, even his bluntness; the tenacity with which he holds on to certain great truths; the little concern he has for what other people think; the sublime indifference to great movements; his perfect satisfaction with himself and his doctrines. A well ordered Hardshell is a man you can live neighbor to a lifetime and enjoy him, and depend on him. Then, a thoroughgoing missionary, a man who believes in it with all of his heart; who spells the "go" in the commission with capital letters, and puts it in the lead of everything in the commission; the man who has no reservations; who is a missionary in heart and practice, all over and all through—he is a delightful man. You will not have much trouble with him anywhere. He is not a kicker. He is a puller. But strike a medium between the Hardshell and Missionary, and get one with Missionary streaks and Hardshell streaks. Now, he flames out as a Missionary under a powerful missionary appeal. Now, he backs off when some objection is made. He is hot now, and next he is cold. If such a missionary mule lives in a place where there are many objectors prodding him, he will spend all of his time kicking. And, as he kicks, kicking becomes more a habit with him and he enjoys it. My father had an old mule that was in such a habit of kicking that she would put her ears back, shut her eyes, and kick at June-bugs if she heard the noise of them. That was in her old age, when much kicking had made a groove in her life along which her perverse nature had a constant flow.

The trouble with Missionary Baptists is not with the thoroughbreds, but those that are just half and half, and don't know very well why they are the better half. A process of evolution out of this condition is the thing that is most needed in our churches. Bring our people to Missionary views, and the kicking will be done.

BY J. B. GAMBRELL, D. D.

CONCERNING CRITICISMS AND LIMITATIONS.

THE right to criticise public men and measures is inherent in every American citizen. It belongs necessarily to the realm of freedom, and it is freedom's greatest safeguard. Free speech is a condition of liberty, and without it free institutions cannot long exist. One able, fearless pen is worth more to a people than a great army.

Among Baptists free speech and a free press are indispensable. For myself, I regard these as such important adjuncts to our democratic free system, that I prefer even great abuse of both free speech and a free press to the least limitation of either. The right to criticise belongs to every Baptist, no matter how humble. It is a fireside right, belonging to all alike. I would not belong to any Baptist body, nor serve any board where this right is denied. In my place as Secretary of the Texas Baptist General Convention, be it understood that any Baptist in the State, or out of it, can criticise me, if he wishes to do so. When he does, if his criticism is just, I will improve. If it is not, I will bear it, or answer it—likely bear it.

But what is criticism? Everything which goes under that name is not criticism by any means. Criticism has in it a fine element of judgment. It implies that the critic has considered the facts touching the case, at least some of them, and delivered a judgment on them. This is a reasonable business and a very fine business, too. It is broadly differentiated from several other employments to which certain orders of human beings devote themselves. Some of these differences invite criticism, so we may have criticism on criticism. In times of loose use of tongue and ink the public mind may be educated by a critical discusion. Criticism in its legitimate use and its abuse, or more properly speaking its displacement by something else, illegitimate and hurtful. At points the abandonment of criticism for some gross counterfeit may be hard to detect. One may shade into the other in such manner as to mislead the un-

The Destructive Critic.

critical mind. In most cases of abuse and apostasy from the high function of criticism to the base use of counterfeits, a reasonably clear mind need not be deceived. Here are some practices known to the public which are fraudulent and do not rank as criticisms.

To make up a case against an adversary out of the odds and ends of things, and represent the other party as holding these things in that form, and then to proceed to criticise him on the basis of your own creation is not criticism, but fraud. It is often a dignified, subtle kind of lying and slander. This is making a straw man, giving him the other man's name, and then tearing him to pieces. This is a common trick of tricky disputers, and they call it criticising the other party. It is mental dishonesty and essential falsehood. Close akin to the foregoing is the practice of interpreting the words of another contrary to their real meaning, and then criticising the false interpretation as the doctrine of the other party. That is, also, essentially dishonest, and is not criticism, but juggling in a lying spirit. There are many plain abuses of the respectable word "criticism," practiced on a long-suffering public. For instance, a man gives columns on columns in his paper to insinuating evil thoughts touching a man or an enterprise. His paper or his speech teems with evil surmises. This is not criticism, It is total depravity, exuding from a debased nature. Bald accusation and robust denunciation are not criticism. A man shooting at another with intent to hurt is not a critic. Likely he is a plain murderer. A man putting a cross-tie on the railroad track to derail the train is not a critic of the train. He is a criminal wrecker. An agitator is not a critic. A man crying "wolf, wolf," when there is no wolf and he knows it, is not a critic. Likely he is a lying idler and mischief-maker. A man seeking to burn a house is not a critic of the house. If the house is useless and in the way, maybe, it ought to be burned; but house-burning is not criticism. There is another name for it. A dog barking at the moon is not a critic, nor astronomer either. He is a howler.

In like manner, people who keep up a howl against things too high for them are not critics. A boy in school who is ever watching for a chance to stick a pin in his fellows is not a critic, but an imp, greatly needing a vigorous rear attack with a shingle or some such useful adjunct to the teacher's equipment. Editors of the painstaking variety are not critics. Objection is not criticism. The man who wrote—

>"I do not like you Dr. Fell,
>The reason why I cannot tell;
>But one thing I know very well,
>I do not like you Dr. Fell"

was no critic of Dr. Fell. He was simply disgruntled.

There is not a worse abused word in the English language than the word criticism. Every ailing church member, who vents his bad feelings on the pastor or deacons or Sunday-school workers, calls himself a critic. Every sorehead in the denomination, who feels like venting his bad feelings on the work or the workers, writes "Critic" on his hatband, and demands recognition as a critic with leave, without responsibility, to drip the filth of his heart over everybody. He don't know himself. Likely he is only an ill-conditioned complainer whose words are echoes from his disordered imagination. Criticism is a fine thing; a disordered heart and mind are bad things. These are wide apart. Bad feelings never rank as good criticisms, no matter how vociferously proclaimed.

In literature critics are classified as constructive or conservative critics, and destructive critics.

A train pulls up to a division station and stops. You may see a man take a small hammer and go along under the side of the train tapping every wheel. He knows by the ring whether there is a flaw in the wheel which would make it dangerous on the next run. He is a conservative critic. His judgment or criticism of each wheel is based on the tone. This is a thoroughly useful man and a sound critic. Here is another critic. He has a sledge hammer. He is bent on knowing all about it. He must see the metal dissolve it, apply acids to test its fineness, and so he smashes every wheel he can get a good lick at with his great hammer. He is a destructive critic, and ought to be locked up in the first police station in the interest of the public. Of these two sorts are our Biblical critics. One tests the Scriptures sympathetically, and to the intent that the Word may be made clearer. He trims the lamp, removes obstructing, human excrescences, that it might shine brighter. The other puts out the lamp and seeks to analyze every essence and element for the sake of doing it. There is a difference between the two. There are critics in the realm of life. One studies the phenomena of life and reasons to a conclusion. The other betakes himself to vivisection and destroys life in the study of it.

The destructive critic is not popular any where. For one, I have no more use for him with the Bible than I had for the boy who smashed a watch with a hammer to see what it was that made the "click" in it. The destructive denominational critic, who wants to upset the old doctrines and modernize theology to suit the age is to my thinking worse than a nuisance; he is a curse. He thinks because he knows some things plain men don't know, it is an outrage on free speech and the right to criticise, that he is not allowed to use Baptist pulpits and Baptist papers in his business. I don't agree with him there, nor anywhere else. His right to speak is granted; but plain believers have a right to protect the Ark of the Covenant. We here strike an important limitation on the use of a right. The man who criticises destructively the doctrines and practices of a church, may do it, if he wishes to do it; but the church is not bound to pay him to do it, nor give him facilities for doing it. There is where I stand. There is lots of room outside of a Baptist church, thank God, for talk, even the loose talk of loose men.

We are right up to the place to make another point on limitations. A church member who criticises the church, the pastor or officers destructively, with the intent to hinder the work of that church, transcends the limits of legitimate criticism, and is amenable to church discipline. A case comes to mind this moment. There was a deacon—rich, supercilious, satirical and bossified. No pastor whom he could not control could remain pastor of that church. When he saw that his control was at an end, he began his destructive criticisms. Nothing escaped. A word mispronounced, the slightest defect in arrangement of the sermon, anything, everything, till the preacher could bear it no longer, and resigned. On the streets, any and everywhere, he lamented the imperfections of the pastor, and bemoaned the low condition of the church. The ungodly were turned away, the feeble-minded were discouraged, the pious grieved, and a general bad condition of affairs brought about. This occurred over and over, till at last the church heroically faced its trouble and brought him to judgment. Was that church opposed to free speech? No; it was opposed to the abuse of it. Was the right of criticism denied? No, the right of the deacon to use his place in the church for the destruction of the church was denied. He could criticise all he wanted outside, and the church would not say a word, but he could not abuse his privileges as a church member by using them to destruction.

The same rule applies to every organization known to men. Any citizen can criticise and denounce the Democratic policies and leaders, if he wishes to do so, but he has no right to employ destructive methods with his party and remain a member of it. This applies to conventions and associations, keeping in mind the difference between the man with the little hammer and the man with the big hammer. Let the man with the big hammer go out and break rocks for Mr. McAdam, rather than pound to bits the machinery designed for use in carrying on the good work of missions. Calling destructive and obstructive methods criticism won't mend car-wheels, nor forward the richly freighted trains of commerce.

Criticism is an inalienable right. It belongs alike to all; but like everything else, it can be abused, and has been, scandalously. It gives no one the right to lie in any form. It gives no one the right to obstruct what he is morally bound to forward. In short, it is closely hedged about by the common moral obligations and proprieties attending human life, and like all privileges, it is to be used to edification, not for destruction.

FURTHER CONCERNING CRITICISM.

THIS article is given as a supplement to the one which appeared last week. It is intended to give a fuller view of an important question. It is not the purpose to develop a logical discussion of the question, but rather to look at certain facets of it.

A critic, if he be sound minded and of a healthy soul, will exercise his gifts to discover and recommend the good, rather than the bad. Every reasonable person is a critic, but he need not be a fault-finder. Ruskin was a matchless art critic. His fine talents were employed in the delightful task of delineating the excellencies of art, and commending them to those who needed the eyes of an art prophet to discover these beauties to them. Pessimism is not to any extent a qualification for criticism. The spirit that loves to find fault makes true criticism impossible, because it perverts the taste and blinds the soul. It turns out that the people most known as critics are mere carpers, who degrade their own senses in response to the impulse of a darkened heart.

There can be no true criticism, except from a proper standpoint. One must really feel the thing he says and understand the thing he criticises. The criticisms of unregenerate people passed on the regenerate are as valueless as the criticisms of men would be on the angels of God. They live in different worlds. They have not the same feelings, and there is no common standard of judgment. It is this that makes the criticisms of widely separated classes of society on each other valueless. They lack a fair basis.

This should put us all on guard, as to our judgments of other people. We can know at most only in part. God alone, who knows everything, can pass final judgment.

Passing from these general observations, and coming to the common use of the word critic or criticism, let us note some important considerations.

The critical or fault-finding attitude of the mind is one of the greatest possible drawbacks to both happiness and usefulness. It robs the critic of a thousand sweets, and utterly destroys his power for good. In a party of ministers the conversation turned on the career of a brother of more than common culture, ability and brilliancy. "Why is it that he has not succeeded better?" was asked. A brother said: "The answer is easy. He is the sharpest critic I ever knew. He criticises everything from a Greek verb to the color of a lady's ribbons. Nothing escapes his keen eye and sharp tongue. Everybody soon expects to be put on the dissecting table every time they meet him and people first fear him, then hate him." There was truth in every word of it. The brother had cultivated a habit of adverse criticism of every thing he talked about. The tone of his mind was like a keen acid. It corroded his spirit and gave pain to those whom he, in all reason, was appointed to help. Such a man was the gifted Dean Swift.

BY J. B. GAMBRELL, D. D.

This habit of adverse criticism, when it becomes chronic, destroys the finer feelings of the critic and disqual-

Did You Notice How He Murdered the Queens' English.

ifies him for seeing and enjoying the nobler and better things of life. It sadly deteriorates the character and works harm, not so much to the things criticised, as in the critic himself. Two illustrations come to mind. I have used them both before this. When that great masterpiece of art, "The Christ" by Corregio, was on exhibition in Cincinnati, two men stood before it, side by side, each holding his own peculiar attitude of mind toward it. It was a marvelous production. The artist had put his soul on the canvas. Approaching the picture, it seemed a rather rough, unfinished work of art; but as you stood before it, the Christ seemed to come out in front of the canvas and beam on you with a look divine. One of the beholders was a soulful Irishman, with a reverent spirit. His bosom swelled with emotion, as he drank in the inspiration of the artist. In the midst of his silent rapture, his companion nudged him, and called his attention to a fly speck on the canvas. In an outbreak of indignation, the Irishman cried out, "Kill him! kill him! kill him!" To what good purpose did the man with an eye for a fly speck see one of the world's greatest pictures? Indeed, he did not see, and could not, because of an awful perverted nature.

Here is the other illustration. It was at a coutry preaching. The congregation was large. A great country preacher had the hour. His theme was as high as the heavens, and he handled it with the hand of a great master. The sermon was great by every rule of judgment, but the preacher having failed of an early education, right frequently made grammatical blunders. Beside me sat a young school teacher. I was lifted out of myself and carried toward the third heaven. The preacher had closed and a profound silence, broken only by the sobs of devout worshippers, succeeded. My teacher brother turned and said, "Did you notice how he murdered the queen's English?" It was horrible. Such a man would starve, if God were to send him bread from heaven by the hand of an angel, unless there chanced to be no speck on the angel or his raiment. A great occasion had come to every soul in that great company, but the attitude of this man's mind was such as to prevent his receiving the least benefit. Is not such a man an **unspeakable** fool with all his grammar?

There are optimistic critics and they **are both** useful and happy. They see the good and go for it with a hearty appetite. L. Q. C. Lamar used to tell of an old maid aunt who always saw the good in everybody and everything. Her habit was never to say a hard thing of any one, nor to complain at anything. At a family gathering, a scheme was formed to make her break her long established habit. The company were to discuss the devil, and finally to force her to give an opinion of him. At the opportune moment Mr. Lamar said: "Aunty, what do you think of **the devil?**" "Well, Lucius, he is a very industrious old gentleman. We might all learn a good lesson from him on that point." They had her opinion, and she maintained her habit.

Where criticisms are just, and should be made, it is often of the utmost importance that we avoid making them till just the right time comes. It is needless to say, that perfection does not belong to humanity. There are no perfect preachers, or deacons, or as to that, church members. It is not hard to find a ground, great or less, for criticising adversely the pastor of your church. If the matters are trivial it is commonly best to let them pass without even letting him know you observe the defects. If it is your duty to criticise him, it will do no good to do this to others. It should be done in tenderness to him. It should never be done in the home before children. Many parents have put it out of the power of the preacher to help their children by thoughtless criticisms made in their presence. It is a thing distressingly common and dreadfully hurtful.

The same rule holds among church members. There are churches languishing today, and thoroughly discredited in the community, because the members have talked each other down. Every weakness and misstep of a brother has been ventilated before the unbelievers till Christianity itself is discredited. It is a great mistake to think that the two main things in church discipline is a keen knife and plenty of caustic. There is not a perfectly sound human body in the world. The healthiest body has microbes in it; but a pegging awl to extract them is not the remedy. Richer blood and better sanitary conditions will beat all the surgical instruments in the surgeon's case, with all the nitrate of silver in the drug stores.

Finally, adverse criticism has its place, and at times we must open sores down to the very bone. But the main function of criticism is to reveal the good in the clearest possible light, and to make it attractive. The world advances on affirmations, not negations. You cannot sweep darkness out of your house; but the darkness disappears the instant you bring in the light.

BY J. B. GAMBRELL, D. D.
PLAIN LESSONS FROM A LOVING WRITER.

ONE of the shortest, most loving and most unique of the New Testament writings is John's third epistle. It covers a very small space. It was written by that apostle who occupies on every occasion a pre-eminence of spirituality. The Gospel by John deals with Christianity in its deep spiritual meaning, and John is always thought of as the loving disciple. He writes this third letter when he is an old man, full of tenderness and love. Nearly all of it gathers around three characters.

First he is writing to Gains, a beloved layman, no doubt. He makes for this faithful brother a remarkable wish; that above all things he might prosper and be in good health, even as his soul prospered. Evidently Gaius was a faithful brother in poor health and the Apostle John is concerned about his health. He commends him because the truth is in him, and because he walks in the truth, and be-love of truth and the faithful performance of truth were the foundation of the excellent character of the beloved Gaius. It was this love of truth that filled him with charity, and gave him such excellent report "before the church," and inspired him to Christian activity. An excellent lesson is taught us here. The love of truth is the only foundation of good character. The man who is thoroughly willing to know the truth and walk in it is saved from a dozen pitfalls, and on such a foundation a bad character can never be built. We greatly err if we seek to substitute mere sentimentalism for downright love of truth, even though the truth may be ofttimes rugged, and always immovable. Nothing will take the place of truth, and it is because many do not come to the truth, and do not want to know the full truth about things and are not willing to walk in the truth, that they drift about and finally come to nothing.

Gaius is a charming character, a model of Christian

faithfulness, broad-mindedness and helpfulness, which we may all imitate with advantage. We can never think of Gaius as even a possible demagogue, offensive, double-minded, double-tongued, half-right half-wrong, and then all wrong. We think of him as a candid, frank, open, straightforward, noble man, whose love of the truth was innate, and whose support of the truth was straight-forward and open before all men. May his tribe multiply.

The next character in the brief letter is Diotrephes, "who loveth to have the pre-eminence among them." His tribe has already increased beyond all the wants of the human race, and greatly to the disturbance of the churches and the hindering of the cause. The brief record shows that the Apostle John had written to the church of which Diotrephes was a member. Certain brethren on a mission were to visit the church, doubtless, to secure help and co-operation in the general work which was going on at that time, aided by the churches. Doubtless also these brethren who were sent were men of mark and of force. They were such men as good people would like to hear; but Diotrephes, looking at the whole matter of religion from a personal standpoint, making himself the center of all calculations, theories, plans and policies, would have none of them. He was on the ground. The brethren who were coming were at a great disadvantage with reference to such a man as Diotrephes. He could work up his crowd, and he did. So, when the brethren got there, they found that they could not get a hearing before the church. They were completely forestalled, and there stood, as the center of a group of malcontents and kickers, this unsavory Diotrephes.

We have an inkling of his methods. He was given to "prating" against the workers "with malicious words." That sounds like an echo of things that have occurred since, and are still occurring. Prating. Stop a moment to think of that word. It means to mouth, and complain and to say much without saying much. It means that human language is used not to express principles or doctrines or truth, but to express bad feelings, and hence the "malicious words." He not only was given over to this mouthing against the workers of his period, but he brought things to the point that the brethren were not received. And, not content with that, he brought it about that those who did receive them were cast out of the church. Here is a picture for you of a self-assertive, mouthing, godless demagogue, using his place in a church of Jesus Christ for his own pre-eminence.

The next character is Demetrius. Not much is said of him, but it is all good. "He hath good report of all men and of the truth itself." That is to say, the conduct and general life of Demetrius corresponded with the truth, and the apostle himself was glad to bear record to his good character. Passing from Demetrius in a few words, the old apostle closes his brief letter with the hope that he should soon see the beloved Gaius and speak to him face to face, with a tenderness and thoughtfulness that is beautiful. His last words are: "Peace be to thee. Our friends salute thee. Greet the friends by name."

Now let us get a few general lessons out of this brief letter, and the first is, that the most spiritually-minded and loving of characters may, and did on occasions, speak the exact truth about men and things. The New Testament is pre-eminently a book of plain dealing. Here was a situation to be met. Here was a church being greatly hurt by one evil-minded man. The most loving of the apostles went into the situation in a thorough-going way to clarify the atmosphere. We make a great mistake when we cultivate nervousness to the point that we can not speak the truth in our churches, or anywhere else, if that truth impinges on somebody. There is no place for people's nerves and feelings in the kingdom of God if they stand in the way of the progress of the truth. In this world the truth itself has the right-of-way.

And here is another lesson. In dealing with situations it is perfectly correct to call names and to award men by name, praise or condemnation, according as they deserve. It is beautiful, John's thoughtful care of the faithful men mentioned in this letter. Paul finishes the greatest of all the epistles, his letter to the Romans, by making particular mention of many, and specifying services, some of them seemingly very small services which they had rendered to him and to the cause. It is right to speak of those publicly, in print, who do well. There is lack of proper care among us for the faithful toilers who are doing the best they can.

Right over on the other side, how straight-forward was the apostle's dealing with Diotrephes! He held him up to the contempt of the ages as a model of a class of men who would infest churches all through time; men who love the pre-eminence, and who are willing to thrust their personalities forward, their personal interests, their personal views, their personal popularity, anything personal to themselves, thrust it anywhere, and do it all in the name of religion. It is time we had an eye on these men, in the churches and elsewhere, who gather about them the most unspiritual and less devoted of the churches, and build up a personal following, and thrust themselves in the way of workers. If Diotrephes, by the pen of an inspired and loving apostle, was held up to all eternity for his conduct, why should not the same thing be done over and over again as often as the conduct of men demand it? Plain speech in the churches today, and in many of our associations as to men's ungodly conduct, in seeking the pre-eminence at the sacrifice of the truth, would mightily clear the atmosphere and make way for peace and progress.

There is great danger of people's getting mixed re-

BY J. B. GAMBRELL, D. D.

garding plain speech concerning evil-doers, as personal wars on men. It may be admitted that the two things may be very easily run together, but it must also be affirmed that a lofty and pure desire to see the cause prosper will compel honest men, who have to deal with ugly situations to come out with the truth about men, and there need be no going around about it. Let the names of the men be mentioned, and truth set down against them, and let it stand there for God and men and angels to read. This would be apostolic. To assail men for personal reasons would be an immense fall from the highest position from which the apostle wrote about this evil-doer in an ancient church. But to make it impossible for evil men to ruin churches is to render service to God and men.

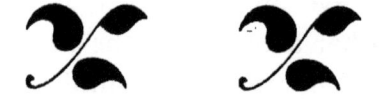

CONCERNING CHURCH GOVERNMENT.

DR. CHALMERS, of Scotland, the most eminent Presbyterian of his day, has been quoted as saying: "The best church government for the ignorant is the hierarchal. The best for people advanced well in self-control is the Presbyterian. The best for those who have attained to full self-control is the congregational. Dr. Broadus said: "The congregational form of government is the best possible for converted people, and the worst possible for unconverted people." These two eminent brethren saw things from different standpoints. Dr. Chalmers had a vein of philosophy running through his thinking. Dr. Broadus put the whole question in the clear light of Scripture. An American statesman—not a politician, a statesman—said: "That is the best government which governs the least possible." Here, then, are three sayings concerning government. The Christian Advocate, after referring to our recent trouble in Texas, says:

"All of these manifestations of strife and discord grow out of the fact that the Baptist church has adopted a system of government utterly inadequate to meet the emergencies now confronting it. It is at the mercy of a few of its leaders, who are a law unto themselves. We therefore see nothing in the system of government practiced by the Baptist church worthy of our adoption. The condition of things brought about by it in that communion is utterly impossible in the government and usage of the Methodist church. If then we are to be accused by our neighbor of The Standard of 'tyranny in the concrete,' we prefer to permit this so-called tyranny to abide with one man, around whom we have placed wholesome restrictions, rather than invest it in an incongruous mob. From the former we get peace and love in the brotherhood; but from the latter our unfortunate Baptist brethren get strife, contention and criminal and civil lawsuits. In view of these things, we are more than ever disposed to look with favor upon the workings of our admirable system of law and order."

Upon this it is pertinent to remark that peace, valuable as we may regard it, is not the chief end of man. There is more peace and order in a graveyard than any other place in this country. And many churches are spiritual graveyards. Our Lord did not come to bring peace, but a sword. It is possible to pay too much for peace.

All of this brings up an old controversy, which, to my thinking, ought to be settled by an old Book. If we could understand it, God has saved us a great deal of thinking by doing the thinking for us; doing it right, of course, and giving us the result of His thoughts.

As between the congregational form of government and the hierarchal, or to come at once to the plane of our good neighbor, the Advocate, between the government of the Baptists and the Methodists, I am ready to admit at once that the monarchical form of government is just the thing for an unconverted church membership, if it is worth while to have churches made up that way. I do not think, however, it is worth while to have such churches. The New Testament, which is a compendium of divine thought on these questions, about which men think so much and so variantly, does not contemplate churches made up of the enemies of God and righteousness, but on the contrary, it everywhere contemplates churches composed of regenerated and obedient people, though not perfect. The Advocate says: "We prefer to permit this so-called tyranny to abide with one man, around whom we have placed wholesome restrictions, rather than invest it in an incongruous mob." If the people composing a church can be counted an "incongruous mob," why, then, certainly, language has come to a bad use. Waiving that, however, the Advocate likes the monarchical form of government in church matters. We shall not quarrel with the Advocate. If he likes to live under a monarchical government in religion, then, that is the thing that suits him, and he has a right to his preference. Many good people do prefer it. However, in his judgment in this matter he seriously disagrees with high authorities, as witness the following facts: When our Lord was teaching on this very question of troubles He gave directions for settling them after a spiritual manner. The offended brother must go to his brother, and if he fails, take another brother with him, and if that fail tell it to the church, and if the offending brother will not hear the church, then his is to cut off. There was no instruction to tell it to "one man" hedged with restrictions, but to the church. Dr. Rankin can find some excellent reading in the 18th of Matthew on this point, all which will go to show that Christ had more regard to the church, the whole congregation, than He had to any "one man," no matter how hedged about. And again, when the church at Corinth was in disorder, the Apostle Paul gave some important instructions as to how they were to do. He did not send these instructions to "one man" with restrictions, but he sent them to the church, and he put it on the church to purify itself. Paul agreed with Jesus Christ in this. Again, in his third letter, John tells us that he wrote to the church about certain men, who were to visit the church, and that one, Diotrephes—an unsavory scamp he was, who loved to have pre-eminence among the brethren—would not receive them, and he would not allow others to receive them, but he cast those who would receive them out of the church. John's instructions very significantly avoided any reference to the appointment of "one man" to take charge of Diotrephes and the unruly members of that church. This shows that John agreed with his Master and with Paul that the "one man" with restrictions was not a remedy for troubles in churches.

By J. B. Gambrell, D. D.

There is another singular illustration of the variance of the apostolic mind from the line of thought which holds our neighbor to his monarchical form of church government. Paul and an excellent brother started out on a missionary tour. This other brother had a nephew, whom he desired to take along with him. This young man had become faint-hearted on a former occasion, and quit the work, going back to Jerusalem to his mother. Paul did not agree to take him. The two had a sharp contention about it. The result of it was they separated. Now, if Paul and Barnabas and the others in that day believed in this "one man" with restrictions, they would have had him somewhere, and this contention between the two missionary workers would have gone up for decision by some hierarch, and the two brethren would have had it settled for them. However, there seems to have been a great lack of the "one man" in that day, and they settled it by parting, just as Baptists have been doing, more or less, ever since. All of these instances are of New Testament record, and will make excellent reading for Dr. Rankin, and may occupy his leisure hours with profitable meditation.

From them it may be most assuredly gathered that God does not sanction the "one man" idea in the church. Obedience to the Divine Word is the fundamental doctrine of Baptists on this, as on all other questions, and so we do not feel under any great burden of thought, and do not consider it an open question any more than is Christian baptism, or the Lord's Supper.

We repeat, God has done an abundance of thinking for us, relieving us of the burden of it, and leaving us more time to obey.

Still, holding fast to the doctrine of obedience as a doctrine never to be waived for a moment in the face of any human reasoning, we may, nevertheless, think upon the question which Dr. Rankin opens up as a practical question among men. Indulging in some meditations on the general question, I would say: I go on record as being totally adverse to belonging to a political organization in any country or to any church organization that cannot have a fuss. Not for one moment would this writer belong to a church that could not have a fuss. Not because he likes a fuss, but he likes the room and the freedom of thought that make a fuss possible. These are essential to the highest development. Any one can see at a glance that the Advocate's doctrine, applied to politics, would commit this government to monarchy. Politically, this writer does not want monarchy in America, and religiously, he does not want monarchy anywhere. He believes more in all the people than he does in any "one man," with all the restrictions that some other men can put around him.

There is a story of an amateur sailor, who, being out on the water, noticed that the needle of the compass kept shaking about. He had an idea that it ought to point directly north, and not move, and, as the needle kept swinging, he became dissatisfied with it, took up the top of the box, made wedges and chugged it in on each side, and then, with great satisfaction, said: "Now, I reckon you'll stay right." The compass was better if the needle did swing than it was wedged in hard and fast. The truth is, the easy swing of the needle gave it its value.

While the New Testament everywhere lays down the qualifications for church membership, and always contemplates a converted church membership, there is abundant evidence that some unconverted people would get into the church, and that converted people would not be altogether sanctified. There would, therefore, be an amount of the world and the flesh to deal with in churches. Now, the real philosophy of self-governing churches is that by a free and equal exercise of all privileges, the tendency is constantly toward purification. A good many years ago I saw

BY J. B. GAMBRELL, D. D.

a cartoon. It was called "Boiling Politics." There was a log fire out doors, and a number of large kettles placed along. At one end they were boiling English politics. Queen Victoria, with a cook apron on, and her prime minister were doing their utmost to hold the top on, and keep everything in. Next was German politics. The old Emperor William and Bismark, with grimaces and contortions of countenance, were doing their best to hold the lid of the pot down, and so all along. But, underneath the edge of the lids of the pots, was an overflow spurting out. At the remote end of the log fire was "Uncle Sam" boiling his politics. He was sitting down with one thumb in the arm hole of his vest, with a pleasing smile on his countenance. The pot was boiling and all the scum rolling off at the top. There was no lid on it at all.

We hope the Advocate will see the point. Baptists have always had fusses. We are going to have more. We commenced with them nearly 1900 years ago. Had them in the apostolic times. Peter and Paul differed, Paul and Barnabas. Diotrephes cut up shines in the church of which he was a member. The church at Corinth got all torn up. Just as long as we are in the world, and especially as long as some of the world gets into the churches, the pot will boil and the scum will go over the top. Everybody will see it, and some will make remarks about it.

I would not be unkind, but, with all the holding down of the lid of the Methodist kettle, there was something that smelt decidedly not very good spurted out from under the edges at Nashville not long ago, and if I read the papers right, good Methodists are sneezing all over the country. We are glad to see how generally Baptists vindicated the Methodists in a trouble that hurt Christianity in general, but one which in no way dishonors that great communion.

Of course it is painful. Some things have happened in Texas in recent years that are painful; but they are very healthful all the same. A great many doctors make the mistake of supposing that symptoms are diseases. Whoever saw a man writhing in pain that did not feel that it is a great pity that a human body was not made that could not be sick. Dr. Rankin, did you ever have the toothache? If you ever did for one half hour you, undoubtedly, thought of the mistake that was made in putting a nerve in a tooth. No. Really it was not a mistake, and the ache was only the warning which nature gave of encroaching and destructive disease. The capacity to suffer is the result of having nerves, but a nerveless body is a dead body.

Beside the purifying effect of commotions among a great, self-governing people, there is another, a decided gain. It is the capacity to die and get out of the way. One of the strongest points about a New Testament church is, that if it gets too much wrong, it dies, and when it dies it falls down and gets out of the way. It disorganizes. The great law of the Almighty Creator, running through all His works, is that disintegration follows death. Two forces struggle in every human body, even the healthiest. One is constructive, the other destructive. When the constructive forces are clearly in the ascendant, there is health. As the destructive forces encroach more and more, there is a lessening of health, and symptoms of sickness. When the destructive forces get in the lead a good time, the vital forces are consumed and there is death. The constructive forces work in two ways; first, constantly throwing off effete and bad matter by the free action of all the functions of the body; and, secondly, by restoring wasted tissues with new matter. That is precisely what comes to a free-acting, self-governing body of Christ, otherwise speaking, a Baptist church.

It would be an awfully unhandy thing if we could not get rid of dead people; if, by some sort of mechanism, they could go on after they were dead, and we had to meet them in the stores and on the streets and on the railroads and everywhere, running by a mechanism controlled by "one man" somehow. Now, it is the glory of the New Testament churches that they can die, and when they die they can disintegrate, go to pieces, and leave room for somebody else. There is no mechanism, there is no hierarchy by which they can be held together after all spiritual life is gone out of them. It is the most appalling fact in all Christendom to-day that church governments hold great bodies of people together without any reference to their spiritual power or life. They are so hedged about, and so articulated that, though they are dead, yet the "one man" can parade the whole thing as a master hand can manipulate a whole bench of dummies. Upon the whole, I am fully persuaded that the divine thinking upon this subject is right.

As to reference to troubles among the Baptists in Texas, they are not the signs of death, but of life. Let the editor of the Advocate see what was done toward missions and education last year. I will send him a Texas Baptist Annual, and he will find good reading in that, as well as in the New Testament. And let him particularly note this: That the great Convention which met in Dallas, which might have looked to him like an "incongruous mob," nevertheless, had its own affairs well in hand. There were messengers freely elected by the free churches of Jesus Christ, from over a thousand churches in Texas, and 74 associations. And when they came to Dallas, having given over $100,000 as their free-will offering to God for the advancement of His cause, they were abundantly able to take care of a turbulent faction. Didn't you observe how it was done, Doctor? The faction was noisy. I will admit it. It was not an edifying spectacle, but, looking away from the faction to the solid, great mass of men and women, upholding the cause of Christ, how handsomely and easily, under a free government, we disposed of the faction! If I were the Archbishop of Canterbury I could admire as fine a thing as was done by our General Convention in the interest of order. It was a great triumph of democracy in religion. A man who could not admire the massive strength of that great, intelligent democratic majority in dealing with an obstreperous faction has not a good eye for a great thing.

The question is entrancing. The further I get into it the more interesting it is, but the article is growing long and I must turn toward a conclusion.

The Doctor is evidently mistaken in this: "All of these manifestations of strife and discord grow out of the fact that the Baptist church has adopted a system of government utterly inadequate to meet the exigences now confronting it." In the first place we never adopted this system of government. It was given to us by the Master before He ascended to glory, and confirmed to us by the apostles, and we have always had it. In the next place the system of government is not the cause of the strife at all. It is an alien and irreligious element that has been worked into the cause, just as Diotrephes got himself into one of the apostolic churches and made trouble. It may be, and always will be, difficult to keep bad men out of the house of God, but subjection to "one man" is not the remedy. The remedy is that which the Scriptures give.

In the next place the Baptists are not only equal to the trouble, but the trouble is uniting us. I feel sure the editor of the Advocate will accept all these remarks in the kindly spirit in which they are made. All of us, whether we believe in monarchy in the kingdom or democracy, need to lay it to heart that it is not churches nor church government that can make good men. Divine grace alone is equal to that. This writer does not agree with Dr. Rankin, nor the Methodist church in its government, but he bears record to the magnificent spirit of the ministry of that great denomination, with which he has been permitted to labor in many ways for the advancement of our common cause. They are men of God, consecrated to the highest purposes of Christian manhood, and I should utterly despise myself if I depreciated them on account of troubles incident to all life. I shall always be ready to lend a brotherly hand in helping them to a higher and better standpoint as to some points of polity and doctrine, but, for their zeal and devotion to what they see to be the truth, I have nothing but unstinted admiration.

And this leads me to a closing remark. There are broad planes of common ground upon which all denominations stand. No Methodist preacher can be hurt in his character and standing without a shadow being thrown upon the ministry of all denominations. No great shame can be put upon the Presbyterian denomination that will not reflect, in the common mind, upon Christianity in general. I have no sympathy with the men in the Presbyterian denomination who have, here and there, at different times, broken asunder the cords of fellowship by introducing doctrines and practices into that fellowship contrary to the standards held by them. I do not believe in the oligarchical or monarchical form of government of the Methodist denomination, but I do not have the slightest respect for any Methodist preacher who, attempting to hold fellowship with that great denomination, makes himself an occasion of strife. If he does not believe with them, there is but one honorable thing for him to do, and that is to get out. And so as to the Catholics. A man who is a Catholic, and has taken on himself the vows of the Catholic church, is in honor bound, on the great principles which govern men in their dealings with each other, to uphold the government of that church, and the order of that church as long as he shares its fellowship. If, in conscience, he cannot do that there is a remedy, and that remedy is for him to get out and go where he belongs. If Dr. Rankin can see the appropriateness of these remarks, and will apply them to the Baptist situation in Texas, at least on that great common ground of Christianity, he and I can stand side by side.

DECISIVE BATTLES IN HUMAN LIFE.

IF ONE is to worry with an enemy on to exhaustion or till one or the other is driven from the field, it is very desirable to seek the earliest advantage and force a decisive battle. This will hasten peace and bring on the era of readjustment. Long wearing wars are followed always by a train of evil influences. They debilitate nations and through continued disorder make the evil results chronic. One great battle would have been vastly better for our country than the four years of the Civil war. The day that saw Waterloo's bloody fray was the best day Europe had seen since the rising of Napoleon's tragic star.

The plan of progress is by epochs. These usually open and close by decisive battles, and this is true in the physical, mental and spiritual world all alike. Growth is by stages. The general truth here discussed is capable of almost endless illustration and application. It invites thought in all its phases; but it is the purpose of this article to discuss decisive spiritual battles. Paul looked on his life as a war. He had fought a good fight. He said at the end of it in the progress of his fighting he had faced nearly every conceivable foe. His fighting was all on one plan. He faced his enemy without faltering and had it out. He never went out of his way to seek a conflict. He was prudent and exceedingly careful to avoid foolish questions, old wives' fables and the like; but when a great moral question was raised he met it in a decisive spirit and settled it.

BY J. B. GAMBRELL, D. D.

Paul's first great spiritual battle was fought on the road to Damascus. The light shone round about him, and brightest of all in his heart. He had believed Jesus an imposter. He was honest in persecuting the saints. There in the road, surrounded by his escort, he was called on to settle the greatest question of his or any man's life. If Jesus was the Christ of God his course was wicked beyond words. He must stop there and then, yea more, he must turn his back on all he had loved and gloried in, on his old religion, his position, his honor, his worldly hopes, his kindred—everything. Was there ever a more momentous time in a human life? The stress was unspeakable. The first and greatest battle in one of the greatest human lives ever lived on earth was there fought and righteousness won the field. The young man saw it all, and conferred not—did not even confer with flesh and blood—but from that hour for him to live was Christ. There was never any vacillation, nor halting till the Roman ax put a period to his earthly life.

The hour of conversion is the most important battle hour in any life. Some seem born into the kingdom feebly, amid doubts and fears, from which they never escape. Life is a long continued skirmish or running fight between the divine and the earthly life. Year in and year out this conflict goes on. The life is a border life, attended with the old-time border experiences of foray and never-ceasing strife.

Christians of this type are ever unhappy and never very useful. They are the pastor's care, not his helpers. They never settled the questions of life by any rule. They shift this way and that, now a little better, now not so good, as the winds blow. Their enemies hover about them constantly. Sometimes the devil tempts them, and sometimes they tempt the devil. They are ever unsettled as to the simplest matters of duty. They are irrevocably committed to nothing because they have never fought selfishness and worldliness on a principle and won the field.

Such unhappy souls ought to have it out on the one point of duty. Let any one once fight his way to the top of the hill duty and plant himself there and all the other battles of life will be easy in comparison. Really duty is the supreme human word. It is the strongest word in the language. Once the heart and mind end all debates with conflicting passions and persuasions by settling down to accept duty, as it appears from time to time, as the rule of life, then the sublimest epoch of that life opens. Here is the weakness of multitudes of Christian lives. They are not formed on duty as the guiding principle of life. They skirmish with the devil around this great center on every separate thing that comes up. Now it is a fight over the theater, now over the ballroom, now over some form of Sunday desecration. It is an endless skirmish; but no decisive victory. Let the fight be on the one great including issue, fidelity to Christ, and when the victory is won all the after life will be better and easier.

I feel to stress this point. Reader, are you committed to do your duty to Christ? If you say yes, then what, if that means going far hence into the darkness of heathenism? What, young man, if it means putting aside all your plans to preach the Word? What, brother preacher, if it means a life spent among the poor and ignorant? Let the principle of your life be settled, and your life formed on duty, no matter where duty leads. This will make a great life, blessed of God, and felt for good by men. If you have not yet settled down on the principle of fidelity to Christ irrevocably you have in your life an undoing element of weakness. Fight one great battle with self on this point. Do not stop till you have gained the victory and when you have won the battle you will find that your life has taken on strength and beauty.

In the course of life we must fight battles to win an open field of action in different directions. Paul came into the apostolic college under great disadvantages, as things go among men. He could never forget that he had been a persecutor and the others would not likely forget it. He had had none of the advantages of the others in personal associations with the Master in his early life. He felt this, for he counted himself an apostle born out of due season. Yet it fell to his lot to withstand Peter under circumstances of peculiar trial. The scene of a memorable conflict was Antioch. The church was deeply affected with Judaistic heresies, brought in sideways, under the color of reverence for divine institutions. The perverts, after their sort, were noisy and proscriptive. Peter, the movable cobble stone, true to his name, was carried away by the Judaizers. Barnabas, devout, tender-hearted, went with Peter and the rest, and everything was going wrong, when Paul came on the scene. An hour of vacillation on Paul's part and this great center of Gentile evangelization will slump into Judaism. There is a right and a wrong side to the business and Paul knows which is which. He does not mince matters. He does not seek to evade the issue. The questions involved go to the heart of Christianity. Paul forced a decisive battle by confronting Peter before the whole company and told him to the face the truth of the business. The victory was decisive. Paul, from that day onward, with Antioch back of him, became the central figure of the Christian age, because he was the fittest man to lead.

Many a pastor, especially in troublous times such as we have had in Texas in recent years, suffers irretrievable defeat the first month he serves the church. There is a silent fight of forces, and the outcome is the victory of a faction, or, perchance, the church itself in a low and worldly condition, over the pastor. He succumbs to bad influences and on to the end is a weak appendage to a lifeless body. Temporizing with evil is an undoing thing for pastor and people. Unless a preacher can command himself to boldly speak the truth in love, he is whipped. Better meet an issue like Paul met the issues of his day and fight the battle to a finish.

Before closing this article I feel pressed to apply the principle here discussed to a matter which gives endless trouble to the churches in these latter days. The money question is an open question with most Christians, and practically all the churches. Giving is a matter of sentiment or preference. Whether to give, how to give, how much to give, are questions around which people and churches skirmish continually. Only now and then do we find a man who has fought the battle to a finish. Giving must be put in the order of scripture doctrine, and not human feeling or preference. Just as long as we skirmish around the question we will be weak and every interest of Zion will suffer. What is needed in every Christian heart and every church is a scriptural settlement. Let a man settle it for good and all that he must work and make money; that he must give regularly; that he must give proportionately; that is a fixed part of what he receives, and then he has settled a long line of troublesome questions all at once. If he wins a decisive victory on the money question he will never again find it hard to give, and he will never get far from God in his business. We need to force the fighting on the money question till the lost ground is all retaken and the old scriptural landmarks reset.

The sum of all this article is that in dealing with the issues of life it is both wise and loving to grapple them with such strength and purpose as will settle them, leaving us free to go forward with added courage and less hindrance.

BY J. B. GAMBRELL, D. D.

GRASSHOPPERS AND GIANTS.

THE Israelites had, through a series of the most wonderful providential interventions, reached the borders of the promised land. Toward this promised land their thoughts had been directed in the infancy of the nation when it was only a family. They had cherished the hope of the goodly country through the centuries of Egyptian bondage. Marvellously had God redeemed them from their task-masters, and marvellously had He led them across the sea and fed them in the wilderness and brought them now to the realization of their hopes.

Camping on the borders of the promised land, Moses, for prudential reasons, sent twelve men, one from each of the tribes, to spy out the land. They were to go through it, and report back what kind of a country, what kind of people, and whether they lived in tents or in walled cities. After forty days these twelve scouts returned, ten of them whipped completely. They made their report, said it was a good country, but proceeded at once to say, also, that it was a country that ate up the inhabitants thereof, and, in the same breath, declared that it was inhabited by great giants. They concluded their report by saying that they were, in their own eyes, among the inhabitants of that country, as grasshoppers, and they were so in the eyes of the giants.

This report greatly disturbed the people. They wept and wailed all night, and, finally, determined on making them promises which they had cherished, forgot everything but an considered great danger, they forgot all the mercies of God, and all His mighty dealings with them, and forgot the a captain and go back to Egypt. In the face of what they impending danger, so mightily did the word of these ten men affect the multitude. Two of them brought another report. They saw the same people the ten saw, they saw the walled cities; but they came back to say to the people that it was an exceedingly good country, and that it flowed with milk and honey; that they were able to take it, and they ought to go at once and take possession; and that, instead of this array of giants being against them, they would be bread for them. They did not prevail, however, with the multitude, for the people were genuinely whipped by the discouragers, and could not get themselves to think of the whole company of Israel as anything above grasshoppers. The divine record tells us what happened. Every one of them fell in the wilderness, and only the two faithful spies entered the promised land forty years later.

How apt and powerful is this teaching when applied to Christians in our time! What a vast multitude of grasshopper Christians we have! Whole churches of them, surrounded by the long-necked Anaks of the world, and intimidated until all their courage oozes out at their shoes. As God utterly discarded the cowardly Israelites, so from that day to this, He has utterly discarded people without hope and without courage. Never in the history of God's dealing with His people has He done anything with cowards. On one occasion, when all Israel was whipped out, God used one courageous woman to deliver His people, but He would do nothing with men who have no courage.

Spiritual cowardice is not only weakness, but it is wickedness. No one has a right to be a spiritual coward. These ten spies, and with them the great multitude, quaked and trembled because they put God out of their calculations. They saw strong men and walled cities, but they did not see God. Joshua and Caleb saw strong men and walled cities, but, over them all, they saw God. They knew that whatever was necessary to take possession of the land would be done through the power of God, and their faith was justified later when the walls of Jericho fell down by divine interposition. Spiritual cowardice has for its tap-root infidelity and a disregard of the divine power. People who think they can do noting, can do nothing because they cut themselves off from the sources of strength. The word of faith is: "All things are possible." The strong point of faith is that it connects itself and connects the worker with the infinite power that can find no difficulties. We need to understand that all successful Christian work is the work of God, through His people, and that there can be no difficulties with God. He can take a worm and whip down a mountain. He could part the sea. He could shake down the walls of Jericho without the interposition of a human hand. The reason everything is possible to faith is because faith takes hold upon God. The ten did not see that, and they misled the multitude.

Let me throw in this observation. These ten whipped leaders set the pace for all their tribe, from that day to this. In a single breath they said the land ate up the inhabitants, and yet reported the land full of great giants. Discouragers don't need to be consistent. A discourager only needs a voice and an unbelieving heart, and somebody to hear him, to get in his work. He can say things on opposite sides, in the same breath, and go right on with his work. The ten tribes represented by the ten spies are well scattered out through the world, and we must have a good share of them in Texas.

It is worthy of note, also, that the giants did not come to consider the ten spies as grasshoppers until the spies had taken that view of themselves. It may be, indeed, doubted whether the inhabitants of the land ever did think it, because, possibly, they did not know how utterly whipped out and done for these men were. But this truth remains: Whenever a Christian man, or a church, comes to feel that he or they are grasshoppers, then the giants of this world will not think of them any better than they think of themselves. If a church takes a mean, low view of itself, in any community, the community will take the same view, and the community will be right. What is a church of grasshoppers worth?

These ten men had at least the aptitude for characterizing themselves. A grasshopper is a very insignificant insect, very uncertain in his movements, capacitated, in great numbers, to eat up a country, but not to build anything. A million grasshoppers will add nothing to the world, and, withal, you can't count on them as to their movements or anything else. They go zig-zag, and are about as likely to hop one way as another, and to light one place as another. A church of grasshoppers, a denomination of grasshoppers, may do to count as to numbers, but that is all.

Let us turn to think a moment about William Carey, standing, a young man, in lowly position, uneducated according to the standards of his time, in the Nottingham Association in England, with men of great repute in his presence, and propounding to them a proposition so far beyond their thoughts that they regarded him as beside himself. Yet undismayed he stood there to preach his great sermon on undertaking great things for God and expecting great things from God. He was not a grasshopper, but a mighty man of valor, and God has honored his courage to bless the world.

There are two churches in this state which serve to illustrate another point. Each had gotten down so low in the thinking of the members that they could not meet the current expenses of the church on the most economical basis. One could not raise a trifling church debt. The other could not raise enough money to pay insurance on an out-of-date wooden meeting-house in a growing city. They were, in their own eyes, as grasshoppers, and the difficulties around them everywhere were giants. In the Providence of God both of these meeting-houses were burned. And now, the point is, God can make men and women out of grasshoppers.

By J. B. Gambrell, D. D.

In the light of these two fires God converted two congregations of grasshoppers into men and women of valor. Each one erected a beautiful meeting-house last year, and greatly increased its work in every direction, all because of the wonderful transformation from grasshopper to hero.

There are a great many grasshoppers in the pulpits; men who walk around about their churches, and into the churches, and up into the pulpit, feeling in their hearts that they can do nothing at all. Here are these other big churches in town, here are the colonels and the bankers and the railroad men, and here are the powerful combinations of evil, the saloons, the gambling places, and here is worldliness stalking abroad in the church, and the preacher stands up before his people utterly whipped. He feels, in his heart, as if he were no more than a grasshopper, surrounded by giants. One of two things will happen with him. He will drop through a crack in the floor some day, and nobody will know what went with him, or else a new spirit will come on him, and he will tower above the heads of the giants, and God will conquer the situation through him. If a preacher feels intimidated and whipped, either he must get out of that by a firm grip on the Almighty through faith, or else he must get out of his place and let a man come. A grasshopper is nobody to lead a congregation of God's people, and he will not do it.

We have 200,000 Baptists in Texas. O, there are so many of them grasshoppers! So many churches that want to depend on boards to help them! So many men cannot do anything unless they are backed up all around! So many men and women in the churches who scarcely can get themselves to the meeting-house, and are just nobodies, to be carried along by those who are trying to do something! If the Spirit of Almighty God would come on these 200,000 and transform every grasshopper into a hero of faith then would the very earth be shaken by the divine power through

God's people. Wherever there are men to pray and men to believe and men to work, no matter how few, nor how weak, if they have come to touch the Divine Hand, they may be an irresistible force.

Brother, what are you? Are you a grasshopper, or a man? What sort of a church is yours, a church of grasshoppers or a church of heroes of the faith? It may be either, and, according as it is one or the other, will it be determined whether there shall be growth or declension.

BY J. B. GAMBRELL, D. D.

SAINTS AND ANGELS.

SOME weeks ago there was reprinted in The Standard an article in which there is an exclamation, "Saints and Angels, help!" etc. I notice that some good brethren question its soundness. Their respectful note in The Standard has put my mind to work on a line of thought much neglected. With regard to the expression in question two very brief remarks may be made. First, it is an exclamation. Second, there is nothing in it suggesting worship of saints or angels. I suppose the exclamation was read in the atmosphere created by the Catholic hierarchy. Catholics have certainly a very erroneous doctrine concerning both saints and angels. They have not only perverted most every doctrine of God's word, but they have filled the world with an atmosphere suited to their purposes of perversion. We need to be doubly on guard lest we either go full length with them in their perversions, or else deny the truths altogether, which they have twisted to their uses. In either case we suffer.

There is a scriptural doctrine of saints as there is of angels. But in each case it is very different from the Catholic doctrine. In having my attention called pointedly to the subject, I cannot recall a single discussion of the differences in all my reading of newspapers. This article is not meant as a defense of the sentence in "Up Fool Hill," but as a brief discussion of the Bible doctrines of saints and also of angels. There is much in the Bible on both subjects. The latter belongs to a realm of thought of which most of us know far too little.

The Catholics make saints by papal power. A person esteemed more than ordinarily good is canonized perhaps centuries after his or her death. It becomes proper then for Catholics to pray to such persons. To these saints are assigned certain duties. One is the patron saint of those suffering from one thing, another the patron saint of those in need of help on some other account. I overheard two young girls talking on a street car in New Orleans. "Where are you going?" was asked. The reply was: "I have lost my ring and I am going to —— church to pray to Saint —— and ask help to find it." Patrick, who was more a Baptist than a Catholic, has been made the patron saint of Ireland. This saint-making and saint-worship is elaborated to almost an endless extent.

Catholocism is a hybrid—part Jewish, part Christian, part heathen. It is an amalgam of Jewish, Christian and heathen thoughts and worship. The ancients had many gods. For every distinct human feeling, hope and ambition there was a deity. Besides, there were gods for the seasons and gods for the great natural objects, as the sun, the stars, the sea, etc. It is plain to see that these were creations of human heads in their efforts to satisfy themselves amid the varying conflicts and experiences of life. When Christianity merged with heathendom the Bible was gradually set aside, and the human mind and heart at once went to work in the old way to make what they wanted. There were inklings of this in apostolic times. Paul speaks of days and will worship, and neglecting of the body, etc., with a warning voice.

Moreover, when Constantine adopted Christianity and decreed it, things worked apace. Not only did these natural feelings find a prepared soil and an atmosphere suited to them, but as these feelings shot out their tendrils, there were crafty men ready to make a trellis on which they could climb. The old heathen festival days were turned into saints' days. It was a compromise deemed helpful to the stability of society. Heathenism and Christianity made up, and we have what we have—Catholic saints galore, with saints' days, until in purely Catholic countries the saints run things. Priests and people stand in awe of the bones of saints, many of which saints never had any connection with Catholicism.

This is a doctrine made on purpose by the Catholic hierarchy. No one can understand Catholicism from an external view of it. It must be studied from the inside, and with the understanding that its never-changing motive is to dominate every man, woman and child in the world, soul, mind and body, in things temporal, as well as things spiritual. The canonization of saints is to this end. So is purgatory. So is the doctrine of indulgences. So is the infallibility of the Pope. So in every part of the vast, complex seeming contradictory practices in the various countries of the world. The girl who had lost her ring would pray to a saint, some human, when she would not pray to the Father of spirits who is a Spirit and can only be worshipped in spirit. It helps to hold her and may secure an offering. This Catholic doctrine of saints is not a Bible doctrine. But there is a Bible doctrine of saints. Bible saints are God-made, washed in the blood of the Lamb and made holy by the Spirit. "St. Matt.," "St. Luke," etc., is a distinction made in that same Catholic atmosphere aforementioned. All the saved are saints according to the Scriptures. Paul addresses his letter to the Romans: "To all that be in Rome, beloved of God, called saints." The words "to be" before saints are not in the Greek. After the same manner his first letter to the Corinthians is addressed to "the church," "to them that are sanctified in Christ Jesus called saints." The second letter is to the church of God, which is at Corinth, with all the saints which are in Achaia." To the Phillipians he writes in the same way—"to all the saints in Christ Jesus." This is plenty on that part of the subject. There are worlds between the Bible doctrine of saints and the Catholic doctrine.

The saints now on earth, in the flesh, are the saints who are needed to take big-headed boys by the hand and help to save them. The like of that is why they are kept in the world. In this work-a-day world disembodied spirits have no work to do. "They rest from their labors and their works do follow them."

Angels are messengers. They belong to the spirit world. But they visit this world and are presented to us often in the Bible in human form. The Bible doctrine of spirits deserves, yea, demands profound and reverent study. The age is materialistic. Physical science has occupied a large place in the thinking of learned people for a long time. The spirit of the world is commercial to a degree to largely displace higher and better things. Millionaires have taken attention away from poets. Oratory has lost its wings, and has taken to the airthmetic. The masses are using the muckrake looking for possible coin. The world is full of voices, but they do not come from the altitude whence the angels sang the annunciation hymn. This is a difficult time to study spirits. But there are spirits, good and bad. There are demons inhabiting the air, and Satan is their Prince. These are wily, insidious, malignant, and they have access to human beings. The Scriptures teem with proof texts to support this doctrine. We do not know enough on this subject or we would not be so ignorant of Satanic devices. Just think how they acted in Christ's day and on. What has become of them? Satan is not yet bound.

There are good angels. In the hour of His agony and betrayal Jesus said He could pray to His Father and the Father would send more than twelve legions of angels. An angel strengthened the Savior in His suffering. There are holy angels, and in the last verse of the first chapter of Hebrews it is declared that they are "all ministering spirits, sent forth to minister for them who shall be heirs of salvation." Here is a great doctrine, comforting, helpful, and in

BY J. B. GAMBRELL, D. D.

accord with the whole current of Scripture teaching from Abraham to John the Revelator.

The doctrine is awe-inspiring. I have no theory about it, but certainly angels have a part in the work of helping and perhaps defending those who are marked out to be heirs of salvation. They are in no sense to be worshipped, but they are to be thought of as helpers in a way appointed. The only trouble about receiving the doctrine is slavery to materialism. The angels are neither dead nor asleep. They are ministering spirits.

BILL MORGAN'S ECONOMY.

ECONOMY is undoubtedly a fine thing. It is commanded in Scripture and was practiced by Christ. It is the law of God in grace and in nature. Waste is weakness and sin. The doctrine of economy goes to everything in life—to time, to strength, to nerve force, to influence and to money also, but to money last and least, for money has no value to itself, but borrows its value from its relations to the higher things of life. There are various views of economy. Taking them all together, they make a fine and profitable study. They carry us over the whole field of profit and loss in every department of life.

When I was a boy my father lived near a man named Bill Morgan. The country was new. Bill was one of the first settlers. He landed in the country when he had the choice of the land. He could select his own home and settle on it for nothing. It was a country of rich bottoms and poor ridges. Bill had a keen eye for a very popular kind of economy. Seeing that the rich bottom lands were overgrown with briers, cane, vines and bushes, as well as very large trees, Bill, to economize labor in clearing, selected the ridge land which had little on it to clear away.

He built with reference to an economy of labor, using small poles instead of large logs, such as his neighbors hewed out with much toil to build their houses. Everything about his place indicated rigid economy, except children. There was a profusion of children—ten in all. In all other respects Bill held one consistent view of economy, and nothing could move him from it.

He made his fences mainly of poles and brush to utilize the waste and save labor. He bought a little pony because it was cheap, and it was too expensive to feed a big horse. His hogs were of the razor-back variety, because they were good rooters and could shift for themselves. He half fed

BY J. B. GAMBRELL, D. D.

Everything About his Place Indicated rigid econmoy.

his pony in plow time, because "corn was too scarce." He plowed awhile and turned his pony to grass while he chopped weeds and dug around his corn. His little scooter plow was made to fit the pony, and hence he scratched the top off the ground and never got deep enough to keep a season in the ground. His cows matched up with everything else. Narrow, slender, always poor, they gave but a scanty supply of very blue milk. But Bill saved their feed. All through crop time Bill was compelled to work out by the day to get bread for his family. There was economy in this, too, for while he was working out his pony could pick up a little and plow a little more when he returned.

In education Bill Morgan was an economist of the most rigid order. It was before the days of free schools, and the charges for tuition were more or less, according to the grades. Bill utterly refused to allow his children to advance to the grammar grade, because it would cost 50 cents a month more, and it was no use, anyway, for folks could "jest naturally talk without any larnin.'" He was never known to pay a tuition bill, but he was opposed on principle to the 50 cents extra charge.

Things went hard with Bill Morgan, notwithstanding his severe economy. Worse and worse matters grew, till at last he sold out, made him a cart with hoop poles for tires, hitched a yearling to it, loaded on a few things, and the last I heard of him he was moving west, the whole family afoot.

Somehow or other Bill Morgan's economy did not cause him to thrive. There seemed to be a weak place in it somewhere. It worked badly. It seemed to go against nature, and certain Scriptures suggest a different spirit. "There is that scattereth and yet increaseth, and there is that withholdeth more than is meet and tendeth to poverty."

I have seen Churches practicing economy after the order of Bill Morgan. They accept as a gift or buy a cheap lot for a church in a town on a back street because it is cheap. They build a cheap house, get a cheap preacher, dispense with the services of a sexton, line out the hymns to save buying books, and wonder why the church does not

BY J. B. GAMBRELL, D. D.

grow. Or, it is a country Church, and the same skimping kind of economy is practiced. The cheapest preacher is

The Cheapest Preacher is Employed at the Lowest Salary, or No Salary.

employed at the lowest salary, or no salary. He is expected to preach Saturday and Sunday for a pittance, and pick up his living beween times like Bill Morgan's pony. The whole policy of the Church is run on Bill Morgan's idea of economy. Everything is little, lean and hard.

It never struck Bill that he could not get out of his cows in milk what did not go into them in the way of feed. He never saw that it was little pony, little work; poor pony, poor work. He seemed to think that nature was a fountain which could be depended on to give what she did not have. Bill was wrong all round. His economy went to the destruction of the sources of supply. He did not understand that whosoever soweth sparingly shall also reap sparingly. That was why he had to leave his crop in the grass and go out to work for a turn of corn to keep the wolf out of his house.

Churches practicing Bill Morgan's kind of economy are no wiser than he was. It pays to pay a pastor and pay him liberally, so that he can buy books, study, and come to his best. It pays to send pastors to great conventions, just like it pays to turn a cow on a rich pasture. No man with starved mind and heart can preach well. If the churches were wise they would treat their pastors at least as well as sensible people treat their horses and cows. That would be true economy. It would bring preachers to their best, and the Churches would get the benefit of all improvement.

The finest economy is the best use of every element of power towards right ends. It aims to develop everything to its highest power and usefulness. Whatever goes out for such a purpose comes back increased. I have known a man to economize in the feed of his horse till the horse lost his working power and market value. He was sold for a song. The buyer reversed the policy, fed well, and shortly had a horse that everybody wanted. He fed high and sold high. The other man fed low and sold low. The world is run that way.

There are hundreds of the Bill Morgan sort of churches

now complaining at their hard worked and underpaid pastors. They want a change. When they hear some well supported preacher, who has studied and can preach with power and life, they say: "Oh, if we had that man for a preacher!" What for? To starve him? He would soon be no better than the man of God you are now giving no chance. Give your preacher as good a chance as you give your Jersey cow and see how he will improve.

This same Bill Morgan style of economy is practiced in mission work. A board gets a man because he can be had cheap. They send him to easy places, on the principle that Bill Morgan located his home on the poor ridge of land. They go around the towns and cities because it will cost more to plant the cause in cities. The cities neglected become powerful centers of evil. The money gathered in them is in the hands of the Godless, and is turned not for, but against the cause of the Master. Bill Morgan made a mistake in not locating on rich land, even if it required work to conquer the natural growth. Equally foolish is the false economy that shuns expense in rightly exploiting any good work. A wise farmer will pay to have land cleared, plowed and prepared for cultivation, even though he knows it will be years before he gets his money back. A wise board will spend money to develop churches and remove troubles, though it will take time to reap the fruits of the labor.

John Rockefeller was asked how his company had grown so rich in the oil business. He answered: "By having the best machinery, the best means of transportation, the best men, the best everything, and paying the best price for everything." John Rockefeller and Bill Morgan would never have agreed in business.

The Scriptures advise that we devise liberal things, and stand by liberal things. It is economy to plant plenty of seed. It is economy to enrich your soil at any cost. It is economy to have good stock and feed them all they need.

It is economy to get the best servants for all work and pay them well. It is economy to have good meeting-houses, well located, though they do cost. Economy lies in the best use of everything, and not in skimping. We get out of religion what we put into it. "Give and it shall be given you."

Bill Morgan left Mississippi forty years ago, coming this way, with ten children. I expect the family has enormously increased, and from signs lots of them must have joined the Baptists.

BY DR. J. B. GAMBRELL, D. D.

PURPOSELESS PREACHERS.

THE highest point aimed at in Paul's life was to fulfill his ministry. Arduous and perilous as was his ministry, he thanked God that He had counted him worthy, putting him into it. He counted not his life dear unto him that he might worthily acquit himself in the trusteeship of the gospel. His conception was that he held the gospel in trust for the world. To default in the trust was to him the most unthinkable of crimes against God and humanity. It was, moreover, a calamity to himself beyond all other calamities short of perdition.

No one can attentively read the New Testament without realizing something of the tremendous importance of the ministerial office. It is, beyond all comparison, the most important calling known to men. Its functions are the highest and the most sacred. It calls for the very highest order of manhood. Indeed, the best men, all their time at their best, must still cry out, "Who is sufficient for these things?" In the Kingdom he is the elect of the elect, a chosen vessel for the highest possible use in the King's service.

The Holy Scriptures describe his character in detail. They mark him distinctly as a man of more than ordinary consequence in the church. In his human relations, in his spiritual endowments, in his ability and common repute, he stands on a high level. No slip-shod man, no come-easy-go-easy, slack-twisted church members may be inducted into the ministry. The churches are put under severe limitations as to the kind of men, who are to be recognized as ministers of the Word. Who can estimate the harm done by overriding the divine restrictions placed around this most sacred office?

Consider for a little while the simple yet unspeakably grave functions of the ministry. The preacher is God's embassador. He speaks in Christ's name. He is to deliver Christ's message and not his own at all. This message is pregnant with the gravest issues of life and death. The highest interests of immortal beings for two worlds are wrapped up in the message of the preacher. Truly he stands between the living and the dead. He is all the time face to face with the issues of eternal consequence.

If the preacher is a pastor, his responsibilities broaden. He must watch for souls as one who must give account—souls slipping away into eternity out of his flock, or congregation. His duty is three-fold. First, to win souls to Christ; second, to feed the flock; third, to oversee the household of faith; to put it another way, to win souls to Christ, to build them up in Christ, to employ them for Christ.

On the minister's faithfulness depends not only the salvation of souls, but all the highest interests of the home, the church and the State. The faithful minister is far away the most important man in any community. He is God's first man in all the ranks of men, the master builder in all the realm of human hopes and endeavors.

Because of the matchless work assigned the preacher, it is ordained of God, that he shall live of the gospel. He is not too good to work at any honorable calling. Paul made tents to preach, not for gain. The greatest preacher living is not too good to farm, dig a ditch, black shoes or sweep the streets. He is not supported because of his dignity, but that he may put all his powers into his work, that he may make full proof of his ministry.

Be it never forgotten for one moment, that the true minister is, like his Lord is, among the needy of the earth as one who serves. And, like his Lord, he needs to be a man of unbending purpose to finish the work given him to do.

The preacher ought to be the manliest of men. How

can human speech sufficiently express a proper contempt for the dilettante man, the purposeless molusk, who uses his great office, and the tribute of love and reverence of the people, to minister to his own ease? The ministerial society man, whom silly women flood with twaddle and smiles which ought to disgust a man of God, living in sight of eternity, is a reproach to humanity and to the ministry.

I believe the greatest weakness in the ministry today is the lack of a proper purpose. It is the source of countless evils and the chief source of the deplorable weakness which makes many preachers mere weather vanes and whining sychophants. It is the cause of the contempt into which the sacred office has fallen in some places. The masses are quick to know the spirit of a preacher.

If a preacher have the right purpose in a scriptural measure, he will gather into his high calling all his powers and make them count for the work of the ministry. The ruin wrought by the purposeless ministry is manifold and appalling. Let us glance at a wide field of desolation wrought by this most inexcusable, blameworthy trifler with eternal things. He has been entrusted by the Master with the first place of responsibility and leadership in his church. Being devoid of a proper purpose, his preaching is without purpose. He preaches to preach. In the pulpit, he is without unction or power. He has no real grip on God or the living oracles. This being true, he has no power over men. From the living ministry he falls by degrees to the level of a very sorry actor. Affectation takes the place of the holy passion of the cross. Nor is this all, or even the worst, the purposeless preacher becomes an unconscious or a knowing hypocrite. He says more and pretends to be more than is true. The downward movement keeps on, usually with accelerated speed. The congregation catches the preacher's spirit. He lets all the twist out. All the services are tame, flat and unprofitable. Then something must be done to fill an aching void. We enter now upon the stage of the artistic. There must be decorations, stately form, hired singers, and all the abominations of death standing where a living preacher would make them impossible. The purposeless preacher has laid the glories of the Master's service in the dust and the strength of Israel has departed.

Nor have things yet reached the lowest level. The purposeless preacher becomes a spiritual coward. He fawns, flatters and cajoles, where he should speak with thunder tones, wake a sleeping church and call it to heroic service. Being a spiritual coward, he becomes spiritually blind also. Then all wisdom has departed from him. He loses his grip and begins to catch onto every passing fad, running with the multitude to keep in with them. He becomes an ardent secret order man, or he joins in with all the outings, hangs around on the street and whiles away the time with small talk, or he gads about from house to house making pop calls, without sense, grace or purpose, except to keep up with the on-moving crowd. He has time to fish a week, or to hunt, or to go on long trips for pleasure, or to do anything except the immeasurably important soul-moving work of the true minister of Jesus Christ.

The life of a purposeless preacher is like a stream, which at first may run strong in the channel made by itself, but gradually slows up, broadens out and loses itself in a waste of barren sands. Such a ministry lets off the tension everywhere and lets on the slack. Under it congregations thin out, earnestness fails, zeal cools, the faithful are discouraged, collections diminish, the worldly flourish, distinctions between right and wrong fade out, the right ways of the Lord are evil spoken of, sinners are hardened in carnal security, the ministry is despised, the Godly grieved, the devil pleased, souls damned, and the Laodicean preacher becomes a castaway.

BY DR. J. B. GAMBRELL, D. D.

O brother preacher, how shall we live or die in peace, if we do not do our best in the great work God has trusted to us? How shall we face the lost at the judgment, if we are unfaithful to our sacred trusteeship? Our great need today is a revived ministry, nerved by divine grace to the highest purpose that can direct a human life, the purpose to finish the work which God has given us to do. A revival of a proper purpose in the ministry means a scriptural revival in the churches, reaching out into every department of the work. It means countless victories on the broad battlefield where Christ wages his Holy War. With a purposeless ministry we are undone.

THE PAINS OF PROGRESS. THE UNREST OF FAITH.

THE SCRIPTURES abound in paradoxes, and there is a strong paradox as to faith. It gives both rest to the soul and disturbs the whole being. It is the headlight of progress, and stirs the world to efforts, making progress possible.

The New Testament is both a book of rest and unrest. The soul finds its rest in Jesus Christ, but the very moment Christ is apprehended, there is set up a conflict between the new life and the old life. Paul described this graphically in Romans. This conflict we are bound to think ends only with the present life. Moreover, faith is a great discerner and has a keen eye all the time for better things. While it is fully satisfied with Christ and with our standing in Christ, by the same token it is dissatisfied with our present advancement in the divine life. He who sees the perfect life will be ever more dissatisfied with the imperfect self, so that faith both quiets and disquiets, because it stirs the soul to constantly seek better things.

Every true interpretation of the scriptures will have its experimental demonstration. We have not really understood any scripture until we have tested it. I take it, therefore, that every real Christian is a witness to the paradoxical power of faith; first, to give rest in Jesus Christ; and second, to stir us to unrest in our present imperfect attainments and surroundings.

What I have just said is only another way of saying that the Christian life is a struggle, a battle for real progress, fight between the powers of darkness and the powers of light. Illustrations of this are at hand on every side. Take the young preacher, who has gotten hold of the fringe of some subject and preached it with vehemence to a people who went no deeper than he himself. There is every like-

BY DR. J. B. GAMBRELL, D. D.

lihood that somebody will persuade him that he has done quite well. As his vision is enlarged and his spiritual understanding increased, he comes to see how little of the real meaning of the text he had gotten hold of. He is profoundly dissatisfied with his old sermon, and makes a new one up to date with his better knowledge. By and by still further study leads him to see that he is yet in the shallows of his text, and he is dissatisfied again. All knowledge satisfies and dissatisfies.

By the same method do Christians grow in the divine life. They go from strength to strength, their outlook ever increasing, their aspirations growing higher and better, and, as the old man perishes, the new man is renewed day by day. The most advanced Christian is the one most dissatisfied with his own weaknesses. There is a fatal paralysis manifest in that kind of holiness, of which we hear much these days, which is perfectly complacent even in the midst of sin and in the enjoyment of sin. It is not a faith holiness. It is a blind holiness, and that means it is no holiness at all, for he who esteems himself perfect in the flesh, is perfect only in his folly.

The New Testament is a hard book to live up to. In the first place, every separate person must think, pray, repent, believe, live for himself. Nobody can put his life off on somebody else. No one can take responsibilities for another. Every one of us must give an account for ourselves to God. A great many people are bothered because they are requested to settle religious questions for themselves. What a convenience it would be if we could have somebody to make arrangements for us by thousands, get tickets for us and ship us to the heavenly world, as great companies of immigrants can be shipped from one point to another, each one giving up the whole matter to the leader. No such easy-going arrangement as that can obtain in the Kingdom of God. Every soul stands for itself, and every soul must meet its responsibilities, must do or fail to do, and finally stand before the Judge of all the earth. No man can have the preacher to tell him how much he ought to give. The preacher may tell him God's law about it, but he must give out of his own heart. All this is very troublesome. It has kept many a soul awake all night and made people pray by the day and week, but all of it is in the line of growth, and without it there is no growth.

Now this means that each person must face his doubts and have it out; face his sins and down them, or be downed by them; face the devil and conquer, or be conquered. It is anything in the world but easy. He who conquers will wear the crown. The redeemed at the last are described as those who come up through great tribulations. Paul when an old man said, "I have fought a good fight," and exhortations abound for striving and fighting and wrestling. It is most misleading to tell anybody that to live the right kind of life, and grow in religion, does not mean the hardest kind of fighting; but it is safe to say that whoever makes the fight will grow by it, enlarge with it, and win eternal glory—not life, for that is a gift, but win the victor's crown.

Let us transfer this principle of rest and unrest to a broader plane. Every church as a body must face its responsibilities. It must deal with the living questions that concern it as a church. It must grapple with difficulties within and without. If it ever gets up it must climb up. A church life is a battle for purity within and progress without, and it is worse than nonsense for people to join a church with the idea that they are entering into a state of heavenly rest, undisturbed by the imperfections and sinfulness of our great mortal state. There be many who think that a church is necessarily a little piece of paradise fenced off. It is no such thing. It is a company of soldiers fighting for higher ground on the great battlefield of this world. Blessed is the church member who is willing to enter into the holy way, and blessed is the church that faces its enemies and God's enemies in the conquering spirit of the gospel. The church which struggles toward higher ground will pass through many tribulations, but it will have exquisite joy. No pastor ought to mislead his church on this point. To do so is to do the church a positive injury, and the cause no good at all, but harm. How earnestly did Paul deal with churches as to the enemies disturbing them. It will be good for all of us if we read the Acts of the Apostles over and the Apostles' Letters. We can get some fine suggestions, especially the pastors, in dealing with the men and things that disturb a church. A milk-sop pastor is nothing short of a downright nuisance.

Let us broaden our application to the denomination at large. We are not to expect to see people doing until they are taught, and let us not mistake this: With increasing light old ideals must be given up and new ones will take their place. A growth is a transition from a lower to a higher state. We are today in Texas undergoing the pains of progress—the profound unrest of faith. Little or none of the present troubles would be on us if we disbanded our work and ceased all our efforts for higher things. But vastly greater troubles would come. For many years ahead, if we anything like do what we ought toward enlightenment, we will suffer many pains in the denomination. The pastors who do not grow, whose ideals are of the smaller and lower sort, will be displaced by men of sturdy growth, higher aspirations and nobler effort. But it will not be without trouble.

I have but a single remark further. Painful as is this unrest in growth, this ever-continuing warfare against the lower and for the higher, however much any one suffers in the struggle, or however much a church suffers, or a great people, every pain, every heart-pang, every tear and every sigh, will have its abundant compensation in the attainments of things for which we strive. Shall we never be satisfied? Yes. A great saint of old said: "I shall be satisfied when I awake in thy likeness." Not before? God forbid. The prayer, the sigh, must be for higher ground.

THE LAST STRUGGLE.

THE BIBLICAL RECORDER says the discontent in Arkansas can not live with intelligence, and that this sort is perhaps the last struggle of it. The Recorder is right as far as it goes. The denomination at large needs to understand the situation in the Southwest. This whole section is infected, and has been for a long time, by small notions, mere exaggerations of the truth, and a spirit promotive of discord and strife.

There is a great uncooked situation. People are here from everywhere, and all have brought their notions with them. I say notions, not convictions. There is a great difference, though many people don't know the difference. This new, rapidly growing country is a paradise for demagogues and the breeders of strife. There is material for all sorts of factions.

The present array of opposition to old-line Baptist principles and practices is composite. It is an Adullum's cave of malcontents. They have no principles to bind them together. It is strictly an aggregation of objectors. In this it is singularly like the Hardshell-Campbellite movement of seventy years ago. The aggregation then in array against the real Baptists were not agreed among themselves at all, except in opposing the forward movement of the denomination

By Dr. J. B. Gambrell, D. D.

The methods employed then were the same as those employed now. Every effort was made to create prejudice. There was then, as now, a ceaseless stream of foul accusation poured forth, with little or no regard for the truth. There was then as now no end of cunning in perverting every possible word and circumstance to the prejudice of the work and workers. Then, as now, every evil passion was inflamed by misrepresentation. Appeals were then made to covetousness, envy, class feeling, malice, evil surmising. The same is done now. Then, as now, the very things done by the opposition were charged on the friends of the work. Then, as now, many good but uninformed people were disaffected and carried away from the truth. For confirmation of this see the rise of Antimissionism in America, by B. H. Carroll, Jr., and editorials of Bebee in one large volume, now very rare. Out of that book every feature of the present controversy can be duplicated in substance, spirit, and, to a marvelous degree, in words and expression.

I have said the leaders have no principles to guide them. One would think, if he were to take them by their words, that they are making a specialty of principles. They are using this pretense just as the Hardshells and Campbellites did.

In Arkansas the split came distinctly and by the open declaration of the leaders, on the Secretary issue. They would have no secretary. In Texas, the seceders have two secretaries. But they encourage each other, and the leader of the opposition in a State further east is for both. He is like the man who could teach the round or the flat theory of the world. The only thing is to hurt the live work. It is easy to show that here in Texas, the opposition have occupied both sides of every issue they have raised. They have no principles, but confound prejudices with principles. Men without the qualifications to lead among the regular forces go out and form a following among the forces of the malcontents. Every Hardshell, every sore-head, is with them, and many good people, misinformed and misled by false issues.

The situation is full of peril and of opportunity. There is great need of wisdom in dealing with it. If no mistakes are made, we may at least write as did Paul, "The things which have happened to us have fallen out rather to the furtherance of the gospel."

They will fail, all of them. Their predecessors in the same line failed. These will fail because their ways are destructive. They will destroy themselves. They can not succeed. Even if everything were turned over to them, they would fail. Negation always fails.

But what is our part in the struggle for denominational progress? The program is simple. First, relieved of the enormous incubus of this heterogeneous mass of opponents, our duty is to give to the denomination a center of unification around sound principles and practices, without even the shadow of a compromise. Much of our present trouble is the leavings of other trouble brought down through compromise. Now is the time to drive down the flagstaff at the right place. We have the opportunity to rally the denomination on higher ground.

In the second place, and with all our strength, we should press the work. We must overcome evil with good. Now we have the opportunity to pitch our campaigns of enlightenment, enlistment and enlargement on sound principles, and to work from a unified center. These campaigns must go on till the masses are educated and the present distemper outgrown. A New Testament order of things has eliminated alien elements. They went from us because they were not of us. In going, they carried many who, at heart, are with us. Gospel work of the right kind will assimilate all sound elements back, leaving the denomination united, sound and progressive.

BY DR. J. B. GAMBRELL, D. D.

While this is going on, care must be taken that the leaders of malcontent do not have an easy time deceiving the people. While we build the walls, we must carry the sword, and see that neither Sanballat nor any of his tribe pull the walls down. We must go to the people with the truth of Christ, in the Spirit of Christ. When we have done our duty in these respects, the long-drawn-out troubles in the Southwest will be ended, and those who come after us will have peace. There is no easy way to end it. Nor is there any quick way. The only remedies worth while are blood remedies. Education, with evangelism, is the only remedy. It will be administered.

QUESTIONS IN BAPTIST RIGHTS.

IN A RECENT ordination, after the examination was finished as to experience and doctrine, a final question was asked: "Suppose that after you are a pastor, say five years from now, you change your views on doctrine and find yourself out of harmony with the views you have here expressed, would you consider it your duty or your privilege to continue in a Baptist pulpit and preach your new views?" This raises a fine question of right and rights. So far as we know, Baptists stand for perfect liberty of conscience and liberty of speech. We would not deny to any one, even an infidel, the right to preach his doctrines. We would be willing to fight that Catholics, Presbyterians, infidels and all sorts, might have freedom of thought and freedom of speech. But when a church is built to propagate the doctrines held by any people, it is no denial of the rights of free speech not to allow that church to be used to propagate other and contradictory doctrines.

There have appeared men in these later days who feel persecuted if they are not allowed to enter pulpits established to uphold a given set of principles, and there overthrow the very doctrines the church is set to defend. There is neither common sense, common honesty nor common decency in such a contention. Men who do not preach the accepted doctrines of the Baptists, have no right in Baptist pulpits, and it is no abridgment of their rights nor any persecution to keep them out. We are under no sort of obligations to furnish heretics with means to subvert the truth.

The same kind of reasoning applies to our denominational schools. Now and then a man in one of our schools finds, or thinks he finds, that the doctrines of the denomination are wrong, outworn, or something of the sort. No one should seek in the least to abridge his thinking, nor his defense of his thinking. The world is open to him. But when he claims the right to use an institution, its money, prestige and opportunities to overthrow the faith which the institution was founded to build up, he passes the bounds of liberty and enters the realm of arrogant license. Common honesty and decency would dictate that such a man resign his place and exercise his liberty without infringing on the rights of others.

In like manner our papers are under no obligation to lend themselves to the support of men who have quit the faith. The editor of this paper has no right to the use of a Catholic paper to overthrow Catholicism.

Coming closer into denominational lines, we have had in another state an illustration of a totally wrong conception of liberty. It is to an extent a question throughout the whole South. Those who call themselves "gospel missioners" (a very misleading name), have supposed that they have the right to use the machinery and instruments formed to promote co-operative work, to further totally different, and, as run, destructive plans, which they approve. For

By Dr. J. B. Gambrell, D. D.

one we admit without the slightest question the right of a church to act independently, to send its money as it pleases, for what it pleases, without the slightest interference by any other church, any association, convention or what not. And we bear cheerful testimony to the worth and zeal of beloved brethren and sisters of that way of thinking. As long as they contend for the privilege of sending their money as they please, we will stand by them. The wisdom of their course is another thing; but their rights in the premises are not to be brought into question. The question is simply this: Have brethren who do not believe in the co-operative system of missions the right to membership in co-operative bodies and in general to use the meetings, the papers, the boards and all the machinery of co-operation to hinder and destroy co-operation? Certainly not. To ask the question is to answer it. If brethren want to give their money independently, they can do it, and, for one, we shall never bring in question that right; but when they ask us to turn over all we have to them, to undo our work, we shall insist that we have a right to control what we have created and for the purpose for which it was created, and that too without molestation from them. It is their right to have all the meetings they want and to have them without molestation from any source. This right is not to be denied; but that is the limit of it.

For Dr. Crawford and his excellent wife, whom we know in the flesh, we have nothing but Christian love. We believe they are not on the best line. We believe they will find what has before been found, that their plan is unworkable to any considerable extent. It is a pity to divide and distract our people over such issues as they raise. But they must be accorded every right and at the same time be kept within their rights, that others may likewise enjoy some rights.

CONCERNING BEING NEARLY RIGHT.

THIS article is in the nature of a companion piece to the one last week. It is intended to enforce the great importance of dealing with absolute thoroughness and honesty with religious matters. It is one thing for an honest seeker after truth to be misled. It is a vastly different thing for one to seek truth with less than a thorough purpose to find it and accept it. Between being exactly right and wrong to the last extreme there is a vast stretch of territory, and one may play up and down in that territory approximating the right more or less and never being really anything but wrong. When we fix the mind on one decisive point of aiming to be exactly right, whoever falls short of it, is altogether wrong and always fails.

I knew a woman once who had been converted several years. She was persuaded that she ought to be baptized, or rather she was fully convinced she ought to be, from reading the scriptures, but she accepted the easy going cheat, that it did not make any difference whether any one was baptized, just so he is converted. This woman had a brother who was going to ruin at a rapid rate. She tried to pray for him. She asked the prayers of many for him, but according to her own word, she really could not pray. Her faith never went out to God, and she had no peace. As she was trying to pray one morning, her sin of omission came up before her, and she resolved there and then, not to be nearly right but exactly right. Then she had access to God in prayer, and very shortly her brother was converted. Baptism will not save one from the condemnation of the law, but it will save one from self-condemnation and from doubts and failures. At last this woman ceased trying to be nearly right and struck out for the high ground of exactly right. If everyone in this country would determine to be exactly right on baptism, we would have great times speedily, and baptism is just one thing. There are others about which we should be equally concerned to be exactly right.

The scriptures furnish us plenty of examples of people who were nearly right, and got left out. There was Moses, the meekest of men. His was a singularly correct life, but he missed it just at one point, when he was to bring water from the rock for the famishing Israelites. Without considering fully, he disobeyed in one particular and the difference between speaking to the rock and striking cost him a place in the promised land. There was a solemn lesson in this. No man may palliate his conscience or make a plea before God because he has been mainly right before God and therefore he may afford to be wrong a little. God has but one rule, and that is to be exactly right.

There was a man who came to our Lord inquiring the way of life. He was a model young man in many respects, moral outwardly, upright, reverential. He stood right on the border line of the kingdom. He was right everywhere but at one single point. He loved money more than he loved God, and being nearly right in his life, and not exactly right, he was all wrong, for he turned away sorrowfully. There is no record that he ever did get exactly right, and so he is all wrong today.

And then there was Saul, the King of Israel, a mighty man in his day, and greatly honored of God. He had a great victory, by the blessing of God. The command was, to make a complete finish of the enemies of the Lord, with all their belongings. Saul committed the mistake that multitudes are committing today. He undertook to do some personal thinking, where God had already done the thinking. To his thinking, a happy notion struck him; he could save the best of the cattle and there could be a great sacrifice and God mightily honored. Saul had gone on all right, until he got right up to the point, and the difference between annihilating the whole business, and saving a little of it, cost Saul his kingdom. Obedience is better than sacrifice, and God intended that Saul and all who followed after, should lay that to heart.

Then there was Achen. He did not take anything like all the heathen had in their city. He just took one golden wedge and a Babylonian garment. He might have taken more, but as it was, he was stoned to death.

There was a Roman judge who heard the Apostle Paul make a tremendous appeal to him, and the judge was mightily moved. He said: "Almost thou persuadest me to be a Christian." He came up to the very door of the kingdom, stopped, and failed to take the last step. Doubtless he went back to ruin. That is what unnumbered thousands are doing today. Almost, but not altogether. It is a common thing in a city to see people missing a street car by a little. They almost reach the place in time but are entirely left.

Taking these examples, and any number of others, which might be presented, the question arises in the minds of many whether one who is so near right should be punished being altogether wrong. Let us look at the underlying principle. Downright honesty in religious matters is essential to any acceptable service. If one be wrong in his heart, every act of his life is vitiated. Because this is so, it is written: "The plowing of the wicked is sin." Plowing itself is a good thing. It would be a great help to the country, if more people were engaged in it but the plowing of the wicked, those whose hearts are not right with God, is sin. A wrong motive will vitiate a proper act. It follows therefore, that to be nearly right is to be entirely wrong. This is enforced by Christ's exposition of the moral law. He taught that whoever was guilty on one point is guilty of all of it, the lesson being that he violates the spirit of the law, which goes through the entire decalogue—the great spirit of love and obedience, without which no worship can be acceptable to God.

There are plenty of opportunities of application. I doubt not that many who read this article, upon a moment's reflection will realize that there is something the matter with them. Many are spiritually weak. Many are in the dark. The exact point from which any of these may have deflected from the straight road, may not be described, but it all began from a relaxation of purpose; the giving up of a fixed purpose to be exactly right, and an acquiescence in something nearly right. Once the soul has given up its high purpose, it drifts, and thousands who meant at the start to be nearly right, find themselves now to be far off from the straight and narrow path. It is easier to anchor one's self by a fixed purpose to be exactly right, than it is to keep somewhere in the neighborhood of the right; for once the anchor is raised, no one can tell where he will drift. I renew my plea for recruits to the exactly-right wing of the army.

CONCERNING DOING EXACTLY RIGHT.

THE weakness of the pulpit today lies largely at a single point. We do need ministerial education, we do need better ministerial support, and we do need in many places a more adaptable ministry, but our supreme need is not at any of these points. The sore weakness of many a pulpit lies in the fact, that the preacher does not try to be exactly right, but only conveniently right—as right as the common run of preachers, or as right as the sentiment of the church will approve. The much abused word "conservative" is wrongly applied to many a preacher. He temporizes with evil and splits differences in theology to keep along with the thick of the crowd, and all this goes under the dignified word, "conservatism." Many of this class of preachers, instead of making a specialty of being exactly right, are engaged perpetually in trying to keep anything from happening. If they can keep everything quiet, they are thoroughly satisfied. How smiling are many of the letters read in the associations! After reporting a long list of blanks, they wind up smilingly: "We are in peace with one another," and that is regarded the acme of church life. In any numbers of cases, the letter might read: "We are at peace one with another, also with the world, the flesh and the devil. Ours is a very conservative church, and our pastor is one of the most 'conservative' preachers in the country." This is the plain English of the situation. In many places, neither the pastor nor the church nor the individuals are trying to be exactly right. To be sure, they would not be willing to be understood as palpably wrong, but the "conservative" position lies somewhere between right and wrong.

Now, I say that this is the abomination of desolation, standing where it ought not. There are preachers who shy from every question involving a palpable right and wrong, and they think they are wise, and fool a lot of people into the same notion. I have known some of this class, who could never be induced to come out straight on the prohibition question. They are opposed to saloons and drunkenness, and in favor of temperance, but when the time comes to put the saloon down and out, they fall back on "conservatism," and that means, so far as they are concerned, conserving the saloon.

What multitudes of preachers trim and flinch and worm around the truth, as to giving. Everybody ought to give. They hope the brethren will feel like it. It is a good thing to give. They are missionary, and go to pieces if somebody intimates that they are not. It is all right to support the orphans and widows, but they do not believe in pressing the brethren on the money question. When they shoot off at all on money, they aim their little guns, not on the scriptural level, but to the level of public opinion. They would not camp with the hardshells, nor will they go up and take the high ground of the scripture, but they buy land somewhere between the highlands of New Testament teaching and the low grounds of downright hardshellism, and live it out there.

And this same tribe does not aim to be exactly right in their preaching on the doctrines of the New Testament. They have great respect for the "feelings" of the people, and the bottom truth about many is, that their main endeavor is not to be exactly right, but to get on the soft side of the people. These preachers lower doctrinal standards. They would not like to press election too far, or salvation by grace alone, or baptism in its place or communion either. They are Baptists in easy places, but they do not make a specialty of being exactly right anywhere. Somewhat right is good enough for them. They are of the pale, pea-green variety, unfit alike for sunshine or rainy weather.

What I want to say now is, that these people are not half as smart as they think they are. They get left. The people who make a specialty of doing exactly right, are the people who always lead and always come out ahead. God is not with the man who aims to be half right, three-fourths right, or ninety per cent. right. He is with the man who aims to be entirely right. The exactly right people have always been the people to do things, and, in the wind-up, they have the respect of the world, although the world may hate them. John the Baptist made a specialty of being exactly right. He could not get along with Herod, nor Herod's woman, and he could not get along with the Pharisees, the religious dudes of that day; but he got along with God and fulfilled his mission gloriously. God gave him a quick passage to his eternal home, and Jesus Christ passed on him the supreme compliment, that no greater man had ever been born of woman. John was a do-exactly-right man, if it made an earthquake, and he landed the cause he stood for at the right place.

Daniel was a do-exactly-right man up to the high-water mark. Moses was a do-exactly-right man, and he got across the Red Sea, bag and baggage. The Hebrew children were do-exactly-right men, and they came out of the fiery furnace in good shape. The do-exactly-right prescription is good against water, lions and fire. Gideon was a do-exactly-right man, and he cleared the aliens out of his country. Luther was a do-exactly-right man on the doctrine of justification by faith, and he turned the current of history. God does not do anything with milk-sops and trimmers.

In a meeting held by one of our evangelists, the leading woman of the place, a member of the Baptist church, who had been hanging on to the world and to the church, concluded, under a powerful appeal, to join the do-exactly-right wing of the army. She went home, burned up all the

BY DR. J. B. GAMBRELL, D. D.

cards in her house, made splinters out of certain gaming devices, brought out her cut-glass wine set and beat the whole thing into bits with a hammer, and then explained to her husband, that from that day on she would give her service to God. She arose in the church and said: "I have lived a double life," asked forgiveness, told what she had done, and in less than a week her husband was converted. One woman known to myself changed the whole attitude of a church on the financial question by doing exactly right and doing it openly.

What the world needs today is a large re-enforcement to the do-exactly-right wing of the army. Half right is not right at all; three-fourths right does not count; ninety per cent. is bad; ninety-nine per cent. is not good. Anything shorter than an honest purpose, fixed in the heart, to do right on all questions as they arise, will not give strength to a Christian life, and about the sorriest specimen of humanity under the sun is the preacher who is trying to make up in tones and attitudes and platitudes for the lack of downright sincerity of heart, which will commit him irrevocably to the right side of every question, as God gives him to see the right.

A few do-exactly-right people in each church will work the mightiest revolution known since Luther withstood princes and prelates at Worms. Do-exactly-right preachers will take counsel of God. They will deliver God's message with no rant or tremor. They will preach in view of the great white throne. Like the do-exactly-right Apostle Paul, when he first appeared before Caesar, they will never stand alone, but will always behold the Lord with them. Under their preaching, Mrs. Grundy will take a back seat, and "they say" will yield to, "thus saith the Lord." These do-exactly-right preachers are the only ones worth their weight in sawdust. And when the pulpits are filled by do-exactly-right preachers, the pews will be filled with do-exactly-right church members. There will be a stiff atmosphere in the churches and the Lord's hosts will be as terrible as armies with banners.

Can't we drum up large re-enforcements to the do-exactly-right wing of God's army? Who will join?

THE GREATEST QUESTION.

AMONG Baptists the Great Commission is commonly accepted as the immovable rock upon which all missionary enterprises are built. Every word of it stands on the supreme authority of him who introduces the document by declaring that all power in heaven and earth is given to him. We may, therefore, confidently assume, that so long as we pursue the policy marked out by the Commission itself, there will be behind us and with us the "All-power" of the Lord himself.

The Commission divides itself naturally into sections. We have first, "Go, teach all nations." Going precedes teaching, and teaching follows going. Baptists have stood against the world, not only for the substance, but for the divine order of this great commission. After teaching, or disciplining, people are to be baptized. Baptism has not only its function, but its place as well, and the Lord places it in the Commission, where he wants it to stay.

Following baptism comes another course of teaching, which, like the commandment of God, is very broad. We are to teach "All things commanded." Every part of this document connects itself back to "go," and it is a missionary document from beginning to end.

A large number of Baptists have steadfastly held to going and to baptizing, but a less number have held firmly to the course of teaching which is to follow baptism. Dr. J. M. Robertson, in a recent discourse in our presence, demonstrated, with great force, that this second course of teaching is just as essentially and truly missionary work as the first; that it belongs to the same great missionary command; that it connects itself inseparably with the go; and that the apostles themselves so understood it and so practiced. With marvelous clearness he showed in the discourse referred to, that while Paul made one tour planting churches, he, himself made two missionary tours, strengthening the churches by teaching them the "All things commanded." He not only made these tours himself, but he sent others on a like mission to the churches; two at a time generally, and sometimes more than two.

Even a casual survey of the field throughout the Southern states will convince any one that we have cut the Commission in twain, and limited its scope to the mere matter of planting churches; while we have left the great and enduring question of Church Culture almost untouched. In this case, as in all other cases where we go contrary to the divine teaching, we have suffered greatly. Our churches throughout all the South are not much more than preaching stations. The church itself is not developed. The purposes of the churches are little understood by the masses, and the obligations of the churches but slightly felt. Taking the country over, by careful estimates made by competent persons, not over 25 per cent. of the churches throughout the South contribute at all to missions. Many old associations do absolutely nothing. The contributions of the contributing churches represent a very small per cent. of the membership of those churches, and the contributions are, as a rule, a mere fraction of what the contributors really ought to give. The result of this lack of church culture, which has come down to us from the fathers through a failure to carry out the commission in its fullness, is exceedingly humiliating. Nowhere in the world do Baptists give as poorly as in the Southern states. Almost a million and a half of us, on a great effort, give about $125,000 a year to foreign missions; whereas it would be easy to find one hundred and twenty-five churches that ought to give more, or even to find one hundred and twenty-five men who ought to give more.

When we consider this situation in all of its bearing, it ought to stir us to the very depths. We have only touched the fringe of the question when we discuss the meager giving of some churches and the no-giving of most of the churches. In case of failure to do right, the reflex influence of the failure on those who fail is greater than the failure itself. Sin is a gun that always kicks back harder than it shoots forward.

What are some of the results, present and prospective, of this condition of things? In the first place, we have very low church life. Low in every respect. So low, indeed, that in many cases it is hardly possible to discover the slightest pulsations of life. Churches that stand entirely out of the order of the commission are churches without divine favor. The membership are weak, poorly prepared to resist temptations; easily carried about with prejudices, and, in general, hard to get along with.

Another result is, the pastors are uniformly not supported. In general, they are compelled to support themselves in some secular employment. They farm about enough to spoil their preaching, and preach about enough to spoil their farming. And so men who might develop into great power as gospel ministers are all their lifetime mere weaklings. They are not only weak, but many of them become subservient and work in harmony with the undeveloped, inactive and prejudiced of their congregations. This is the systematic, or rather, unsystematic way, which starves them first, and then the churches as a result of their starvation.

Another serious result is, that these churches, undeveloped, inactive and disobedient to the divine command, are a

By Dr. J. B. Gambrell, D. D.

dangerous force in the denomination. The idle are dangerous to themselves and others also, and those who are doing nothing good are almost sure to be doing something they ought not to do. They are a constant peril to the order and progress of the denomination on all lines. They become a great obstructing force. They can be used by men who have a use for them. They are subject to spasms of excitement, and by reason of their weakness in Bible knowledge and spiritual life, are a great burden and care upon the more active in their own churches, associations and conventions. No great forward movement can be projected that does not have to overgo the opposition of the inert, uninterested, untaught and prejudiced part of the denomintion. We stand in jeopardy every hour throughout all the Southern states from this great mass of inactive, do-nothing Baptists.

We do not take the view of many pessimistic writers that they are unconverted. The mass of them we believe to be converted, and they are less to blame for the present state of things than those who have been placed by divine Providence in the forefront. Our denominational policies have been narrow, insufficient, and far short of the scope of the divine commission of our Lord. The trouble that looms up dark and forbidding, before the mind of the thoughtful Baptists is that these churches are a nesting-place for the unnumbered hosts of do-nothing Baptists in the time to come. It puts a nightmare on our spirits to think of generations of Baptists throughout this, the greatest Baptist country on the face of the earth, and only a small per cent. of them doing anything, and that small per cent. doing only a small per cent. of what they ought to do.

This is the situation and not a dream. No wise man among us will shut his eyes to it. It is to be considered as it is, and dealt with in a practical way. Practical men, not dreamers, are needed to change the front of things, and bring the whole denomination in Texas, and elsewhere, nearer up to the New Testament standard. It is said by men who oppose practical methods for changing this state of things, that these churches have pastors who ought to train them and lead them in all practical missionary work. That much is granted. But the churches planted by the Apostle Paul had pastors. He had given orders that elders be ordained in all the churches, and it was done; but, notwithstanding that, he provided for the visitation of the churches to bring them to the proper standard of usefulness. We shall hardly see the time when we can improve on the divine method of doing things; and there is at the bottom of this opposition to apostolic methods in developing churches, an unworthy spiritual conceit, which runs into a monstrous spiritual deceit. Let us face the situation. One hundred years have gone since the cause was planted in some parts of the South, a half a hundred since it was planted in some parts of Texas, and yet, the oldest churches having had pastors all these years, many of them are among those who do nothing at all. The truth of it must be told. This is no particular fault of the pastors, but is a result of their environments. They have not been taught. It is no humiliation to any man of God to say to him that there are things that he ought to know that he does not know. There is only one kind of preacher in this world, that we thoroughly disbelieve in, and that is the man who thinks he knows enough.

Now, if this situation has continued for all these years, and is growing rather worse than better, when will it mend itself? Is it not time that the denomination broaden its plans to compass the whole design of the great commission? Just as certainly as we live this work of righting the inactive, or poorly developed churches is the work before Texas Baptists today. It is the cure-all remedy. Right these churches and teach them all things commanded, and a strong church life will be the best possible safeguard

By Dr. J. B. Gambrell, D. D.

against wordly temptations, the best safeguard against heresies; a guarantee of pastoral support; a guarantee of co-operation in our mission work, and a guarantee against the disturbances that so often hinder the progress of Zion.

Even from the financial standpoint it is the greatest problem to be worked out. In Mississippi, some twenty years ago, many of the associations having completed, as they thought, their associational work, had dropped entirely out of all co-operation in the spreading of the gospel beyond the preaching in their own meeting houses. One of the largest associations in the state, numbering about 2,500 people, living in an excellent country, gave habitually less than $100 a year, which was distributed in a loose way among some broken-down preachers in their own association. The state board employed some of the ablest men in the state to teach the "All things commanded" in these churches. Among them was that heroic spirit which went from New Orleans the other day to glory—Dr. D. I. Purser. We have in mind at this writing the work he did in the above mentioned association. A few months was spent with the churches, the association came into hearty co-operation, and for the years succeeding has given perhaps $1,000 a year for the spread of the gospel. This is but one of the many instances known to the writer. In nothing was the financial wisdom of the board in that state so demonstrated as in its effort to bring to the support of all missions the inactive associations and churches, and that ought to be the leading business of our board in Texas until there is a new face put on things in this great state.

That objections will be raised is absolutely certain, and it is certain that these objections will come, mainly, from those who have studied the matter less, and need the work the most; but no amount of objection should turn a great convention away from an honest effort to carry out the commission of our Lord in its fullness.

WHICH WAY, THIS OR THAT?

ONE of the chief of the debaters advises that "Dr. Gambrell" get up some debates as a means of uniting the brethren. He has had a little debate with a Campbellite debater, and he says all the Baptists lined up together. Likely those present did. But unhappily for the suggestion, the brethren who do things to much account were not there, and will not be at the next one. The Campbellite with whom this debater came the best part of a thousand miles to debate told us that the trouble with him had been that he could not get a debate with a representative Baptist. This will be his trouble next time we see him.

I do not insist that debates never do good, or that it is never wise for a Baptist to take part in them. I have a feeling to the contrary of this, though I have never seen the time when a greater victory could not be won by not having a debate. Hence, though challenged repeatedly in the past, I never saw my way as a minister to do what the flesh and the world would delight in, take the "cuticle" off an obstreperous belligerent. I knew it could be done, and had a feeling that there would be some satisfaction in it; but there was no market for Campbellite and Pedobaptist "hides." And, besides, I preferred to take another course and get the "hides" and the people in them all in the Baptist churches in a comfortable state of mind, soul and body. Thus I have missed some fine chances for debates. Still it may be that now and then a debate would do good.

This article is directed against the professional debater, his spirit and methods. I have a long, painful, unsatisfactory acquaintance with the subject in hand, having seen the cause suffer many things at the hands of this unhappy class. Are they or their ways helpful toward denominational unity and co-operation? They are not. I could write down the names of the leaders of the tribe and show that severally and collectively they are the most factional, turbulent sowers of discord within Baptist ranks. This is notorious. They have the contentious spirit and must fight on till death, and fight they will. Turned into pugilists by their debates, they lose interest in other things, and must turn everything into a fight. Well did Dr. J. B. Moody turn away from a course, which was rapidly disqualifying him for higher, holier and better things. To secure unity with such a spirit and such methods, the denomination would have to be like them, and that would be to turn our whole working force into a perpetual prize ring exhibition. Look at the very heroes of the debating arena, and they are in one eternal round of fights, with outsiders and insiders. The less unity on that line the better.

But I have well matured convictions on the subject, going to particulars. It may help us to a fair understanding of the matter to state some of them.

1. Speaking now of the professional debaters, I risk nothing in saying, that of all men among us, they are poorest representatives of New Testament Christianity. They are extreme in statement, lopsided in doctrine, and off tone in spirit. They are the unsafest guides in religion, being extreme at this point, entirely blank there, and in spirit trash, and of the world, the flesh and sometimes worse. Read their papers; read the accounts given by their admirers of their performances, and see the coarseness, the vainglorious spirit, the utter absence of that spirit which breathes through every page of the New Testament. It is the spirit of the bully and the prize ring, not the spirit of the Nazarene. Can this sort of thing win for Jesus? No. It is a reproach to the cause and a curse to the Baptist people.

2. These debaters and debates infect the denomination and the public with their vainglorious spirit. They make contentions and strifes in communities to the detriment of

the spiritual life of God's saints. They never dispose the people to prayer or praise or to any of the sweet charities, which are the strength and chief ornaments of religion. They are, as they go, fruitful of many small questions which do minister strife rather than godly edifying. They have turned multitudes, even whole churches, away from the main things and set them off into vainglorious wrong, while the last are neglected.

3. These debates harden sinners, as well as saints, the way they are commonly carried on—a battle of gladiators without tenderness or love; without grace or unction. The communities where they are held become spiritually dead and barren, like spots where log heaps or brick kilns are burnt. The results in many cases are such as to appall any soul devoted to the chief thing for which Christ lived and died and rose from the grave and intercedes on high, the saving of the lost world. They are schools for the deceitful handling of God's Word.

4. They are not favorable to the propagation of the Baptist faith; for they commence in an atmosphere of oppositiou, and men's minds are set against the truth. The conditions are bad to begin with, and nearly certain to get worse. Both sides nearly always report a victory. The world, the flesh and the devil have a fine chance at an ordinary debate where the "fur flies" for the fun of it, and where sinners lost are made partisans touching things beyond them. This is not the place for truth to have the best chance. Without one shadow of a doubt, I believe the professional debater a burlesque on New Testament Christianity, and an awful curse to the cause of Christ. If a time came when some Goliath must be met, let the churches select some spiritual pastor, well rounded in his theology and Christly living, and let this man, in lowliness of spirit, care for the cause, and then take care that he be not infected with the spirit to go about and seek whom he may get up a

debate with. And let him be careful not to be beguiled into starting a paper to exploit his views, so as to catch things coming and going.

What is the best way to unify our people? I answer: Lift up a standard for the great thing nearest the heart of Christ, even the rescue of the perishing. Not hold debates, but hold revival meetings, blood warm; God has given every redeemed soul a love for this. A revival will heal more bickerings, more strifes, more heartaches and heart breaks than anything ever set agoing among men. To see the lost coming home to God, will lift a man or a church higher than anything else this side of heaven. A great revival will burn out the dross, purify churches, and clarify the atmosphere. It opens more hearts than anything, and disposes more people to receive the truth and walk in it. It makes the finest possible conditions for preaching Bible doctrine, and results in baptizing more Campbellites and others than all the debates ever held. Moreover, it associates strong doctrine with Christly spirit, and puts no stamp of reproach upon the Baptist name, as the average debate does.

"Dr. Gambrell" is distinctly in better business than holding little, pesky debates. To preach to a little congregation in a school house, as I have been permitted to do lately, and to hear the shouts of souls born to God is immeasurably more glorious than all the pitched battles of all the debaters walking the earth today.

I may be extreme, but I can't even imagine Paul quitting his great missionary work to hold a five days' debate with Diotrephes at $100 a debate. I must close with this remark additional: We owe something to God's people who are not Baptists, and it is bad to give them a stone for bread.

THE LAW OF THE HARVEST.

SOWING and reaping is the world's work. We go a ceaseless round in this common employment. It is seed time now, and then harvest. The farmer, having regard to due seasons, plants, and in the fullness of time gathers into his barns. The merchant buys and sells and gets again. The capitalist invests and collects. The politician canvasses and goes to the legislature. so all the world toils in ceaseless circles, all sowing and reaping, some in sorrow, some in joy.

The laws governing the harvests are the same in temporal, intellectual and spiritual things. We are all under these laws and must do our life work under their inexorable sway. They are fixed by the hand that made the world, and the fulness of it. They reach to every square inch of man's kingdom, and they take life out of the realm of chance and give to it a fixed rule of action.

The first feature of the law of the harvest I mention, is that all are sowers, whether they wish to be or not. No man liveth to himself, and no man dieth to himself. In this life a man cannot be a Mr. Nobody. He is somebody by virtue of living, and his life is a continuous seed-sowing. So intensely true is this that every human life affects the moral level of the world even as every drop of water affects the sea level. This imparts to every human being an unspeakable value, and ought to deeply impress us with the importance of looking closely after the very lowly. A neglected girl, left parentless by an epidemic in New York State, became, in time, the mother of a generation of six hundred criminals. Society sowed neglect, and reaped a harvest in kind. This neglected girl lost the State $3,000,000, to gather the tares and prevent further ruin. Society, as well as individuals, sows and reaps under the law of the harvest. We sow saloons and reap murder, gambling, poverty,

BY DR. J. B. GAMBRELL, D. D.

squalor, social disorder, wrecked homes; temporal, intellectual and spiritual ruin. The politicians concern themselves in such matters with trying to curtail the harvest.

The Unlettered Negro who Digs His Living out of the Ground is Wise Enough to Plant What He Wants to Gather.

Statesmen, knowing the law of the harvest, concern themselves with the sowing.

The law of the harvest, furthermore, is that the sowing and the reaping is the same in kind. Even the dullest farmer knows this. The unlettered Negro, who digs his living out of the ground, is wise enough to plant what he wants to gather. He does not plant at random, just anything his hand finds. For corn he plants corn, for potatoes, he plants potatoes, etc. This is the law: "Whatsoever a man soweth, that shall he also reap." In the natural world we have natural demonstrations of this truth in such an endless series that no one questions the absolute certainty of the law. But this same law holds all through life, in the intellectual as well as in the spiritual. There is no difference. The eyes of the world are holden that they cannot see this. They sow evil and expect to gather good. They sow darkness and expect to reap light. They sow hatred and expect love. They sow folly and expect to reap wisdom. They sow strife and expect peace. Everywhere everything produces after its kind. Under the law of the harvest, seed multiply, some thirty, some forty, some a hundred-fold. This law of increase is limited by conditions. The yield is larger in rich soil prepared for the seed. Seasons also affect the harvest. But the law of increase holds. There is a story of two Scotchmen who, upon leaving the mother country each resolved to bring with him something which should perpetually remind him of home. One brought the seed of thistle and the other a colony of bees. The thistle rapidly spread over a large section of America to the grief of every farmer. The bees have spread, also, and furnish honey for millions. True or false, the story illustrates the law of increase. One evil word produces others, and they others still, until a whole community is convulsed with strife. We are planting saloons in our new possessions. They will multiply and curse the races we have set our hands to bless and elevate, and this government can no more escape the harvest than can an individual escape the harvest of his sowing. We are sowing blood-guiltiness, and the harvest will be the blood of our own people.

Applying the law of the harvest, Paul said to the church at Corinth: "They that sow sparingly shall also reap sparingly." This, in temporal things, comes home to the common sense of every one. He is an uncommon fool who economizes in seed corn, when a single grain planted is likely to produce hundreds of grains a little later. But in spiritual things such folly characterizes whole churches and even whole denominations. Herein is the weakness of many. They sow sparingly and expect to reap abundantly. They skimp in all the work and ways of the church, and then lament the leanness of the church. The individual withholdeth more than is meet and expects to increase. "There is that scattereth and yet increaseth, and there is that withholdeth more than is meet, and it tendeth to poverty," says God.

From these general remarks on the law of the harvest, let us draw some lessons profitable to individuals and churches. It is easy to see the folly of the notion that young men must "sow wild oats." If they do, they will reap wild oats, and the likelihood is the crop will constantly reproduce by grain left on the ground. Wild oats is another name for tares, and tares are dreadfully hard to eradicate from the soil, once they take root. There is every reason known under heaven why young men should not sow wild oats. Paul, in parceling out advice to different classes, admonished young men to be sober-minded, the Greek being wise or reasonable. If a man is to sow wild oats he ought to wait till he is old, so as to shorten the reproductive period. The real foundation of future success is laid by men in early life. The seed sown reproduces in the character of the person, and he becomes like the things he does. Besides, early good deeds reproduce in others to our life-long advantage. The sheaves are brought back and fill our barns in old age. To sow economy and industry in early life is to gather a harvest of plenty in old age. To sow kindness early is to gather staunch friends amid the gathering shadows of age. Kindness reproduces from father to son, from friend to friend. How often do old men meet the young and hear them say, "I have heard you spoken of by my father or my mother, perhaps it is my grandfather or grandmother who loved you for the good you did them."

The sower must commit the seed from his hand to wind and weather, not forgetting that God rules both wind and weather. No one can tell which grain will prosper. We must sow beside all waters, at morning, noon and evening. The Lord of the harvest keeps watch o'er all the seed and will reward the sower.

It comes to pass often, that one sows and another reaps. The Sunday School teacher sows the seed and years after in another place perhaps, a pastor or evangelist reaps, and both rejoice together. The mother plants the seed in her child's heart and dies. When the great harvest home comes at the end of the world, she will reap what in tears she sowed, but did not live to see spring up and bear fruit. None of us can labor in vain in sowing the seed of the Kingdom.

In spiritual sowing we are just where we are in temporal sowing. In both cases, the increase is of God. No man can make corn grow. The light and the moisture are of the Lord. In the natural world seed time and harvest, under the good providence of God, do not fail. It is so in spiritual things. Churches and people who go forth sowing with tears, do reap, though there is much about it mysterious. The idle churches fail. The sowing churches reap. There is amid all the uncertainties of it, a divine certainty. Faith sees it, and withholds not its hand.

BY DR. J. B. GAMBRELL, D. D.

EVANGELIZING THE FAR WEST.

SOME years ago, Pastor Bunting, then of Pecos, backed up by that church, and aided by religious people of different denominations, who desired the religious welfare of the scattered people of that section, began the Madera camp-meeting. Like most great things, it began small, but has grown, year by year. The place is 500 miles west from Dallas, 45 miles south of the Texas and Pacific Railroad, up in the Davis Mountains. If anyone supposes that there are no mountains to speak of in Texas, he is mistaken. The whole country in the west is high. The boasted mountains of New England, put down out there, on a sea level, would make deep holes in the ground. On this elevated plateau, there are real mountains. Up in a deep canyon in these mountains is the spot where the great cowboys' campmeeting is held. To get there you must go on purpose. It is not on the way to anywhere. The mountain pass opens into a wider place, a valley of a few acres. A mountain stream comes down to supply water for cowman use, and an excellent place for baptizing.

John the Baptist was fond of the wilderness, and he stuck close to Jordan, and other places where there was "much water." Madera would have suited him exactly. Encircling this open space are the lofty cliffs rising hundreds of feet perpendicular. It is one of the most picturesque spots the eye ever beheld.

Last year there were about 300 campers; this year between 400 and 500. They were there from Houston, San Antonio, El Paso, Dallas, and other remote points. Some came 400 miles out of the country, taking trains at their stations, coming part of the way, and then traveling 180 miles in their private conveyances. The diameter of the campmeeting circle was full 400 miles.

People came for one great purpose—to seek their soul's good; not every one, but that was the predominant thought. The cowboys were there in great force, manly, respectful, and reverent. The great ranch men and women were there with their full force. Peoples of many denominations were there, broad-minded and tolerant, all co-operating up to the point of agreement, and no further, yet without bitterness, when they could go no further.

These ranch people are great. The average person from the East must revise his judgment of the ranch people. They are uncommonly intelligent, thoroughly orderly and self-respecting. They have cut out the rowdy and the scrub. There is no more place for them among these high-minded people. There were large numbers of young people present, and during the entire time, we noted not so much as an indiscretion.

The hospitality of the people is boundless. The finest beef one ever ate is provided; and all the campers are invited to help themselves. People turn in and eat anywhere. The social feature is not left out by any means; but it is not foremost.

The one large feature of the meeting was its intense religious purpose. That seems fixed. One ranch woman, standing as practically alone for Christ on her great ranch of more than 400 square miles, brought her entire establishment, except one negro woman, to keep the place, hoping that salvation might come to her house. And it did. Every one was saved, and she went before several of them into the baptismal waters. One man, 73 year old, who had spent much of his life on the waters, but who lived in the mountains alone, walked 20 odd miles, with his heart set to seek the Lord. He was baptized at the very last. People from remote parts were careful to bring the unconverted, hoping they might find grace and salvation. Some entire camps went away rejoicing in the Lord.

By Dr. J. B. Gambrell, D. D.

How many were saved? God only knows. Almost every service some came over the line. One of the first converts was a man of great strength, whose wife said at the very start: "I am here to see my husband converted;" and speedily it was done. Then she wanted everybody saved. What a noble dissatisfaction does this soul-winning create right in the midst of the highest joys heaven gives to mortals here below!

There were mountain top meetings, hours "when heaven came down our souls to greet, and glory crowned the mercy seat." Some of these were quiet and heavenly, when the dews of grace fell gently on our hearts. Then there were great conquest meetings, resembling the irresistible onslaught of a conquering army when the vanquished throw down their arms and come under the flag for protection. At one such meeting 23 surrendered; at another, 28, and, perhaps, more. They came singly, and in groups, under the powerful pleadings and solemn warnings of Pastor Truett, who was the principal preacher of the meeting. The preaching was strong and thorough. The converts were admonished to take their stand and to obey Christ the Lord, and not man at all. Things went on very much after the New Testament fashion. Twenty-one were baptized in the beautiful stream hard by. There were 4 baptizings, one at midnight. Some cowboys were to leave next morning, and, having found the Savior, desired to follow Him that very night. There were 4 of them. There was water and no one could forbid them. Not a few will join Baptist churches at home, and numbers will join other denominations, according to their several views. There were not less than 75 professions, and many backsliders were reclaimed, and won to a higher life.

Some evenings the girls formed companies and marched up and down the camp singing sacred songs. Then men and women broke into groups and went to the mountain sides to pray and labor with the unsaved.

One of the best features of the meeting was the deepening and maturing of the religious life of God's people. There was a drawing in all round. The sublime possibilities of Christian faith were brought out strong. The power of the gospel to save, and save the worst, and to save at once, and to save eternally, gripped many hearts. There were at least a dozen preachers present, and I believe not one failed of a great blessing helpful toward a new order of preaching.

I cannot help believing that one of the best features of the meeting was its utter openness and candor; its relief from all unnecessary restraint. People spoke out freely, even boys and girls. Men came seeking salvation and said so right out. Everything was easy.

Eminent ministers were present belonging to other denominations, and rendered efficient service. Among these were Pastor Moore, of the First Methodist Church, San Antonio; Dr. Little, superintendent of missions in Texas for the Northern Presbyterians, and Pastor Bloyse, of Fort Davis Presbyterian Church, whose praise is on the tongues of all good people in that entire section.

These notes must be brought to a close, though multitudes of things crowd on me, all worthy of mention. Camp was broken at noon Monday, and the people moved out of the canyon on to the wide prairies, separating here and there, making for their distant homes, many with new hopes and all in love. One of the wonderfully beautiful things about these glorious western people is their love for each other. It is beautiful beyond words. The long caravan looks like an army train; 75 or 100 stopped the first night at the Cowan ranch, after a drive of 25 miles, made in about 4 hours. The horses in the west don't know much about walking. A beef is killed for all to help themselves. The

By Dr. J. B. Gambrell, D. D.

"church wagons" are opened and the cooks, Negroes and Mexicans, go to their work. After a while one cook cries out: "Here it is. You had better come and get it, or I will throw it out." Men and women, boys and girls, all come up and take a tin plate, a tin cup, knife, fork and spoon, and go and get what they want. They sit down on the grass, tailor-fashion, chat and eat. There is some hearty and wholesome romping out on the open. The shadows of the evening fall on the wide plain. The campers gather in a group, sitting on the grass, and one after another quotes a passage from the holy Book of God. A girl leads in a song. Then there is a prayer, "God be with us till we meet again" floats out on the air, then another prayer, and every one prepares to sleep the sleep of peace. The beds are spread out on the open plain in groups by families and we lie down. Looking up to the clear sky studded with stars, the 19th Psalm comes to me with a strangely happy meaning, "The heavens declare the glory of God and the firmament showeth His handiwork."

It is morning, and the cooks are rekindling their fires. With breakfast over, we break camp piece meal, and go our several ways, to meet next year, if God will, all expecting, praying and willing to work for much greater things when we meet again. It is worth a trip across the continent to be in such a meeting.

CHURCH SOVEREIGNTY AND DENOMINATIONAL COMITY.

THESE two questions lie close together. It is quite easy for us to press either one beyond its proper limits, and thus interefere with the other. There is nothing about Baptists which are more thoroughly agreed than church sovereignty; that is, the right of each separate church to govern itself and to regulate all of its affairs after its own mind without any interference from the outside. Once upon a time, in the heat of a popular discussion, we struck off this statement, which presents the case about like it is: "A church is a complete institution in itself; it is finished off and tucked in at both ends, and has no contrivance for attaching itself to anything else." That is the truth in a figure.

While the church sovereignty is universally accepted among Baptists, it is also widely understood that a church has not sovereignty in the sense that it can do anything it pleases, but rather, that it is under limitations of the law, and that Christ is the head of the church. It is not a legislative body, but an executive body; therefore, there are limitations upon church sovereignty.

First: No church can exercise in any such way as to go beyond its own sphere. Outside of that sphere it has no power, and in fact, no existence. The limitations of church sovereignty are the bounds of the church itself. All matters pertaining to more than one church are regulated by denominational comity.

Second: The simplest kind of truth is that one church cannot press its sovereignty to the point of depriving other churches of equal rights with itself. To illustrate: If one church should exclude a member, or depose a minister, another church could on its bare authority immediately restore the brother to membership, or to the ministry; but, it would have no claim in the world on another church to recognize the act, or to co-operate with it; other churches having an equal right to an independent judgment.

The Scriptures unmistakably show that sovereign churches did co-operate for the support of the gospel and for the maintenance of sound doctrine. We may, therefore, follow the apostolic churches in these particulars, but all questions concerning co-operation go not on sovereignty, but on comity. A council composed of messengers from churches can never be invested with the slightest degree of church character. It is at this point that a great many otherwise sound Baptists fall into the heresy of Presbyterians and Episcopalians. It is altogether within the power of the sovereign church to send messengers to a council, as the Antioch church did send messengers to Jerusalem. But no church can claim anything of their messengers in council on the score of church sovereignty, because the transaction is carried entirely beyond the limits of independent churches, out on the open field of inter-church or denominational comity.

On this broad platform the plans for co-operative effort in denominations are wrought out. Here the messengers from the churches ought to stand on equal footing. Here there should be mutual confidence and respect; openness and fairness, and consideration for the welfare of the one common cause. The church which will not enter this field of comity except with the understanding, that the other churches shall yield to its judgment, ought, as a matter of common fairness and decency, to refrain from sending messengers. A council necessarily implies freedom to hear and discuss and determine. A body of messengers absolutely fixed cannot be a council at all, and so if we fall into the practice that some of the churches have recently adopted of instructing their messengers to our great denominational councils, and putting them beyond all counsel that should at once bring the whole matter of associations and conventions to an end.

There is one thing immeasurably greater than a great convention, however large it may be in numbers, however imposing in the character of the messengers present, and that is the spirit in which a convention ought to be held. If there be not present a common respect, and a willingness to confer in the spirit of brotherliness, then a great convention may be lowered to the level of a group of caucuses, each working to secure a definite end, without reference to the spirit of deliberation. From such a convention, in the language of the prayer book, "The good Lord deliver us."

"SQUIRE SINKHORN'S" MISTAKE.

I ONCE heard Dr. J. R. Graves, in my house, greatly interest and instruct a number of preachers by relating, in the way of illustration, the following story:

Somewhere in Kentucky there lived a magistrate by the name of Sinkhorn. Of course he was Esquire Sinkhorn. A lawyer returning from the state capital to the county where Squire Sinkhorn administered justice met a constable, whom he knew, with a citizen in charge. He inquired where the constable was taking the man, and was informed that he was taking him to the penitentiary by order of Squire Sinkhorn, and that he was to be committed for two years on charge of horse stealing. The lawyer said to the constable: "You had better take that man back. If you put him in the penitentiary on the order of Squire Sinkhorn you will be in trouble." The result was the man returned with his prisoner, accompanied by the lawyer, and the case was reopened before Squire Sinkhorn, the lawyer telling him it was beyond his power to send a man to the penitentiary. Squire

By Dr. J. B. Gambrell, D. D.

Sinkhorn averred that he was acting within the law, and at once produced the code and read that part of it which provided that for stealing property to a certain amount a man should be sent to the penitentiary for any given time within certain limits. This man, Squire Sinkhorn averred, was undoubtedly guilty of horse stealing, and therefore he had sent him to the penitentiary. But the lawyer said: "Give me the book." And he turned and read the section of the law providing that every one so charged should be tried before a jury of his peers, detailing at length the manner of trial. Squire Sinkhorn was greatly astonished, and woke up to the fact that he had not read far enough. This Dr. Graves used to illustrate how certain persons have fallen into a great error in discussing the 6th of Hebrews by not reading far enough.

Squire Sinkhorn's mistake will illustrate the mistake of many others who read only in patches and snatches, and never get a full view of any question which they seek to discuss. Indeed, Squire Sinkhorn stands at the head of a great procession of men in law, in politics, in science, in religion, who come to hasty and vicious conclusions by not reading far enough.

A little learning has been declared to be a dangerous thing. It is very dangerous in law, as illustrated above. It has been amazingly fruitful of perils in science, where little snatches of truth have been taken, and men have built up theories on a single segment of truth. But in no sphere has Squire Sinkhorn's mistake been so fruitful of evil as in religion. The whole theory of Universalism is based on a few passages of Scripture taken out of their connection and away from their meaning. The Universalist does not allow the Bible to speak on the whole question, and so almost every false religion is built up on some select passages taken out of their true meaning. The cure for the evils of a partial view of the truth is the full view of the truth.

At an association in Georgia, where a number of preachers were gathered in a large country home, one brother animadverted severely on the fact that the congregation was invited to stand for prayer. He regarded it the abomination of desolation, standing where it should not, and said that he had denounced the custom all over the country as unscriptural. When asked the ground of his denunciation, he referred to the fact that Paul and the elders of the church at Ephesus kneeled down to pray. A brother present, taking a Bible as the conversation was going on, selected and afterwards read many passages touching the question of attitude in prayer, and from them altogether it was seen that sometimes people stood, sometimes kneeled and sometimes lay prone upon the earth, and from a full view of the subject it was evident that the Scriptures put no emphasis on the attitude, but all the emphasis on the condition of the heart. When the reading was through the brother who had condemned standing said that he ought never to preach again as long as he lived. It was suggested to him that the remedy for his mistake was not to quit preaching, but to find out all the Bible said on any question before making up his mind. He had simply made Squire Sinkhorn's mistake. He had not read far enough.

This mistake is notably the mistake of the Arminian. He reads only those passages which teach on the human side of religion, and from them he makes up his conclusion, leaving God a very small place in salvation, and some of them no place at all. The Antimonian reads all about predestination and hardens it into fatalism. With him there is no place for human action. His entire mind is directed to the God side, and because he will not read the other side he has a perverted and hurtful view. A notable example of this was the brother who took for his text "The grace of God which bringeth salvation hath appeared unto all men." He laid the stress of his sermon on the grace that bringeth

BY DR. J. B. GAMBRELL, D. D.

salvation, but did not even look to the end of the sentence, for the doctrine of the text is, that "the grace of God which

"Squire Sinkhorn"

brings salvation," is a teacher of duty. So, if he had read far enough, he would have seen that the grace of God runs right out into human actions, just as the sap passes through the fibre of the wood and makes leaves and fruit.

Our so-called "Gospel Mission" brethren are much given to Squire Sinkhorn's mistake. Their whole effort is to prove the separate action of churches. They commence with the action of the church at Jerusalem which sounded out the word through Judea, Samaria and the regions roundabout, and from that argue that a church, single and alone, ought to be a missionary force. They next take the church at Antioch, which was in that day the second great missionary center of the world, from which especially sounded out the word to the Gentiles. They read how, in obedience to the Spirit, Paul and Barnabus were sent out as missionaries from that church, and deduce from that very correctly, that a church is thoroughly competent to send out missionaries. Here they stop. But there is more. For instance, it would appear that Jerusalem and Antioch held a council and thereby laid the foundation for all councils between independent churches. If they would read on further they would see that Paul, whose membership was probably at Antioch, arose to the position of a great missionary leader, and that he brought about co-operation among the churches in the support of missionary enterprises. If they would read over in 2 Cor. 8 they would see the divine method of rounding up a great collection and of carrying out a common purpose among the churches. Three things were done: (1.) Paul wrote letters to Corinth about this collection, just as our secretaries today write letters to our churches, soliciting collections and co-operation. (2.) Paul went to what would be regarded now a prodigious extreme. He sent a number of brethren to the church at Corinth to help work up a collection in that church after they had already promised it. This was a system of agencies in the churches on a very strong scale. (3.) There were a number of men selected by the churches to take charge of the common fund and to distribute it. The reason for this was that nobody might be blamed. Now this is exactly what is going on today, only we do not put in on it as strong as Paul did.

If the brethren would keep clear of Squire Sinkhorn's mistake and read far enough they would see that while Paul and his traveling companion preached, and planted churches, and ordained elders, that afterwards they went back over the same ground and taught the churches and helped the churches. They were missionaries to the churches.

There is a great deal in reading far enough. The short sight is not as good as the long sight. Part of the truth is not as good as all of the truth. And the man who believes his theory, or accepts his doctrine from a partial view of the truth, is constantly in danger of being upset by more truth.

A good many men need today, as Squire Sinkhorn did, to revise their findings, finally making them to conform to the whole doctrine of God's Word.

PRINCIPLES UNDERLYING CO-OPERATION AMONG BAPTISTS.

(Outline of Lecture delivered at Baylor Summer School.)

BAPTISTS stand pre-eminently for personal obedience to a personal Saviour. With us, in the realm of religion, the family is lost. Each individual soul must repent for itself, exercise faith for itself, make a personal confession of Christ and be baptized for itself, and on his own faith and confession. Following baptism is an endless series of duties; every one of them is to be performed as a personal act of service and worship.

This, of course, implies the principle of voluntary service. There can be no coercion in religion. Every act from the beginning to the end must be of good will, not by constraint. In delivering his people from the bondage of sin, our Lord has made them his own free men and endowed each one of them with high and holy prerogatives.

But this does not imply that each one is to live a separate life. That is, to stand apart from his brethren in acts of worship and service. It implies, rather, that these individual free men shall come together in the unities of the gospel and stand together in helpful relations for the carrying out of the will of their common Lord and Master in the world.

It ought to be spelled large that liberty is not license and it is not foolishness and it is not separation. Liberty limited by law is the formula of all spiritual and civil progress. Whoever comes into the liberty wherewith Christ makes us free, at that moment goes under the laws by which that liberty is limited. The laws of the spiritual kingdom tend, all of them, to unity and co-operation. The very Spirit of Christ which reigns in his kingdom is a spirit of harmony. So all through the New Testament the spirit of strife, schism and opposition is discounted.

BY DR. J. B. GAMBRELL, D. D.

The individual Christian finds in the church the place where he can most successfully co-operate with his fellow Christians in the work of the Master. Let us pause a moment at the door of a church and contemplate the conditions of admission to its sacred fellowship. Whoever comes into the church must, by the very act, bind himself to the laws governing the church. He is committed to its hight and holy purposes, to its great mission in the world, of spreading the gospel. He is committed under the laws governing the church to seek the peace of that body; to live up to the covenant founded upon Scripture teaching and to co-operate with his brethren in that church to fulfill the will of the Master.

This means that within the realm of law he is to submit his individual judgment to the judgment of the church expressed in a scriptural way. No false idea of independence can be successfully urged to justify the individual member of the church in his opposition to the church, unless the church depart from the doctrines of Christ. There will be in every church many things which will test the spirit of each member. There will be many things about which there will be diversities of opinion: The pastor's salary; who should be the pastor; work to be undertaken by the church, the methods of the work, the workers, and a hundred things will arise to test the great Baptist principle of submission of the individual mind to the mind of the church. It is not too strong to say that within the realm of the church and within the limits of the teachings of Scripture, every individual member is bound in all good conscience and reason and Scripture, too, to submit his individual judgment to the judgment of the church rightly expressed.

It follows that no member has a natural or spiritual right to remain in the church unless he will co-operate, for churches were ordained of God for the very purpose of promoting co-operative work among individual Christians.

Our churches, as a rule, are far from maintaining their tendencies of ovegrown and altogether unscriptural personal independence which sets the will of one man against the law of Christ and the will of his brethren.

Let us go one step beyond this position. The churches are independent of each other, but, like the individual, not independent of law. We greatly need to emphasize the fact that the independence of the churches is itself limited by the laws which create them and assign them their places and work in the Kingdom of Christ. The stars in the heaven are entirely independent of each other, in that each one of them is a complete entity and separated from the others, but they belong to one great siderial system, and are all under general laws which regulate their courses in the heavens. So Christ has set his churches in his kingdom, each one a complete body, endowed with all the attributes of self-government and all of them together subject to the laws which govern in the kingdom. Here again the formula of liberty limited by law applies. When we open the Scriptures we are not long finding that under the inspired leadership of the Apostles, separate and independent organizations did co-operate for the carrying forward of the work of their one common head. They united in the support of missionaries, and in the support of the poor and gave their consent, judgment and united support to the establishment of sound doctrine against heresy. The churches of today need not hesitate to follow in the wake of the churches of the apostolic time. There is one example in the Acts of a council of churches. The initiative in this council was taken by the church at Antioch, by sending messengers up to the church at Jerusalem. The occasion for calling this council was some disturbances concerning doctrine in the Antioch church. The example is good for the modern practice of councils for the churches. We have these councils now under the names of associations and conventions and in them the basis of an inter-church co-operation is formed.

With regard to these general bodies there are several things to say:

First. They exist entirely outside and beyond the sphere of the churches. And in that sphere they have all the authority that there is or can be to regulate and control themselves in matters of membership, etc. The churches occupy a sphere to themselves and these two bodies, entirely dissimilar in nature, can have no authority at all in common. The churches have a divine constitution and order and are executors of the laws of Christ in their realm. The general bodies are absolutely without ecclesiastical power or character and can only exercise powers within their circle and which concern the matters for which they are formed.

Second. The churches gain no added power by affiliating with general bodies. It is possible for a church to exist in completeness, endowed with all the functions of a church and live entirely to itself. While this is true for a church, it is equally true that it is impossible that the local churches shall delegate any of their powers to a general body. It is an axiom well established, that delegated powers can not be re-delegated. We must therefore think of the churches as being above the general bodies, and in no way subject to them. In its sphere, the weakest little negro church in Texas is greater than the Southern Baptist Convention.

We stand now at the parting of ways with respect to the relation of local churches to general bodies. The theological thinking of the world has divided into two lines: First, it is held by many large and influential bodies of Christians that the local churches merge themselves into the general bodies so that, in fact, the general body, by whatever name, association, convention, presbytery, synod, or what not, is the sum of all the smaller bodies. That is the Episcopal and Presbyterian view. The other line is that these local bodies do not and can not merge themselves into general bodies, but that they affiliate with the general bodies through messengers. This is the Congregational or Baptist view. Under this doctrine, the local churches are bound always to be independent. It is impossible that they can put themselves in any position where a general body can control them. They can not, in fact, strictly speaking as churches, become members of a general body, because if they became members, then on every question of division we would have the majority controlling the minority and the independence of the churches would absolutely and forever disappear. It is worth stopping to remark that in every self-governing body, where questions are debated and finally put to vote, it is impossible in the nature of things, that any part of that body should refuse to be governed by majority. Now, if local churches, as such, do become actual members of general bodies, then they subject themselves, beyond peradventure and beyond remedy, to the control of an outside body. This is repugnant to the principles of congregationalism, and has been repudiated by every Baptist writer who ever treated this question.

The churches through these general councils control the co-operative work in which they are engaged. This is done by messengers from the churches who sit in council and reach conclusions by submitting the questions to vote. The only way that churches can ever control any co-operative work is through their messengers who are supposed to represent their feelings and convictions in the general bodies having control of the work. It is clear to the smallest comprehension, that if any church affiliating with a general body is to have any voice in controlling the work of that body, it must do it by messengers, not through any direct action.

It must always be assumed that the churches are not in law bound by anything that a general body proposes. In other words, an association or convention can not hand down decisions which will bind the churches, but the influence of these general councils must always be great, and if it is found by any church, that it can not submit to the conclusions of a general body, its remedy is to cease to co-operate.

There is another question which goes beyond the one I have just discussed. What are the limitations of the powers of these general bodies That question is answered by the constitution of each separate body, as we have them organized for missionary and educational purposes. They have complete control of the work in their sphere. To illustrate: A convention of messengers from the churches with a constitution providing for a mission board, and arranging for the prosecution of missionary work would have full control of the co-operative work in its realm. The money contributed to a general fund would be dispensed under the rules and regulations governing the body, but it must be borne in mind always, that while a board may employ a man to preach, it can never ordain a brother and can never do any of these acts which are assigned specifically to the churches.

Baptists have always guarded with scrupulous care the independence of the churches. It is the fortress of our safety and the strength of our work. Sometimes, however, we have not equally guarded an extreme to which we may go in the opposite direction. Some have supposed that the independence of the churches necessarily carries with it the doctrine of the isolation of the churches. Some have supposed again, that a church affiliating with a general body might, because of its independence, govern the action of that body in which other churches are as much concerned as itself. No church, as such, may assume to control any work in which other churches are interested. The other churches are also free and independent.

I close with one simple statement. We must never

forget that a church occupies a circle to itself and occupies all of that circle; that no other body can intrude itself within that circle to the least extent and that no church can go beyond that circle, and we must remember that those bodies which are voluntary are alike beyond the circle in which the churches exist, has a sphere of its own and in that sphere it is just as free and independent as the churches are in their sphere. It is impossible with right-thinking to have the least conflict between those two bodies.

STACKPOLE UNIFICATION.

THE function of a stackpole is well understood by farmers. The fodder or oats or whatever is to be stacked has no cohesive power in itself. It is purely passive.

The stackpole makes a steady center around which the passive bundles may be piled. It gives steadiness and a measure of strength to the helpless mass of material lying around it. If the pole is strong the stack may be a fixture. If the pole rots at the ground or should be removed for any purpose or in any way, there is a calamity to the stack. It begins to fall to pieces and wastes.

Analogous to this is a kind of unification in many churches. Some pastors have the knack, if not the design, of unifying the people around themselves. Their method is to create a personal following, and by personal influence hold their place and do whatever they accomplish. Their following may be large and enthusiastic; but the pastor is the stackpole. If he remains and does well, and nobody with more personal magnetism appears on the scene, good reports may go up to the association or convention, or get into our wide open papers. But, if he leaves, or some winsome evangelist comes along, or if he should make a bad

By Dr. J. B. Gambrell, D. D.

break, there is at once a falling away, and it is made plain that many people joined the pastor and not the church; that they have not grown into the body of Christ, as members one of another; but have simply attached themselves to the man, as a dog attaches himself to his master, to bark and bite at the master's word, or to be fed by him.

This was the weakness of the Corinthian Christians. They had more than one stackpole. One said, "I am of Paul," and another, "I am of Appollos." The great-hearted servant of Christ refused to be a stackpole of these weak, carnal church members. In the intensity of his loyalty to his divine Lord, he exclaimed, "Who, then, is Paul, who Appollos, but ministers by whom ye believe, even as the Lord gave to every man." They were at the most only servants, and whatever success they had was not of themselves, but was given. Study the lesson in I Corinthians, third chapter.

A more contemptible thing than a pastor's building up a personal following among church members can hardly be conceived. It is the prostitution of a great and sacred office to a very low and little ambition. A man of such mind should quit the pulpit and take to ward politics.

When one of these stackpoles is removed the church falls to pieces. Any succeeding pastor finds around him a heap of human rubbish, which refuses to coalesce with the vital forces of the church. They literally cumber the ground. The master builder constructs on Christ and around Christ, and leads, not for himself, but for Him whose he is. He roots and grounds the people in the truth, so that, whether he dies or lives, remains or moves, the church, unified in the truth, holds together and goes right on.

This stackpole unification extends beyond church lines and the pastoral office, out into the wider fields of human activity. We would name more than one noble institution of learning which came near being wrecked by a retiring president or gifted teacher. It is a crucial test of a man's devotion to the cause and to a trust committed to him when

Some Pastors have the Knack of Unifying the People Around Themselves.

circumstances make it needful that he retire from an honorable position. It tests, to the core, the work he has done.

By Dr. J. B. Gambrell, D. D.

If he leaves the friends of the institution united and strong for the work, he shows himself a man of high qualities.

There are two states in this Union in which the Baptists have suffered ills from which a whole century will not relieve them, because prominent men divided the brotherhood on themselves. The men who did it are, no doubt, in heaven; but their mistakes live.

If grief and sorrow and repentance could be in heaven, they would bewail the effect of the partisan spirit infused into the brethren on earth.

We have been a reader of Baptist papers forty years and now give it as our firm conviction, that personal leadership has given Baptists more trouble, impeded their progress more, weakened our churches more, disgusted more good people with us, and, in general, done us more harm than all the enemies we ever had on the outside. The words personal leadership are used in contradistinction to a leadership of principles.

Personal leaders of factions have for forty years been thrusting their private affairs on the denomination, gathering partisan followers and distracting the brotherhood with issues which are of no manner of concern to the great body of disciples. Private property interests, which have taken on a semi-denominational importance, have been back of an untold amount of strife and personal war.

In Texas we want unification, but not stackpole unification. We can never agree about men; it is not needful that we should. God has graciously relieved us of the responsibility of that burden of holding the great judgment. He will attend to that. That leaves us free to do his work.

We want unity around the cause and the institutions of Christ. Here all good people can agree. Questions about men have always been distracting. But Christ said, "And I if I be lifted up will draw all men unto me."

We do really wish pastors and all who read these lines would consider this matter and resolve that there shall be no personal domination in our churches or in our denomination, that the cause of Christ for its blessed self shall have the right of way, and that men shall not distract Christ's servants with their personal matters.

A Southern brother once attended a meeting in Massachusetts. It was a wide open meeting for a talk, and the brethren and the sisters, too, got off on the war, on Grant and other men. They went to a great length. After awhile the Southern brother was called out to speak. He reluctantly rose to his feet, hardly knowing what to say. Finally he said: "Brethren, while you have been talking my mind has been busy. I do not believe much you have been saying; a great deal of it I know is not true. You and I will never see the war alike and we will never get together on it or the questions growing out of it. On many of them I have personal knowledge and deep feelings, and am sure you are totally wrong. But sitting here listening I thought of what I wrote my wife yesterday. I said "these people love Jesus just as we do. They love his Word." I was just now thinking, too, of Paul's words to his brethren at Phillippi: 'I thank my God upon every remembrance of you for your fellowship in the gospel from the first day until now.' We will never agree on Lee and Grant, on Sherman or Stonewall Jackson; but can't we agree on Christ and have fellowship in him? He is the great unifier and peacemaker."

At once the tone of the meeting changed and as the brother went on to speak of the great Captain of our salvation, as any one might have done, there were tears and later, warm hand clasps and fraternal greetings. The lesson is plain. Let us lay it to heart and practice it.

BY DR. J. B. GAMBRELL, D. D.

THE BATTLE GROUND FOR MISSIONS.

EVERY church is an ever-continuing battle-ground for missions, or should be. For missions were the churches formed. For missions in their varied forms, do the churches exist. They are not worth the name unless they are doing the things commanded in the great commission. Missions is the true mission of the churches of Jesus Christ. They stand for what Christ stood, for the life, the doctrine, the work, the Spirit of their Head. Each several church is a body of Christ. Its members are His tongue, His hands, His feet, His heart, all conjoined to carry out the will of Him who is the Head over all.

Missions involves going. Christ sends, we go, go on His errands, to evangelize, to baptize, to teach the all things commanded and to do them. The commission outlines the sphere of the activity of every church, both as to duties and extent of territory. Each church must stand for all the commission or fail to respond to the authority of the Divine Head.

The battle for missions must be fought out to a finish in the churches. The issue must be made on the authority of Christ, and there should be no modifying of His broad ed right or it will be lost in the pitching. It is not a question of preference, nor of feeling; but of obedience. Every church member has joined an army of conquest. He must play the soldier, and soldiering is not easy. The enlisted man must, first of all, learn the lesson of subordination and self-sacrifice. He must obey. This means that he must give, for he is so commanded. It is not optional. The pastor is God's leader of the host. He should magnify his office, by making full proof of his ministry. It is his bounden duty to see that the work is done, for the Holy Ghost has made him overseer of the flock. The avaricious must be taught, admonished, urged, pressed to give. There is no more reason why a member should be indulged in covetousness than in drunkenness.

This seductive sin has long had the right-of-way in the churches. In the battle for missions this is Satan's stronghold, his chief fortification in the King's country. It must be taken. Men and women must be confronted with the authority of God's Word and crowded to do their duty. With the Word of God their hearts and pocketbooks are to be opened.

Their chief obstruction to the development of many churches is a few leaders who are covetous. And in the face of God's Word they are tolerated. Christ will not honor a pastor or church thus dishonoring Him.

The battle must be fought clear out to the edges. Now only a few give and fewer give up to the divine rule. The problem of the future is to be solved by enlisting all in every church in the great Christ-ordained and Christ-led missionary movement. This is the work of the pastors as leaders in the churches. Missionary secretaries can not do it. They may help, but the pastors must work it out in their churches. This can be done, not instantly, not easily; but it must be done if Zion ever puts on her beautiful garments and goes forth to conquer as she should. This is our supreme problem today. To its solution every energy of the denomination ought to be divided with increasing prayer and unfailing zeal.

The churches are the heaven-appointed missionary forces. They cannot transfer their work, nor their responsibilities to conventions, associations or boards. It is to be deplored that attention should be so much directed away from the churches to extra ecclesiastical bodies. And it is to be still more deplored that any one should consider that in some way churches may blend in general bodies for missionary purposes. We need to come back to a clear conception of primary principles, lest we lose out in the main fight in the churches, where alone victory is to be won. No matter what conventions or boards initiate in counsel, it must all be referred back to the churches for their sanction. This is the true "initiative and referendum," which ever presses the whole question of missions back into the churches, and leaves it there, where Christ placed it, and where the battle for progress must be constantly fought against the world, the flesh and the devil.

Boards do not do mission work. This needs to be kept clear. If one hundred men give a hundred dollars each to build a meeting-house and employ three men to see that it is built, the three men do not build it. The one hundred build it, and the three are only their instruments or agents. "The messengers of the churches," spoken of in second Corinthians, did not relieve the saints in Jerusalem, except as the servants of the churches contributing the fund. The real doers of the work were the churches. They were the sources, the "brethren" were the channel through which they wrought. They were a "board," but Paul pressed the work in the churches, because it was pre-eminently the work of the churches. This is the model for all time. Into the churches, every one of them, from the greatest to the least, with all of Christ's work. The battle for progress must be fought out in the churches, and the pastors should lead.

The churches must not only do the work, but they must direct it, each one directing its own gift. Whatever plans are proposed, or agencies, by counsels, the matter is up to and into every church to direct its own funds. It may use a board or not. It may do work alone, if it choses; but no church can lay down its individual responsibility in the matter of doing Christ's work.

This year should be made memorable by a mighty renewing of the missionary effort in the churches. Plans should be devised to reach every church and every individual in every church. This will help the churches, honor Christ and bless the world.

GREAT MEETING, AND SOME REMARKS.

I HAVE been intending to say something about the Palopinto Campmeeting for The Standard readers. Since the write-up of the Madera meeting, out in Davis mountains, I have had letters from many places, some of them far away, indicating a quickening on the subject of a sound evangelism. I write this for the encouragement of a movement, happily now widespread, and still spreading.

Palopinto town and county have suffered much for lack of harmony and the tender, faithful preaching of the gospel of the grace of God. A brother, not a Baptist, said for years it had been a battle ground for all sorts of wars over inconsequential questions. Christians had been greatly hurt, and sinners hardened. Large numbers of the strongest people in the country were unsaved, and many of them abandoned to eternal ruin by those who had ceased to pray for them. There is no temperate language that will adequately characterize that method of preaching which bruises the sensibilities of God's people, vulgarizes the gospel, and turns the lost away from the gates of heaven.

But all about these were God's reserves, who waited and prayed for salvation to come to the people.

Preparations were made to care for all who would come. The meeting was widely advertised by Pastor Clouse and his co-workers. Christians of all denominations co-operated beautifully, and with the full understanding that it was to be a Baptist meeting, yet hoping and expecting, that it would be thoroughly Christian in tone and purpose. The attendance was good, notwithstanding some special drawbacks. Here, again, it was proven that difficulties, drawbacks, etc., do not count where a few get right with God. Ring it out again and again, there are no difficulties

By Dr. J. B. Gambrell, D. D.

with God, and we end our difficulties always when we reach God with them.

The meeting was a series of direct attacks on the powers of darkness. The preaching was strongly doctrinal in the deep and blessed sense of the Word. The foundation of hope was made bare. The great doctrines of grace were proclaimed with love. It was a doctrinal revival. It was understood and accepted by all, that we were to preach out of our hearts the whole counsel of God. We all went together as far as we could, and there was no friction, but thorough respect and the tenderest Christian love where any differed. The whole meeting ran on a high plane, and the natural thing happened: a great conquering, triumphant revival, with a blessing for every hungry soul.

There were hours, tragic in their crucifying power, hours there were of great prayer, when men and women went to the depth for those they loved; there were hours as heroic as one ever saw on a battlefield; there were hours when, faith having conquered, rested serene in a holy confidence, as soldiers lie down to rest after a victorious battle; there were hours so triumphant, that men and women were swept, as if by a whirlwind from the mountain tops of glory. Pentecost returned to bless the earth again, and men and women shouted aloud with uncontrollable rapture.

Pastor Truett delivered his soul one night on sinning away the day of salvation. In all my life, I have never heard an appeal that had in it so much of the very essence of life and death. It was directed to those who had long withstood God. Their ranks broke. White-haired men were moved. The strongest appealed for prayer. Men fell like dead men. It was a terrific hour. As the preacher plead, men and women prayed, some aloud at intervals. When the break came, shouts went up like the shouts of a great army, when a difficult position is taken on the battlefield. It was not an hour of surrender, but of conviction to be followed up. Some fought out during the silent hours of the night, and came in happy next morning. Another great hour was when a strong man, much honored by his countrymen, after a silent struggle, came forward and appealed to know if Jesus would save the worst sinner on earth. Being assured of it, he cried out, "O God! the worst man in the world surrenders," and he did. In a few minutes he was testifying, while old friends rejoiced around him.

The baptizing scene was glorious, and well worth description; but I must turn to another feature of this article.

What were the results? The one broad, general result is the carrying of the whole cause of Christianity up on the upland. If I am not mistaken, the religious life of the country was greatly elevated and strengthened. There were scores of conversions, and about 25 additions to the Palopinto Church; others will join other denominations, according to their faith, and churches around will receive accessions. This, however, was not all, maybe, not the greatest good. The religious thinking of the country has been largely changed on many points. This is but a restatement of what was said there. The bitter, acrimonious preacher of small "pints" will have a hard time in that part of the moral vineyard. And the sentimental, sloppy preacher, who never goes into anything over his shoe tops, will find a people who will call for something more solid. I can but believe the Baptist cause was greatly helped, by being associated with preaching unctious, rich in grace, and disassociated from such preaching as some have heard. The best doctrine in the world ought to preached in the best way. The real spirit of our State work was born to the people of that great section in the tender, spiritual, powerfully persuasive preaching of Pastor Truett. It will heal and help.

The enlistment of strong men in the aggressive work of the denomination is a gracious feature of the meeting. Oh, what strong, noble people we found out there! How

BY DR. J. B. GAMBRELL, D. D

hungry for bread warm from the great Father's table. How joyous in their conscious fellowship with the mighty, conquering army of God all over Texas. They had not felt the sweet influences which have so blessed other places less remote. Large reinforcements are coming into line, as a result of these inland meetings. And my own heart was wonderfully blessed and enlarged. I came back to put more spirit into our great State work. Hardly ever in my life, did souls seem so precious to me. I am certain our public men need to be caught up in these mighty currents for the sake of their own work.

One distinct result will be the fixing of a great camp-meeting ground, where thousands can come from the regions round about and remain away from the cares of life for a few days, to hear the things of the Kingdom discussed by men given to them, heart and mind. Who can measure the advantages of such meetings for salvation, indoctrination, edification and training? There is a diamond mine out in the Palopinto Mountains, richer in those fine young people than all the hidden wealth of South Africa, which provoked the Boer war, that cost England $1,200,000,000, and tens of thousands of lives.

There is coming to me new visions of spiritual conquest as I see how, as of old, God's word and Spirit triumph wherever the gospel is faithfully preached. It is the old story new again, as it was when Peter, fresh from penitence, and from the throne of forgiving grace, preached at Pentecost, and sinners of all degrees, there and then, threw down their arms of rebellion, and rushed under the white flag of the King for salvation. Such meetings and such scenes as I have so imperfectly described, bring into the soul a new faith in the power of Jesus to save to the uttermost, and to save at once.

Pastor Buntin of Gordon, is chairman of Committee on the New Camp Ground. This means it will be well done.

TEN YEARS IN TEXAS

BLESSED BE BOOKS FOR THEY ARE A BLESSING.

I HAVE just read The Standard of July 3, and see that my very good brother, A. J. Harris, has been charmed away from the use of tobacco. As from

I Would not be Very Particular as to What Induced a Devotee of Tobacco to Quit.

by Dr. J. B. Gambrell, D. D.

time to time I had observed with what zest he wasted fragrance of the cigar on the desert air, I had supposed him one of the incurables, but he has quit. Beloved, do not quit too often. Let this time suffice.

I would not be very particular as to what induced a devotee to tobacco to quit its use. If he quit in disgust, if he quit out of deference to his friends, if he married a wife and quit; oh, there are a hundred good reasons for quitting, but some of them are better than others. Pastor Harris, oblivious of all other inducements, quits because he cannot buy books and smoke cigars. That is good. With a mental appetite equal to the natural appetite of the shark, he was compelled to decide beteween a degree of mental starvation and a kind of regrettable physical comfort. He chose the better part.

What a thing is a book to charm people to higher and better living, and this reminds me of myself when I was a boy. What great things a book did for me. I was not addicted to the tobacco habit, having smoked only once in all my life, and that had the happiest effect on me. I quit. I was addicted to the dog habit. My soul went out in tenderest longings toward every dog I saw. I loved dogs for what they were, and for what they could do. I had accumulated a large assortment, fox dogs, coon dogs, squirrel dogs, rat dogs, deer dogs, fighting dogs, trick dogs, and then quite a number unclassified—just dogs. To my boyish mind every dog had in him great possibilities of something useful in the dog line. I never had enough dogs. It was a constant struggle for room for my dogs, and a long suffering mother endured more than she ought to have endured. Like Brother Harris and his cigar, I had a natural affinity for dogs and was a great hunter. I went with my brother and father one night to a Board meeting and met the colporter. I had always had an idea a book was a pretty good thing, but had never fallen in love with them. Having sold two coon skins, I had two dimes, and among the boys in that country I ranked as a captitalist. As I looked over the books I wondered if there was one for two dimes. Selecting one I thought would suit me, I asked the price. It was twenty cents and a trade at once. I put that book under my jacket with my hand on it and ran home, touching the ground at high places. And I sat up with that book until I read it through and through and knew it all. It was a book made for boys. Great vistas were opened. I saw mountains and seas and ships and armies and great statesmen and scholars. It worked in on me. Then I came to the same place, as a boy, that the distinguished pastor of the First Baptist Church, San Antonio, reached. It was books or dogs. Oh, my dogs, how I did love them. Trayler, Ranger, Watch, and all of them, but I could not know what a person ought to know and keep up with all those dogs. It was a square case, one or the other, and with a sense of suffocation I sent word to the Negroes and boys that the entire lot of dogs were at their disposal. They came with ropes and took them away. I had many a cry over it, but I held to that book and got many other books. My mother was delighted. That book was an epoch in my life. I did not love the dogs less, but books more. To this day no man can beguile me into a fox chase. I would hear horns and dogs for weeks to come in my sleep and waking. I would not be able to drown their voices for the sake of hearing the church choir on Sunday. No, I have quit dogs. I quit forty-five years ago, and have not gone back to them since. Let me hope that Brother Harris will hold out forty-five years.

Now let us come back. How many people in Texas are smoking and following dogs and keeping sorry company and wasting all their time because they have never fallen in love with books? And they have not fallen in love with books because they never had a good taste. Mothers and fathers are wondering that their girls and boys are so giddy, that they do not love home, and that they keep idle company. They expect their children to give up every foolish and low thing without any substitute, without any higher or better motive or impulse. I do not know any greater folly than that exhibited by thousands of men all over this country, who have great homes, great farms, horses and buggies for their children, and no books. The boy who falls in love with good books is nine-tenths saved from every form of vice. Whoever loves good books loves good people, and good things, and is walking along the enchanted galleries of the past, communing with the great souls who have lived before, and looking far out into the future, catching always the first gleams of sunlight on the mountains ahead. And good books are so cheap. Anybody can have books. A few dollars expended every year will soon make an accumulation of good books in any home. Neighbors can exchange, and there is not a community in Texas so poor that every boy and girl in it, to say nothing of the men and women, might not feel the exaltation that comes to one in the reading of good books.

And more. If we read good books we become like the things we read about. If we read of great men, the tendency is for us to become great. If we read of great things, we grow to be like them. Good books are a sovereign remedy for a thousand ills. Why in the world don't people buy good books?

And still more, many a soul has been won to God and heaven by reading a book. A thousand times a dull soul has been set aflame by a single book. If I were a pastor I would look after the reading of the people. I would sell books, lend books, do anything to induce people to read good books. A good book is a shining lamp in the home that never goes out.

LOPSIDEDNESS IN MISSIONS.

THERE is not another enterprise under heaven known among men so well calculated to stir the human heart as missions. Every real missionary movement sets two currents to running in opposite directions. One flows outward and the other inward. One is the spirit of altruism, and the other selfishness.

The mission enterprise awakens the noblest enthusiasm but it is often beset by many human limitations. Once it is allowed that we may in any way be influenced by mere human considerations or feelings, we are involved in endless questions of preference. Missions stand in the authority of Jesus Christ. They are a doctrine, not an expediency. For instructions concerning missions, we must go to the law book of the Kingdom, the New Testament. From this source we may most surely learn what we need to know, as to this livest of questions. There are some things we may gather with unerring certainty from the living oracles, and these certain things must be our guides amid the complexus of conflicting opinions which divide people into small groups of missionary advocates.

I leave out of consideration in this article the antimissionary and the omissionary, both obnoxious to the plain teaching of God's Word. I shall discuss lopsidedness in missions, and there is plenty of it to discuss. Before entering on the discussion, I desire to make a few preparatory remarks.

Missions must always be considered from the standpoint of the whole world's conquest to the obedience of faith. The far-reaching meaning of the conversion of any soul is the conversion of other souls, reaching on to the consummation of all things. Every convert belongs to this army of conquest, which is never to stack colors till the reign of Christ is completed in the earth, till the annunciation hymn of the angels shall be a reality. Any view of missions which detaches one part from another is insufficient; any conception which gives to one part a supremacy is worse than insufficient, it is bad. Any plan which limits the efforts and prayers of God's people to a man or a single section is hurtful. The Christ view—"all the world," "every creature"—is the only true view. No Christian, no matter how little or poor or weak or ignorant, can stand for less than all that Christ stands for—all of it, to the outer limits.

But there be many who are for associational missions and no more. These say such is our work, and so it is; but not one particle more their work than is the work in China. To a very great extent our present crippled condition, as a people, comes of lopsidedness in the training of the young churches. The churches concentrated on associational mission till the territory was dotted over with churches. Then, having made no connections leading outward, they ceased their efforts, remained undeveloped and many have perished as the result of lopsidedness in missions. If we are at all wise, this monumental blunder will be carefully guarded against in the future. Every little mission church of today, from its infancy, should be trained for world-wide missions. If the conversion of one soul means the conversion of other souls in an endless chain of influence, grace and salvation, so the establishment of a church today means other churches, till over the whole wide world churches shall grace every landscape and welcome earth's children to the fold of the good Shepherd for rest and safety.

Some go as far as State missions and stop. "Is there not as much as we can do in our State?" May be there is vastly more than we can do; but, if our eyes are not holden, we will see that we can do the work near far better, if, in our spirit and purpose, prayers and efforts, we go full length with Him who loved the world. The outflow of the mission spirit to China, to darkest Africa, will make the current swifter nearer home, provided it be in deed and in truth a genuine mission spirit.

We need a proper standpoint from which to look at the whole question. That standpoint is the Cross, where Christ died for the world. From Calvary all nations, tribes, kindred and tongues are equidistant. A world lost in Adam is to be saved in Jesus, through the preaching of the Cross. The races of men were made of one blood, and are to be redeemed by the one blood. Territorial divisions do not count in Christ's purposes of grace.

But this round, full New Testament view of missions is sorely marred by lopsidedness in the thither view of things. Foreign missions have to some an attraction, not unmixed with the heroic. There is a charming heroism in people's going far hence on the sublime mission of winning the heathen. Besides this there are various and very specious arguments advanced to show that foreign missions should have a pre-eminence in all our plans for world-wide missions, all of which is very short-sided and lopsided, having neither scripture nor common sense to support it. Dr. Edward Judson, a son of the apostle to Burmah, in a missionary address, in the interest of foreign missions, said, with great fire, good sense and point:

"We must be sure, however, that our foreign missionary spirit is genuine and not a mere fad. The sure test is whether we are interested in everything lying between the heathen and ourselves. To many of us distance seems to lend enchantment to the view. We burn with enthusiasm over the miseries of people far away, but are limp and nerveless as regards suffering close by. We find ourselves greatly interested in foreigners when they reside in their own land, so much so in fact that we send our best men as missionaries to them and pay their traveling expenses; but when the Lord puts it into the heart of these same foreigners to come to our shores, paying their own traveling expenses, instead of rejoicing over their advent, we are sometimes inclined to turn away from them in despair. They do not look so picturesque near by. This is only the semblance of the true missionary spirit—a counterfeit, not the real coin."

There is considerable lopsidedness of this sort among us. It lacks the tone and substance of genuine New Testament missions.

Sometimes workers in one department of missions, home, foreign or State, become so immersed in that particular part of the work that they can see nothing else. The common sense of the masses of God's people must save us from lopsidedness in one direction or another. Sometime ago a brother seriously proposed that all foreign mission money be collected without charge, or that the expense be put on other departments of the common work of Christ. This is sheer lopsidedness. Another would induce everybody to give nearly all to foreign missions and only a pittance to home missions. Still another will give largely to State missions and hardly at all to home or foreign. All of it is hurtful even to the favored mission. No severer blow could be struck at foreign missions, for instance, than for an effort to be made to leave home missions out or nearly so. Where are the funds to come from to support foreign missions? From the home field, of course. Suppose we lose our home field, how will that affect foreign missions in the future? No prophet is needed to tell.

Turn it round. Suppose we concentrate on missions at home. What then? We will have denominational stagnation, and, in the end, death in our home churches. The New Testament is luminous along the whole line of operation. Churches were planted and nurtured through courses of training, not only for themselves and the regions near by, but as sources of supply for operations further out. The two went together, lengthening the cords and strengthening the stakes. Woe be to those who despise this order.

Undoubtedly the general policy of the Convention is the wise one. It only needs to be made effective in the all-round development of our churches to stand four-square to all the demands of the gospel to the ends of the world. If we will unitedly follow the true conception of a rounded development, Texas Baptists, in this generation, will stand for more than all the South does now for the evangelism of the whole world. Lopsidedness, whether in one direction or another, will hurt the one great mission enterprise in which are wrapped up the hopes of humanity.

TWO LARGE EXAMPLES, WITH LESSONS.

WHEN Phillip the Second came to the throne of Spain, he came to the greatest empire then in the world. It looked as if Spain would rule the world, and that was in the Spanish mind, just as it is in the Russian mind today to dominate all Asia, and, later, the world. It was an hour for much Spanish congratulation which degenerated into national vanity and conceit. The monarch fell under the bad influence of the current feeling, if, indeed, he did not lead it. He decreed that no Spanish youth should leave Spain to study abroad, and no teacher should be imported into Spain. This decree was based on the conception that Spain had nothing to learn from abroad. It was that spirit of pride which goes before a fall, a spirit so deep and all-pervasive that till this hour it dominates the Spanish mind.

When Phillip decreed the insulation of the Spanish mind, he laid an ax to the root of all Spanish greatness.

by Dr. J. B. Gambrell, D. D.

It was as if a man put an iron band around a growing tree. Either the tree, by its growth, would burst the band, or the tree would die, not all at once, but surely, little by little. With Spain the inevitable happened. The nation did not burst the band, but decay began at once. Through weary centuries national decay has marked the course of that once powerful people. Her colonies have fallen away from her like dead limbs from a falling tree. The last were Cuba, Porto Rico and the Philippines. Little is left that decrepid, laggard nation. Her people walk in a vain show, hugging to their bosoms ideals long since outgrown.

Spain fell by taking a wrong mental attitude toward the larger world of truth she counted herself to have attained. She scouted the truth not home found or developed. Her attitude was a facing in. She practiced involution, not evolution. Having a wrong mental attitude, she could not learn. Her dismal history of bigotry, arrogancy, intolerance, persecution, priestcraft—all of it—had its taproot in her mental attitude, unfriendly to the wide world of truth. As a man thinketh in his heart, so is he. People individually and collectively are as they think. Phillip the Second wrought the ruin of Spain when he faced Spain in. This is a large example of the working of a principle.

Let us take another example, looking the opposite way. Fifty years ago Japan was insulated, along with Corea and China. Her people were not allowed to go abroad. Her emperor, representing the oldest dynasty in the world, reversed Phillip's policy and Japan's, too. He faced his people out by giving them a new mental attitude towards universal truth. The brightest of the youth of the empire were sent abroad to learn. England, Germany, America and France received relays of Japs, of both sexes. They came feeling their mission to be torch bearers. Nor did Japan stop at this. She brought to her great national university the most eminent teachers of the world, and paid them salaries which would create an uproar in America. She imported men to reconstruct her whole civilization, putting everything on the best known basis. She saw that her ships were outclassed, and forthwith set about constructing her present up-to-date navy. Her army was reconstructed throughout. Her armaments were of the best. Her public school system was organized to reach every boy and girl in the empire. Missionaries were welcomed. The mental attitude of Japan is: "We are doing the best we know, but if you know better tell us."

What has been the result of this new attitude? Ask Russia. But the world knows. Hardly ever was there such an awakening. The Japs are the leaders of a third part of the world. A new life thrills the nation from its ancient throne to its utmost borders. Her people are standing flooded with the sunrise of a new and glorious life. From peasant to prince, there is enlargement, and an all-conquering spirit of achievement. The whole people are assimilating to higher ideals, and Japanese greatness is written in letters of light, as across the vault of heaven.

Now for some lessons. No greatness is possible without a proper mental attitude. This comes with tremendous force to Southern Baptists. The South has been badly environed for fifty years. The effect of Southern environment

By Dr. J. B. Gambrell, D. D.

has told on Southern thinking. With respect to the Negro, we have been in a defensive attitude. With no intention of entering the domain of politics, I feel nevertheless constrained to say that our strenuous president has done the South and the nation a grievous wrong by reviving the race question. The whole South needs to face out and blend harmoniously in the national life. This is the need of Southern Baptists. In some way our young people, for their own enlargement, and for what they can do, ought to face out, and feel their responsibility for the spiritual life of the whole country and the world. Two-thirds of the Baptists of America can't be shut up to one-third of the people of this great country in their thinking and efforts. We must face out.

The same lesson is good all along the line. The church which faces in will follow Spain to the shades of death. The association which lives for itself will die to itself. The preacher whose thoughts and efforts revolve around himself and his church, will circle in and come to a dead standstill at the center.

These lessons ought not to be lost on our people. If our boys and girls think great thoughts, they will be great men and women. If every Baptist in Texas could feel that he or she belongs to a great army of conquest, which is to reach every spot of the globe and bring the lost tribes of earth to the obedience of faith, our churches would rise gloriously into strength and world-wide usefulness. Our supreme task now is to bring our people to a right attitude toward the whole world.

THE PASSING OF THE BULLY.

THE BULLY is a product of society in its crude, unformed state. He belongs to the period of razor back hogs and long horned cattle, and he disappears with them. Over most of the country, all three of these primitive products have gone the way of all crudities of an overgrowing civilization. The places that once knew them know them no more. But here and there a specimen remains, more curious than valuable.

The old time bully was a great man in his day and generation—in his own eyes and in the eyes of his sort. He was on hand at all meetings, political speakings, and wherever the people congregated. It was his self-appointed duty to regulate everybody. He was always looking for somebody who needed whipping, and was wonderfully lucky to find what he was looking for. But he was careful not to find the wrong one. There was a fighting frenzy in his blood, and it took plenty of fighting to make him endurably cool.

The bully was soon known, and nice people avoided him. Gentlemen did not attend public meetings to fight. They kept apart from the bully for the sake of peace. The bully was quick to see this, and that was taken as a concession to his powers. His set saw it, and gave it out that they were "skeered" of him. A good deal is allowed to some animals simply because they are disagreeable—who wants to fight a skunk; a biting dog is avoided because nice people can't afford to bite all the dogs that would bite them.

Whoever wants to see the bully depicted in all his vain glory, should read "Georgia Scenes." I have seen it all in my day, Ransey Sniffles, and all. The big bullies soon have in their train a lot of little bullies, all having the same spirit, but varying in size and strength. They are an amalgam of coarseness, brutality, cowardice, impudence and self-conceit, with the inevitable brag and noise. They can strut standing still, and all life is a strut with them.

"And It's Fight You Are Wanting, Is It?"

The bully is allowed much liberty, but he always reaches his limitations, sooner or later. I knew one, a powerful man, physically, who had beaten many men brutally, having forced them to attack him by his coarse abuse. One day he thought he saw an Irishman in need of his professional services, and he began his preliminary treatment in the way of abuse. The Irishman was small, but he said, "And it's fight you are wanting, is it?" It was agreed to, and they went into the ring. It was soon over. The bully never touched the Irishman, but he hit the ground as fast as he got near the little son of Erin. The Irishman was a trained boxer. The bully was in bed three months, during which time he indulged many profitable meditations on the cruelty of fighting. He joined the church later and always regarded the Irishman a means of grace, one of those righteous providences employed to bring in the elect.

This man made an excellent citizen and church member. Two minutes with that Irishman took the frenzy out of his blood. I knew another bully to be cured in a half minute, by a boy with an ugly knife in his hand. Not a drop of blood was shed, but his blood congealed as the boy moved toward him, and it never got hot again as long as he lived.

The political bully is a strain above his common street brother. He has the same qualities, the difference being the arena of action. He may be educated, but that in no way changes his nature. I have seen an educated hog, but he was a hog all the same. The gravest question of statesmanship, requiring careful handling, and needing cool discussion, are treated by the bully as matters personal to his opponent. He aims to win, and does win, with some, by low flung abuse of his opponent, and by making himself so disagreeable that no one wishes to meet him in discussion. He clouds every question, and odors men out of competition. His brazen effrontery goes for courage; his bald assertions for truths; his vehemence for convictions; his billingsgate for arguments as strong as "holy writ."

The worst of the tribe of bullies is the religious bully.

BY DR. J. B. GAMBRELL, D. D.

He is the street bully joined the church, bringing into the church his old spirit and manners.

Every bully is a coward. Courage is considerate. The religious bully has the finest field in the world. He deals all the time with people, who neither have the spirit, nor desire to meet him on his chosen field. Moreover, the men he employs his arts upon have in charge great interests, which they must preserve. Even if they desired to do so, they cannot afford to punish the bully. An Irishman could find no place for his gifts in the chosen field of the religious bully. All that can be done is to avoid him. Educate the masses and wait for his passing.

In all circles the bully is passing. Social order eschews him. Patriotism abominates him. Religion abhors him. He is thinning out. The progress of civilization is leaving him behind. The future dominant factor in civil life must be a statesman, reasoning and reasonable. The religious leader must be religious and a gentleman. Discussions must go on principles. Abuse of men will influence only the very low, and that in ever lessening degrees. The progress on all lines is away from the bully, to the man of good manners, sound reason and sane spirit. The bully is passing, and the mourners are few.

A LETTER TO A YOUNG PREACHER.

YOUR letter is before me. There is nothing that I have undertaken more difficult than to advise a young minister in his starting out. It is only on the general lines that anyone can speak, because God has a special work for each one of his servants and he brings them into the work in a way that neither they nor others can know. I may make the following suggestions with safety:

Commit yourself fully to the Lord and remember that it is absolutely safe to do so. You cannot know where he will lead you, nor how he will lead you, but he will lead you by a way that he knows, and it will be, without doubt, the right way. Looking back over my life, I see now how unfounded were all my early fears, and I see, also, of what little account were the many precautions that I have tried to take. Commit your way to the Lord and he will bring it to pass.

In the next place, remember that it's not intended for you to see far at a time. I was greatly helped when I started out in the ministry by what an old brother told me. He said: "You are a young man, and I want to tell you something from my experience. All my life in the ministry, now for more than fifty years, I have been able to see but one step at a time. Much of the time, it has seemed to me that I was coming right up against an impassable wall, but when I took the step that was before me, even and clear, I found that it either brought me to where I could turn the corner, or else the wall was removed; and, so for fifty years I have gone on preaching, and have had enough to eat and all the work I could do."

It was a very helpful message to me, and one that I found to be true in almost thirty years of ministerial life. Therefore, my advice would be to take the step that you can take. If you feel called to preach, preach; preach in school houses, in a private home, preach at all times, preach to little congregations, preach anywhere; and always preach, not to preach, but to do good. Aim at saving somebody or helping somebody, and it will be a delight to you how things will get out of your way and fields will open before you. I do not have a shadow of doubt, that the Lord has use for every minister, who is set to do his will, and he will carry him through, and make him a success, if he will trust the Lord and go forward.

It is hardly necessary, I would think, to advise against hunting places, for the tone of your letter indicates anything else but such a spirit. And yet it will not be amiss in this letter, while I am writing to say that place-hunting, a desire to get up in the ministry, has kept many a man down in the ministry all his life. I have been much with young ministers in my time, have tried to help them and have watched their course much. I have seen those who sought places where they thought they would be respected, and could live easy, and I have seen those who sought to do the work and thought little or nothing of the places, going out into the backwoods, going among the negroes, preaching to little congregations and pouring out their souls in preaching to the poor and the neglected and the ignorant,—I have seen these two classes for years, and I have seen the man who wanted to go to a big town and preach in a big church fail in his work, become soured and profitless to himself and to the cause. I have seen the man who went to the country, and thought only how he could best do God's work, set all the country places afire and have men write to him and come after him to go up higher. Some of these are now in the greatest pulpits in the whole country. Spurgeon's great ministry began this way. He preached out in a little village, a few miles from Cambridge, and the people were too poor to pay the ferryage across a stream for a cart that was to carry him out to his preaching place, so he walked out to the stream, went across at less charge, and rode to his place of preaching in a cart; but he set the village afire up there, and the world knows the rest.

You wish to know, without doubt, whether you are called. If my own experience is worth anything, and the experience of many others with whom I have spoken, you are liable to have doubts as to your call to the ministry about as often as you get cold in the work. God never intends that his people shall have the joy of assurance about anything outside of the path of duty. The path of service is the shining way that shineth more and more unto the perfect day, but whoever forsakes that path will have more or less of doubt about everything religious. I think I can tell your experience in advance, and it will run this way: When you have been much in prayer and are very humble in your feelings and take hold upon the promise of God and preach in the power of the Holy Spirit, you will not have any doubts about whether you are called to preach. But if you grow worldly minded, neglect prayer, get puffed up about some previous success and preach in your own wisdom, you will be apt to get out of the pulpit with some very strong doubts as to whether you have been called to the ministry. I do not know any way in the world to live above doubt except to live a high spiritual life. The clouds shadow the low lands.

Now, my brother, if you have in your heart a longing for souls and a drawing toward the work, and if these experiences are stronger when you are more religious, go right into it and your faith will strengthen, your capacities enlarge and you will pass through your ministerial life with perhaps about the same ups and downs as all the rest of us.

BY DR. J. B. GAMBRELL, D. D.

BEAUTIFUL FIGHTING.

AT the first battle of Manassas the Southern troops were all new, and really, according to the rules of war, were whipped all day, but were not enough trained in military tactics to know it. The writer, with nearly everybody else on the Southern side, fought practically without officers. We never had the least idea in the world that anybody was whipped while he had a gun and cartridges and room to load and shoot. But, nevertheless, we were falling back in a kind of wavering way, and the officers who had better ideas of military affairs, realized the seriousness of the situation more than the soldiers did. It was really this ignorance of the technical points of war that gave us the victory later on. Along in the evening General Smith came on the field with recruits. We were all glad to see them and the enemy were sorry to see them. They came up in double-quick, and having made quite a distance from the depot, they were worn. One of the generals who had been holding out all day, rushed up to the first line of recruits and said: "Fall in, gentlemen, fall in; there is beautiful fighting here anywhere." And they did fall in and the Federals fell out, and we had the victory.

Now, in Texas we have a great battle line, and the fight goes with varying success at different points, but it is safe to say to every true soldier, that, if you will just fall in, you will find beautiful fighting anywhere, plenty of the enemy, and not very far to find, with a good cause and all the enthusiasm that a living faith in the Captain of our salvation can give us. We want the spirit of fight in us, not of fighting each other, but of fighting the enemy.

A brother recently said to the writer as we were discussing the late war: "A great many of our men were killed by their friends." We all recall that the immortal Jackson fell, wounded to death by his friends. Let's take care how we fight. In every great fight there is more or less of confusion; we cannot fight in blood earnest with perfect precision. It was that sort of thing that lost one

"There is Beautiful Fighting Here Anywhere."

hundred battles to Napoleon. The generals on the other side were so punctillious and nice that they felt that battles

By Dr. J. B. Gambrell, D. D.

had to be fought out on certain plans and by certain rules, or else they were not decently won. The old Austrian general claimed that this young Frenchman did not fight according to any military rules, and, therefore, he was not entitled to military recognition. But, all the same, he got the Austrian's cannon and his bagage and his men, and sent him out of Italy in very bad military plight. It won't do in a great fight to stop and consider every little point. It's no time in a charge to stop to sew on buttons; a great many things will be regulated after the fight is over.

Now, in Texas, we want to have a great fight this year, we've got plenty of fight to satisfy the most unreasonable along that line. Let's not stop to settle little points till we win the victory. Men who have wounds and bruises and sores and divers troubles of one sort and another ought to keep them out of view, until we have gone through with our great battle. A great many things will come right easy enough, if we only work toward the right point.

In this fight let everybody come in, no matter what he thinks of men, nor what he thinks of past battles. If he wants to see the Baptist cause succeed and men saved, let him put that to the front, for that's the thing to fight for. A good soldier fights for his country in battle without any reference to whether he likes his officers or not. A good Christian strives for the mastery of this great Captain's sake, and he will not abandon the cause, nor hurt the cause by stopping to complain of personal troubles between himself and some fellow soldier.

The fact is, we have often noticed that soldiers, who would fall out in camp and fight each other in camp, while they were doing nothing else, would not only go in, side by side, in a great battle and fight like heroes, but they came out with mutual admiration for each other's courage, and their personal animosities were sunk in their love for the cause for which they both fought, and they became fast friends.

A great year of missions, in which the fighting will be forced from one side of Texas to the other, would do more to uplift us, unify us, settle personal animosities and dignify the Baptist name in Texas than anything else we can do. There is such a beautiful chance now for everybody, for the old veterans, for the women, for the young people, for the children's bands, for the new disciples—such a good chance for everybody to have a share in a good fight that we hope that not a person who bears the name of the great Captain will be sulking in his tent during this year. Just fall in; there is beautiful fighting all along the line.

BY DR. J. B. GAMBRELL, D. D.

DREADING THE PROCESS.

I HEARD Dr. Geo. Needham relate a story of a strong man who hung on the edge of a meeting, evidently deeply interested but refusing to do anything. When pressed in a personal interview, he admitted his deep conviction and longing to be a Christian, but said in explanation of his conduct, I dread the process. Here was a mind misled, likely by false teaching, or, maybe, by false deductions, from his own observations. It is quite easy to preach too much about the plan of salvation. As to that, it is not impossible to preach too much about Christ. There is a distinct difference between preaching Christ and preaching about Him. The first is saving preaching; the second may be far from it.

The best preaching and teaching is that which brings the sinner, by the shortest road, to look upon Jesus by faith, that keeps all thoughts of mere process out of the way. No sort of process should be allowed to crystalize in a church. No special form of service should be held to, until it becomes the force of unwritten law. There is much in recognized slavery to a fixed order. This applies to every part of public service, to preaching not less than other things. For in effectiveness, I believe there is nothing worse than the regulation service, with the regulation sermon, made out with the precision and fixedness of cut flowers. Lawyers are bound to do better or quit, and politicians would not get on at all, if they went under the yoke after the fashion of the regulation preacher.

"The process" has a deep grip on the average mind. Indeed, it has stifled that openness of heart and mind, that ready response to truth, which marked the conversions of the apostolic period. Of all the pictures of a real conversion given us in the divine records, not one is so instinct with life and action as the parable of the prodigal son. Here is a sinner, a real hard case. He has played the fool to a finish.

He has gone far beyond all respectability. He has gone past the dogs and reached the hogs. He has gone far off into a strange land. Then in his dirt and rags and hunger, he thinks. Like the prophet would have us all do, he thought on his way and turned. Sorrow wrung his soul. He made up his mind what to do. He would return to his father's house. He rose and struck out. There was no parleying, no hesitation, no delay. To put it in the graphic words of Sid Williams, "He hit the grit in the middle of the road, and never stopped till he got there." It was soon done, this settling of the whole question, and as quick as time would allow, he was sitting at his father's table, well dressed and eating the best in the land.

As we go back and read of the conversions of the New Testament, we can hardly fail to be impressed with the simplicity of the whole business. In a short ride, the Eunuch, being an honest seeker, came into the light. And forthwith he obeyed in baptism. That the conversion was genuine, there can be no doubt. The chariot seat was a mourner's seat; but he never thought of it. He thought of no process. The Master called Andrew, and he followed, the spirit working inward grace. Andrew went and told his brother Simon, and he came, and believed. The woman at the well, half heathen, outcast, dark in her heart, her mind and her life, steeped in vileness; yet in one short interview, she repented, believed and went flying back to town saved, with a message of hope to the hard men of the town. Many of the men believed through her word, and that right away.

The thief on the cross, hardened in sin, disgraced, outcast, amid the agonies of crucifixion, in a short hour, heard, saw, his heart melted, he confessed, believed and his ransomed spirit shot out of the horrors of that, the world's darkest hour, to be with Christ in paradise. How quick, how simple, how certain it all was.

In studying it all over, I have been deeply impressed that

we need to get back in our thinking, our faith and our efforts to the simplicity of the better times. Preachers can afford to be excentric. What is an excentric? Why it is something which moves out of a circle. The doing of the same thing the same way by everybody all the time, has great weakness in it. It brings about a psychological stagnation. It has all the weakness of a written ritual, without its good English and flourish.

If we ever come to our best, we will have far more liberty than we now allow ourselves. Where the Spirit of the Lord is, there is liberty. Look at Pentecost. That was a day when Mrs. Grundy quit the grounds. Men and women, too, spoke as the Spirit gave them liberty. "The process," what was it? Repent and believe, right now on the spot. Thousands did, and were saved. Nobody thought of any process; they thought of the truth, poured out of warm hearts by tongues of fire.

Quite recently I have been watching the developments of the growing revival spirit among us. Two cases occurred, one in each of two Dallas churches, where people heard, repented, confessed all in an hour. In another service one heard, repented, believed, confessed and was baptized all in a single service. Why not?

It will be a great time when preachers get the "process" business out of their own minds and preach for immediate results. It is a sublime scene when a preacher grapples his congregation with the truth and presses men to immediate decision. This hour of victory will be greater when churches look for it and pray for it, even while the word is spoken. What an era will that be when soul-winners have faith to crowd the unsaved and bring them to forget processes, surrender, believe and live. It looks like we are somewhat emerging from slavery to processes and attaining to a more heroic faith. Processes may well be dreaded when they take the life out of us.

A FINE EXAMPLE OF ORGANIZED EFFICIENCY.

THE military organization is the most perfect known to men. No matter how large the army, the individual is still the unit of organization. The individual is never lost sight of for a moment. On any morning each individual can be accounted for, if the situation is normal.

In the whole scheme of organization, two things are held constantly in view: First, making the most of the individual, and, second, making the individuals support each other for the highest efficiency. These are the primary ideas in military organization. They are at the base of all the larger organizations, such as regiments, brigades, division corps, armies. No matter how large the army, its efficiency depends on the faithful application of the two primary principles just named. If the companies are incoherent, ragged, loose; if the units be spiritless, and untrained, there can be no efficiency in the subdivisions of the army. The strength of the units will determine the force of the organization.

For all large undertakings large combinations of units sub-organized are needful. Yet no army can ever rise above the general average of its individual soldiers. And this principle holds in all organized society. Hence the necessity to keep close to the heart of things in dealing with large forces. The home, the school, the church, are the real makers of America. The statesman combines and directs forces created for him.

We have before us today, a demonstration of what has just been said on a large and imposing scale. It is the second demonstration on the same field of action within 10 or 12 years. It is now conceded, even by the Russians, that the Japanese army is the most powerful military force afield on any part of the earth. It easily whipped China a few years ago—40,000,000 Japs against 400,000,000 Chinese.

By Dr. J. B. Gambrell, D. D.

It has, from the firing of the first shot, shown its superiority to Russia. The great empire of the North is learning a lesson its military men ought to have known, and all its leaders as well. Numbers do not count much against some other things. The countless hordes of Xerxes were as nothing against the disciplined, high-souled, trained Greeks, who, on the immortal field of Marathon, locked shields, 10,000 of them kept step, sang their peans, and bore down everything before them, as each soldier stood in his place, and supported every other soldier. The army of Japan has every element of strength developed to a very high degree.

To begin with, the individual soldier is intelligent, high-spirited and patriotic. Ninety-two per cent of the Japs can read, and they are perhaps, the greatest readers, taken altogether, in all the world. Intelligence will win on every battlefield, and let us lay it to heart. Almost 92 per cent of the Russians cannot read. Which will whip? Which ought to whip?

Add to the intelligence and patriotism of the Japanese private soldier perfect military organization, from the lowest form to the highest, and you will begin to understand why things are happening as they are.

But there is still another great element of success, not to be lost sight of for a moment, and that is the leadership of this splendid army of spirited, alert, dauntless soldiers. Their officers, from the lowest subalterns to their great Field Marshal Oyama, are trained, devoted and courageous to their finger tips. Many an army has gone to pieces under indifferent officers.

Note one other element of power in this conquering army: They are willing to suffer. Private soldiers as well as officers are willing to endure hardness as good soldiers. They expect it. They are all, to a man, on their country's altar. They are willing to live or to die for their country.

They believe in their country, in their Emperor, who trusts them. They count it an honor to die for their country. Their friends and relatives at home share this high view.

Added to all this is the skillful leadership of the army. Their generals are selected solely for their ability. There is no favoritism in the army or navy. The prince of royal blood fights under an officer educated and trained out of the thick of the population. It is all different with the Russians.

I have been transferring all this to our Baptist people. Paul dwelt much on the military features of a Christian's life. "Endure hardness as a good soldier of Jesus Christ." He himself was a great soldier. He fought to a finish the good fight. He counted not his life dear unto himself. In no area of human action is there a call for higher soldiery qualities than in the realm of Christianity. The whole life of a Christian is a series of battles for the conquering of the enemies of the King eternal. The world is the battlefield and every disciple a soldier.

In the army of King Jesus, every soldier is a volunteer. There is no conscription, and there is no compulsion. Volunteers are always the best soldiers. The motives for service in this army are the highest that ever moved intelligent beings. Love, immortality, glory fadeless and transcendent move us to service.

Under the voluntary principle we may have the most perfect, flexible and efficient organization the human mind can conceive, all of it resting on the individual as the unit and following the perfection of military organization, in which the individual stands for all in him, and each stands for all, and all for each. It is given to us to demonstrate on a large scale what the voluntary principle is worth in the Christian warfare. We may put to shame all the "strong church governments" by the no government of the New Testament, which leaves individuals free to co-operate for the glory of our common Lord on principles of love and consecration. The campaign we are in ought to do it. It will, if each one will stand in his place, and do his duty; the individuals, the pastors, the associational workers, the women, the Sunday School officers. Such a demonstration on so large a scale, will be worth an untold amount to the cause we represent in Texas, now and hereafter. Texas Baptists may, and I believe will, to a large extent, demonstrate in Christianity what Japan is demonstrating in war. We will give a fine example of organized efficiency, and do it this month. May every soul thrill with high and holy purpose, and may the spirit of the living God brood over the great army and lead us on to a victory of love, faith and consecration.

THE PROBLEM OF DENOMINATIONAL PROGRESS.

WHAT is the problem of denominational progress? It is men. Our supreme need is men—men, of course, of the right sort. With the right kind of men, and women to match, all things are possible. The best plan of doing anything is a man. President Faunce, at Waco, struck the keynote of progress when he put the emphasis, in his great speech, on man. "Let us make man" is the text for all the times. "Let us make money" is a small thing to say. To raise the whole denominational level, we must raise the level of Christian manhood.

By all odds, the chief glory of any country is its people. This is true the world over. The Scotch have an exceedingly rugged country, but they are a glorious people, because they are religious and devoted to education. No equal number of people in the world exercise a wider or better influence over every realm of human activity.

The value of the right kind of men to a country can never be computed. A man may easily be worth millions of dollars to a country. Governor Joseph Brown, of Georgia, has been worth many millions to his State in actual money, by his practical wisdom in directing the public mind of that State. Ben Franklin largely created the industrial North.

Let us transfer all this to our denominational life. Men are our great want; men who are wise to see what Israel ought to do; men with visions of the future; men of lofty ideals; men embued with the spirit of the New Testament; men willing to serve in any place, and whose highest conception of life is to serve.

At this very hour Texas Baptists need 100 equipped men, not to fill places, but to make places. Wide is the difference between the spirit of the man who wishes to fill a place and that of a man ready to lay himself out to make a place. Our want is place-makers. Paul had the greatest spirit, because he was ready to put his whole being into foundation work. He had the true vision of glory. You can see the brass globe on the top of the church steeple much further than you can see the foundation stone, but it is not one-thousandth part as important.

We have a vast field, rich in possibilities. There are mines of human wealth in Texas richer than all the diamond mines of the world. These are waiting development. They are waiting the coming of the right men and women. If worked, they will enrich the world, intellectually, religiously and materially.

Our present need is a reinforcement of men, apostolic in spirit and in labors. These men are wanted to go to needy sections and devote their lives to building up. If these men can be had, the future is safe. But they must be adaptable, as well as devoted. It is ideal to have a pastorate,

By Dr. J. B. Gambrell, D. D.

preach regularly and have an ample income. But all that belongs to an advanced condition. Places are not made that way.

During the Civil War I met, in East Virginia, a young Baptist preacher, Rev. J. F. Dean. In that part of the State Baptists were weak, and, in the main, they were held in derision. They were few, poor and unlearned. There was no one to lead them up and out. Young Dean was from Columbia University, from which he graduated with credit. He determined to devote himself to building the Baptist cause in East Virginia. To do this, he began teaching and preaching. He established himself at a small village in the very heart of the country he wished to lift up. Year in and year out he went on with his work, teaching and preaching. Twenty-five years went by, and a great transformation had come. He had sent relay after relay of students to Richmond College from his Windsor Academy. The Baptist cause was redeemed and the country greatly blessed. In that section great churches have grown up, and are led by an intelligent ministry and laity. He did not suffer for a living. A few years ago the teacher-preacher died, and thousands rise up to call him blessed. His works do follow him. He made a place and made men.

Let us come nearer this way. Shortly after the war I had many talks with Gen. M. P. Lowery, who had come back to his home in the hills of Tippah County, one of the poorest counties in that State. We talked of the future of the whole south of our State, to which we were both devoted, and especially of the north end of it. It was clear that nothing would redeem it but sanctified intelligence. He had many calls to important fields, but determined to devote himself to that section of his State. The question of a school was much discussed. I urged him to found a school at his home, far interior, and thus make an intellectual center, from which a new life should go out to bless the country. He urged me to undertake the enterprise. He questioned his mind whether a preacher should teach. At last he reached a conclusion and began his great work. Blue Mountain College is the result, and it is one of the greatest schools in the South. Its influence is more than State-wide. The whole land has felt its uplifting power.

Things like these can be done in many places in Texas. The opportunities are many. They wait for men and women with minds and hearts and a true vision.

But we may look another direction with equal encouragement. There are scores and even hundreds of churches in Texas rich in all sorts of possibilities of good, only waiting the coming of a pastor who will commence on a bare living and work constantly toward larger and better things, It is all a mistake that every young preacher must be fully provided for before he should enter upon a pastorate. A hundred young men of the right type can establish themselves in ever-growing pastorates in Texas, if they will commence right and go on right. This was done by Pastor Ammons, of the Tabernacle Church, Houston. To do after this sort will make character, and character is strength, and strength is success.

To a large extent, we look to our schools for intelligent leadership. Consecration is the very heart of Christian education. We are rightly concerned for the culture of our rising young people. There is even more room for anxiety that they put their culture to the highest use, by serving where service is most needed. The preacher who makes service second to position is spoiled. Service will make position, and it will grow men. But position of itself will not make men.

Our whole problem of progress is to be solved by developing men and women of the true type. There is not any more need for consecration in China than in Texas. Our development is arrested in many places for lack of heroic leaders. There are noble men and women ready for any service, if only they can have leaders, intelligent, courageous, self-sacrificing and adaptable; men and women above class and race feelings; men and women who will not look at the ministry from the social and financial standpoint, but from the standpoint of the cross. The right kind of preachers can do well anywhere, for God will be with them.

I cannot close this article without a word to preachers' wives, and to those good women who expect to be preachers' wives. A preacher's wife may greatly help or hinder him. If a woman expects her husband to use the ministry to promote her and his social position, or for ease, she makes an unspeakable mistake from every conceivable standpoint. The glory of the ministry is service, and no wife can have any glory separate from her husband. Alas! for a worldly-minded, self-serving preacher's wife. She will prove the truth of that scripture which teaches us that whosoever will save his life shall lose it. The royal road to all good, and to the greatest honor, here and hereafter, is the way of service consecrated by the footprints of the Son of God.

LIZARD KILLING.

SOME years ago a brother was visiting the state convention of a sister state and heard a prolonged discussion on a very small point of parliamentary law. It seemed that every brother present was especially strong on parliamentary order, and had an opinion to give on the question in debate. This was characteristic of the state, in a measure, for many years. Under the lead of the paper most read among the people, they had turned their religious meetings into debating societies, and had discussed all manner of questions, without any regard to their importance or to the appropriateness of the discussions, or to spiritual conditions. It goes without saying, that in such a state, the practical duties of Christianity would be very much neglected. Next to nothing was done for missions, and still less for education, but no people were busier, none could become more enthused, or annually had greater discussions, but they were all about things that were trivial.

When this brother saw an opportunity, he got the floor, and after talking in a semi-humorous way for quite a time, until he had turned the whole convention into sympathy with himself, he began to come down closer and closer upon the practice of wasting life on questions that gendered strife rather than godly edifying, making his discussions as serious and severe as he could, not to irritate his hearers too much. Toward the close he related the following incident, which really occurred within his knowledge:

"A gentleman sent his son after dinner one day to lay by a promising piece of corn. About the middle of the afternoon, the father walked down to the field to see how the plowing was going on, and to his amazement he saw that Charley was running and thrashing and making a great effort evidently to kill something. He had already beaten down and destroyed about a half acre of corn and he called out, 'Charley, what in the world is the matter?' Charley explained that he was lying down sleeping, a lizard ran over his face, he got up, ran after it and intended to kill it. His father said, 'Now, see what you have done; you have lost half the evening, and destroyed half an acre of corn, and what is the use of killing the lizard anyway? If you kill him he is worth nothing, and if you don't kill him, he will do no harm.' Charley replied, 'I don't care; I am going to kill him, if I lose a crop.'"

"This," said the speaker, "represents many a Baptist. He goes to sleep until some little question that has no good in

BY DR. J. B. GAMBRELL, D. D.

it—and no harm either—is sprung, and then he is all wide awake, ready to settle that question, if the Lord's work is

Charlie Kills the Lizards and Ruins the Corn.

utterly neglected." Waiting a moment to allow it to strike in, he continued, 'I neglected to say that Charley was the son of a Baptist, and was half idiot.'"

The anecdote did its work. One of the brethren who had been a leader in the discussions rose to his feet, waving a ten dollar bill and said, "I want to do something." The money was turned over to education, the trend of the convention changed, and for many years the whole state has been on the up-grade. The same speaker told the anecdote in his own state convention, and a young brother, attending the meeting for about the first time, heard it. Soon afterward he went away to the Seminary, and in a few years became Secretary of Missions for the state of Tennessee. He took up the lizard anecdote and went from one end of that state to another, employing it with fine effect to illustrate how Baptists were allowing the Methodists and other denominations and the devil to take the state, while the Baptists were discussing little questions among themselves, and questions, too, which amounted to nothing, no matter how they might be settled. It served him many a good turn, for he told it with inimitable effect.

At the B. Y. P. U. convention in Wilmington, N. C., one of the speakers, to the great amusement and evident instruction of the great audience, brought forward the lizard anecdote again, and told it, not as it was originally told, but in substance. It carried the point, and was much spoken of by those who heard it.

This is the history of the anecdote, and that was one lizard which really did good in the world, albeit, it never intended to do it. Really, may not the lesson of the story have a wide application? Are there not many questions debated among us of such trivial importance, that we may well compare them to the chasing of a lizard, and isn't it really true that some of our preachers, some of our churches, too, have lost more than one crop chasing lizards? There is an old proverb which illustrates the same point, "The game is not worth the candle." In the common affairs of life men always consider whether the thing they are after is worth their time and trouble. Why should we not be equally reasonable in religious matters? Isn't it a thousand pities that able men will so often throw away life with all of its opportunities on questions that are trivial?

There comes to my mind at this moment a very able preacher who threw away the latter half of his life discussing a very abtruse and unsolvable question relating to religion and science. And we all know how earnestly and often in the not-long-ago people discussed Melchizedek, always ending where they began, in a midst of darkness. There are minds that delight in the mystical and the curious. There are people who spend a great deal of their time on puzzles, and if they can get a religious puzzle, then they are in the heighth of their glory. Of one of this class a man with a genius for characterization said, recently, "He is a donkey braying in a deep mist."

We all might study with a great deal of profit the intense earnestness and practical good sense of our Lord and his apostles. One of these curious people came to Jesus once with a question: "Will there be many saved?" Our Lord did not answer his question, but he did for him something a great deal better; he gave him some practical advice as to seeking for himself to enter the kingdom.

Let each one of us see that we do not resemble Charley, who only stirred himself out of sleep when the lizard crawled over his face, and then lost all regret at the failure of a crop in his intense desire to kill a harmless little animal, and if we have any proclivities in that direction let us remember that Charley was not of a sound mind.

TWO CHAPTERS ON MONEY AND METHODS.

THE TWO great chapters in the New Testament on money and methods are the 8th and 9th of 2d Corinthians. Nowhere else can we learn so much as to methods of co-operative work among the churches. The immediate occasion of the writing of these instructive lessons was the rounding up of a great collection for the poor saints at Jerusalem. This was partly missionary and partly benevolent. The Jerusalem saints gave largely, many all they had, to keep the Pentecostal revival going. Then came wasting persecution. Jerusalem was a great center of evangelism. It was of the utmost importance that the church be supported that it might carry forward its work.

It appears clear that Paul was conducting this campaign among the churches. From this it is certain that the Holy Spirit sanctioned the common sense idea, that somebody must look after all business of consequence. The notion that the large affairs of the kingdom, involving co-operation among the churches, must be left without human superintendence, has no support in reason or scripture; but is flatly negatived by both. No one can read the 8th chapter without being convinced that, as in all other things, religious, the Holy Spirit uses men who employ common sense methods.

It is perfectly clear that separate, independent churches co-operated in the one great move. It is just as clear that co-operation was voluntary, not by compulsion. Paul in every expression appeals to their love, their devotion and never once to his authority. They are to give of a ready mind, not grudgingly. All his appeals go to the heart and consciences of the saints.

We learn, also, that in matters financial it is right to use the force of example to influence those who need to be lifted to a higher plane of giving. Paul tells the church at Corinth of the noble giving of the churches of Macedonia. Why should we be so squeamish in using common sense methods in the great business of inducing each other to give, as we should? Here we have apostolic example, falling in with common sense.

We may furthermore learn, that it is right to send men to churches to urge them to do their duty. Paul sent, not one simply, but more than one. Here again common sense and Holy Scripture coincide. Indeed, the whole modern notion that collections must go by spontaneous combustion is completely exploded by Paul's teaching and example, as shown in these two chapters. They are marvels of common sense and practical wisdom.

It appears further, that it is right for a church to make a promise. Paul commends the Corinthian church, because it was ready to undertake and promise. But Paul, led by the Spirit, did not leave it at that. He urged them to go on and complete their collection. He had been boasting of them, and he urges them not to put him and themselves to shame by falling down on the collection. He went further and sent men to look after it. He knew the danger of cooling off.

And the marvelous wisdom of this divine plan is displayed in the rule of giving. Every one and every one as the Lord had prospered him. The poorest could give as well, though not as much, as the richest. Besides, the giving was all to go on the underlying fact, that all prosperity, great or small, comes from God. This is the very cream of the whole matter. This should be the unbending rule in every case.

The 8th chapter particularly settles one great point never to be lost sight of in managing money given for religious purposes. Paul associated a number of brethren together, selecting tried men and men of the highest repute in the churches to receive and administer this fund gathered from the several churches. He tells us why, and his reason is good. He would avoid blame by "providing for honest things, not only in the sight of the Lord, but also in the sight of men." He would so manage the fund as to hold the confidence of the brethren and the churches. Where there is no power to compel, there must be confidence to win. This is God's plan. These "messengers of the churches, the glory of Christ," were not messengers sent by the churches to some general body, but a board or committee traveling with the fund of the churches. There is here revealed a great principle in the management of denominational finances. It is at this point that what is called the gospel mission plan breaks down. It is neither according to scripture nor common sense, because it does not safeguard denomination finances. I have recently had a letter from Mexico which informs me, that a meeting-house built by the gifts of the churches sent to one man is now rented for a dance hall. The brother took title in his name. He is now in this country and collects rent from the property. Because this method has in it no safeguards and can never appeal to the common sense of the plain common sense masses, it will never have anything more than a spasmodic existence. Paul's principle should never be sunk out of sight. It is vital to all large success.

It appears from a study of these scriptures, that the churches severally, each for itself, chose the messengers to travel with and administer this bounty. A convention may name a number of brethren and recommend them to the churches to administer a common fund, but after all each church must choose or reject these men, commonly called a board. They are only the messengers or agents of as many and of such churches as chose to employ them to disburse their funds. This is a point as vital as the co-operation of the churches on the one hand, and the independence of the churches on the other. Whoever tries it will search the scriptures in vain to find one example of two or more churches "through messengers" to a general body choosing men to administer their funds. The choice was direct, as is shown in the wonderfully instructive scriptures under consideration. A convention may nominate men; the churches, each for itself, must choose. This was the method wrought out under divine direction. It is a marvel of simplicity and common sense. Within the limits of these principles lie our safety and our success. These prnciples define clearly how co-operation on the widest scale may be practiced with perfect safety to the independence of the churches. They also show how co-operation may be powerfully promoted.

These are but a few of the lessons contained in these two great chapters. They are a compendium of revealed wisdom and plain common sense touching religious giving and financial management on a large scale. They are worthy of profound study. Whoever understands these will not go far wrong on the general question of church finance and denominational management. They mark out the King's highway, leading to the largest success. The great bulk of the denomination has always kept within the limits of truth and safety. Only within recent times have we had men advocating the doctrine that churches can transfer their authority through messengers into a general body, and thus give a board church authority to do church acts. And what is called "gospel missions" on the other hand ignores scripture example and common sense. Keep in the middle of the road.

CONSERVATISM AND CORNS.

AN ENGLISH wit tells of a man who, being applied to by a corn doctor, refused an offer to have his corns removed, exclaiming: "What! them corns; twenty years have I kept them."

Here is one kind of conservatism for you. And it is the kind very much lauded by many whose thinking is only in the bark of things. Conservatism may or may not be good. Corns gain no value by their age. They are a kind of belonging not desirable, and the longer one has them the less use he finds for them. A man of ordinary judgment will be ready to part with this kind of property on short notice, and pay something for the privilege.

Nevertheless Douglas Gerrold's conservatist has many close kinspeople in America, as, no doubt in England. They cling to what gives them trouble for no better reason than that they are used to the thing that way.

Spurgeon tells us of the great trouble he had to get a grotesque, high and thoroughly unholy pulpit removed and a sensible one put in its place, all because the nonsensical one had been there a long time. Dr. Gill had occupied it. It was associated with his long ministry. Why should it be removed? It counted for nothing, that for real preaching, it was wholly unsuited. It was a corn not to be sacrificed to comfort or sense. I have myself had a similar experience with a pulpit, and only succeeded in removing the old one by promising to use the material in it to make a new one.

Not a few churches hold on to a set of old leaders, deacons and others, after they have long been a burden on every member of the church. These effete leaders are most known as not leading. Like veritable corns, they locate themselves on the body, and make it very uncomfortable if they are rubbed. They are like corns in that they are ex-

BY DR. J. B. GAMBRELL, D. D.

crescences. They have no vitality in themselves. They add nothing to the strength of the body; but they won't put

What! Them Corns? Twenty Years Have I Kept Them.

up with any pressure. Their whole force lies in making it uncomfortable when not let alone.

A man with corns on his feet very soon learns the value of room for them. He never fails in buying shoes to remember his corns. He makes ample provision for them, not because he loves them, but because he will hear from them if he does not give them plenty of room, and let them have due prominence. They will retaliate without mercy if any repression is used.

It is even so with some men in the churches. Hard and horny, without tenderness or consideration for others, they occupy chief seats, and have their way for no other reason than that the people dread to touch them. They can turn the pleasantest occasion into a terror and they will do it remorselessly if they are rubbed the wrong way. People put up with them for no other reason than that it is troublesome to do anything against their wishes. These excrescences, like thorns, preempt their places, and serve notice that whenever they are crowded there will be a row in their neighborhood.

In many churches these disagreeable, not leaders, but setters, are permitted to annoy and pain the church for no better reason than the Englishman refused to have his corns removed. They had been there a long time. We read of a knave in the Acts who controlled the people because of a long time he had bewitched them with his tricks.

Coming back to conservatism, let the question always be asked whether the thing to be conserved is worth having, or whether a better thing might not be had in its place. Conserving corns is a poor business. There are some other things not worth conserving. The old Latins asked a pregnant question: What good? What is the good of corns? If none, then let them go by the best means at hand. My experience with them is that you can afford to swap them for nothing and pay boot. Equally certain is it that many churches can afford to dispense with a so-called leadership even if, at the cost of a temporary tumult. I have seen people who could do very little besides sit up and nurse a collection of corns which, on the slightest provocation, put their owner on a rack of pain. Without adding a thing to the force or happiness of the body they claimed special attention, and gave the owner no time for much else than trying to keep them from making trouble. And in scores of churches the whole body is occupied trying to keep a few useless members from destroying the happiness of all the other members.

My deliberate judgment is that corns are good property to part with by the quickest and easiest way possible, no matter whether you have them a week or twenty years. They do not improve by acquaintance, and like the deadly tongue, no man can tame them. And many churches can well afford to part with an element which only remains to give trouble no matter how old or how young these people are. The Irishman, who had an ailing tooth extracted, and remarked to it as he laid it aside, "Now, ache as much as you please," was a philosopher in his way.

Here I drop the subject, inviting the reader to work it all out to his own satisfaction, only remarking that conservatism is a good thing if the thing conserved is worth the trouble.

A CASE OF APOSTOLIC SUCCESSION WITH NOTES.

THAT waste is a sin there can be no doubt, if we consider the matter in the light of the scriptures. Our Lord, exercising divine and limitless power, multiplied a few loaves and fishes, till they were sufficient for a great multitude. But in the midst of the abundance of divinity, He taught a lesson of economy by commanding that the fragments be taken up, that nothing be lost. Nature, reason and religion all abhor waste, and, I believe that the greatest sin of our time is waste. It is a sin of which the churches are fearfully guilty.

But in considering the question of waste, we need to be careful to know what real waste is. Judas felt he made a strong point on Mary when he objected to the anointing of Christ. The exceedingly precious ointment would soon perform its function and be gone. It might have been sold for a round sum, and the proceeds given to the poor. Judas was a type of a class in the churches today—a rather large class, it is to be feared. Covetousness was at the bottom of this objection. Judas did not care for the poor, but he did love money; and, in his soul, he did not like a liberal example of giving set before the people. Moreover, he did not have the face to come out square and open before the Master and his fellows and oppose honoring the Savior, but he made a fictitious display of a concern he did not have, and set up one good cause against another. This is an old trick still in high favor with Judasites. It is always something else. If it is a foreign mission collection now on, they are taken with a great spasm of concern for the heathen at our doors. If it is a home mission collection, they are for sending the gospel to the millions, who never hear of Jesus. If it is for both of these in one collection, they remember that the pastor's salary is behind. This is the way of the Judasites.

But there is another phase of the question of waste presented by Judas, head of a tribe in Israel. When Mary's warm heart and keen spiritual vision prompted her to do the thing which filled the world with a sweet fragrance, Judas put in where he did not belong. It was not his money Mary was lavishing on her Lord. It was Mary's own money. By this mark is a real Judasite best known. He wants to regulate other people's money while he keeps his own. Much of the din and confusion of the Christian world is kept up by those who are simply objecting to what others do. Let the readers make a note of this, and consider the objectiors in his part of the moral vineyard. The likelihood is, he will be surprised at the similarity of what went on in Christ's day and what is going on now. The successors of the noted Apostle Judas have the tribal mark well set. Some of them are mixed, to a degree, with other apostolic tribes; but blood will out, and they show themselves, with more or less plainness, every time the question of money is up.

There is a feature of the apostolic economy of Judas that should be noted with care. While objecting and commending a proper consideration of the poor, he was keeping his real motive under cover. He wanted the money himself. Back of all the talk was self. And the scriptures are very bold, for they do say he was a thief. What is thievery but getting what does not rightly belong to you?

The successors of Judas are not smart. They have their own personal interests to serve, and they try to head off and capture every move, so as to turn it their way. If there is a great mission move agoing, they tell the people there is too much ado about money. Better keep clear of the thing, or it will cost too much, and a lot of the money is wasted anyhow. A Judas pastor shunts missions aside because they might absorb his salary. Poor fool, he is like his apostolic predecessor, or playing his double game against God, who has said that whosoever will save his life shall lose it, and whoever loses his life will find it.

There have been Judasites who took to running papers for a living. They are for economy. Elaborate plans for spreading the gospel fill them with dismay. My, the expense! They do not know what it is to throw themselves into the great work unreservedly, and sink or swim, survive or perish, live or die, with the Master's cause. And if the people get caught up into a swelling tide of missionary zeal, they will get left. Then begins the working of the Judas spirit. They will not come out and tell what is in their hearts. But they begin to object to what other people are doing with their money. They raise the cry of waste. And in the meantime they have their own schemes wherewith to turn contributions their way. They cut up shines, get up counter-movements and pose as defenders of the faith. One of this tribe charged $100 for a three days' debate, and gave it to the secretaries for loving money. Another has kept the hat passing for himself while he cries waste of mission money. This has been the cry against every great movement for Christ and His cause from the days of Judas till now. The great givers have had joy in it, and the successors of Judas have been active in opposing. Likely it will go on this way till Christ comes. What ailed Judas, that, with all the light around him, he drove on to such a dismal end? Spiritual blindness was his trouble. Mary saw what he could not see. She saw the Christ in His death and resurrection glory. With such a vision filling her soul, she could think of herself and of her money only, as she and it might honor the Lord. To love and faith, to withhold was to waste all. Hers was the true vision. All life and all treasure can only be rightly estimated by looking at them from Mary's standpoint. Love has good eyes; selfishness is as blind as a bat.

By Dr. J. B. Gambrell, D. D.

From the true standpoint, we are to study all economic questions in the kingdom. Let me suggest a few. Here is a pastor with a warm heart, longing to be useful in the ministry. He serves a church anxious to secure his services for as little as possible. They keep him in a financial strain. Here is waste, grievous waste; because with a little more, the man of God might employ all his powers for the main thing. This is a waste of heavenly resources. In hundreds of cases 25 per cent added to the pastor's salary would double his efficiency. But Judasites likely will not see it.

Many think to strongly equip missionary forces is a waste. Get weak secretaries, put them in a corner, withhold resources, or else do away with secretaries entirely. What is this but waste of all that is best? It has been demonstrated 100 years. Last year our State Board raised in Texas $176,000 in round figures and expended it at less than 5 per cent. Four thousand, four hundred and eighty-four people were baptized, 114 churches constituted, and over 8,000 people were brought into the churches under the faithful labors of 259 missionaries. Yet with some it was counted that money was wasted. More than $40,000 was raised for home and foreign missions by our board, scores of meeting-houses were built, and a great upbuilding work done in the churches. All this was done while the cry of waste went up from multitudes doing not a thing, but objecting and trying to tell other people what to do with their money. They are the true successors to Judas.

There is another view, and a very solemn one, too. Here it is. Under the mistaken view of saving, many are hoarding unneeded money, piling it up, adding house to house, farm to farm beyond any possible need. Two men live neighbors. One lives to give. The other lives to keep. The first has sent his money in streams to preach the gospel over the world, to help colleges, hospitals, to help God's cause everywhere. He dies. Has he wasted his money? The other kept all and dies leaving a large estate. Has he saved his money? A man dying requested his friends to put this on his tombstone:

"What I gave I have; what I kept I lost."

There is such a thing, and let us never forget it, as laying up treasures in heaven. The rich man of the scriptures died poor indeed. He wasted all by keeping it.

The greatest thought of all is, that this life extends itself into eternity. We can only be rich toward God by giving as Mary did. She saved all she gave and brought a vast revenue of glory to her Redeemer.

Multitudes ought to ponder this question of waste. It goes to money, to time, to influence, to everything. All is wasted that is not used for the honor of Him who is Lord of all.

THE EVIL OF THE FIGHTING SPIRIT.

JUST this morning I was reading in the third chapter of James and came on these words, beginning with the fourteenth verse: "But if ye have bitter envyings and strife in your hearts, glory not and he not against the truth. This wisdom descendeth not from above, but is earthly, sensual, devilish, for where envying and strife is, there is confusion and every evil work. But the wisdom that is from above is first pure, then peaceable, easy to be entreated, full of mercy and good fruits without partiality, and without hypocrisy, and the fruit of righteousness is sown in peace by them that make peace." How wonderfully apt are the words of Revelation, how true to nature and suitable to all ages. These words have their application in our times and are full of instruction for us.

The object of this article is to call attention to and

emphasize the wickedness of the spirit of fighting. Let us remember that there is a spirit of truth and there is a spirit of error. Sometimes truth is disassociated from the spirit of truth. There is such a thing, and it is not as uncommon as it ought to be, as preaching the truth in the spirit of the devil. It is quite possible for a person to advocate truth in a spirit which altogether destroys the truth.

Of course, fighting has a prominent place in the Bible. There is a great deal of militarism in the New Testament. The Christian life is reckoned a constant warfare. Strange as the expression may seem in print, it is easy to fight in the spirit of peace; and this is the only way in which it is lawful for Christians to fight at all. Our Lord was the Prince of Peace and yet he is the Captain of our salvation, and the Leader of his own people against the powers of darkness. He fights in the spirit of peace and love. He fights not to hurt and wound and kill, but to save. That a good many people in modern times who bear the name of Christ, and are fighters, do not fight in that spirit does not need any proof. There is oft against the spirit of peace in contending for the truth and for righteousness, the spirit of strife, the love of fight, the disposition to hurt; a general spirit of antagonism which shows itself in the writing and in the speaking of men, who, in their own thinking, are set for the defense of the gospel.

It is this devilish spirit of fight that has brought the preaching of baptism into such disrepute in many quarters. Some brethren who have felt themselves specially set for the defense of the ordinances of the church, and the church itself, have gone to battle in these great interests in the spirit of the prize ring. They stand ready to crack every head that pops up, and they do it in the spirit in which men contend for the mastery in worldly things. There is little wonder that a great many pious people uninstructed, have turned away from the preaching of the truths of the gospel in disgust, because they felt and recognized the spirit of fighting, the utter absence of the spirit of love, and felt that any preaching done in that style was unfit to hear and wholly unsafe to believe.

Looking back now over a good many years of strife and fighting, I give it as my deliberate judgment, that the spirit of war, of contention, of worldliness, which has characterized very much of the preaching of the doctrines of the Baptists has done us more harm than all the preaching of pedobaptists in the same length of time. It is not a pleasant thing to say, but a very important one for us to think upon.

And then when we come to our denominational discussions, what a vast amount of all the writing in our papers and the discussions in our public bodies bear the unmistakable mark of the spirit of contention. Even the common people are not satisfied except for a short season. They know when a preacher is seeking to reach a sound conclusion with his brethren, and they know by a spiritual intuition when he is characterized, in his utterances, by a wicked spirit of fight. This spirit is every way wicked and devilish. It is of the earth earthy and, it appears to me, one of the very worst things about it is that it associates the sacred interests of Christ's Kingdom with the lowest and worst passions of the human heart. Even the world understands its own spirit and recognizes it in those who contend on whatever ground and for whatever cause in this wicked spirit. Who has not seen a whole community of sinners turn out to hear a fight in a church where this spirit unmistakably reigned? The same class of people would go to see a prize fight or a dog fight, or any other kind of a fight. They recognize their own spirit and are drawn by it, to the great shame of Christianity.

There are few more deadly things than the association of that which is holy and good with that which is low and mean. Those who are animated in their perpetual fighting by this wicked spirit are always loud in their protestations of deep concern for the cause. Generally, they hold themselves up as being willing to sacrifice themselves for some cause for which they are fighting, when, in fact, they are contending for the mastery simply as men would in a political arena. People are not very long deceived by such professions and always, in the end, turn away with a less opinion of religion than they had before they met such champions.

This wicked spirit of strife readily diffuses itself among the unspiritual, to their very great detriment. It is not hard where religion is at a low ebb, for a few men to divide a whole community and array them in parties, one against the other, about a thing in which not one of them has a particle of interest. We have known a whole county, a whole state, and even several states, to be involved and wrought up to fever heat by the contentions of a few men about matters personal to themselves, with only the thinnest veneering to cover their sefishness. There is much that is partisan and fleshly in the average Christian. He is, for a season at least, good game for such a spirit as works in the hearts of those who contend for the mastery in the spirit of the world. Churches, associations, conventions have been paralyzed by this spirit. The Apostle says, "Where envy and strife is, there is confusion and every evil work." Only turn this spirit of strife loose and get it a-going among a people, and every evil work will result. Suspicion, lying, backbiting, evil surmises and all uncharitableness will be the fruitage. What a miserable and deadly thing it is. Confusion and every evil work is the result of the spirit of envying and strife.

This spirit works its greatest ruin in those who entertain it and act under its dictations. Some men are naturally combative, and if they yield to the spirit of combat, they will find that more and more they will grow in that direction and less and less they will like the things of peace.

Confusion and Every Evil Work is the Spirit of Envying and Strife.

and love. Some have gone so far already within our knowledge that they can not enjoy peace. Everything is too dull, unless there is a fight of some sort. They do not like to go to church, if there is nothing but praying and singing and ordinary preaching. They will go long distances to hunt up somebody who will pitch into somebody else, and the man who will pitch in most will have most of these unhappy souls to hang to his ministry, at least for a season. Nothing more completely ruins a preacher than harboring and cultivating the spirit of fighting. Not a few men of our acquaintance have practically ended their ministerial career even before middle life, because they were everlastingly fighting somebody.

Some, indeed, are so fond of fighting that they will hunt through the papers and find something, perhaps a thousand miles away, to pitch into before their congregations. Some foolish thing that some woman said in New England or in Old England, some little figment of error from the brain of a German who has smoked his old dirty pipe until he doesn't know the difference between Bismarck and Melchizedek. He is taken up and pounded to smithereens before his people. Such men, if they lived in Ireland, where there are no snakes, would have snakes shipped to them just for the sake of killing them.

There is a limit to the endurance of good people along this line. When people have borne, perhaps, with some pleasure at the start, the fighting, when they turn away from their busy employments which have wearied their bodies and minds through the week and go up to the house of God on Sunday and instead of finding rest for their souls in the promise of God and food for their souls in the bread of heaven, have all their passions lashed into fury by some fightitive preacher, such turn away from him and seek somebody who will feed them and give them the real blessings of the gospel. Alas, for the preachers today who have fought themselves out of work, fought the world, the flesh and the devil and their own brethren until they have lost all spiritual power themselves, all love for the sweeter and better things of the Bible and have become so dry and unprofitable that the people turn away from them. In every such case the people are right.

It would be for us all a most profitable study of our own hearts to find out how far, even in our contentions for the truth, we are animated by this evil spirit of contention and strife. Some of us need to be especially guarded. All of us need to separate ourselves from men who are undoubtedly of this evil spirit. Not one of us is so strong as not to need the spiritual help of his brethren and it is not good for us to be with those who are constantly seeking to make us like themselves—strife-mongers.

As we love our own peace and growth in grace, as we love the work of our Master and would seek to be useful in it, as we love our brethren and desire to help them, as we love the lost world and desire to save it, let us cultivate the spirit of peace and pursue it.

PAUL, THE TENT-MAKER.

IN the abundance of mail coming to my office, nearly every phase of denominational life is revealed. It is impossible to read many of the letters without tears, such heroic devotion and suffering, as well as joyous consecration, do they reveal. I have been led to compare what is going on among us now with what happened when Christianity was just rooting itself in human hearts and in human society.

If is often said, and yet scarcely need be said, that, next to the Master, Paul was the mightiest personality of the apostolic period. He was colossal in his mind and in his character. He was unmatched in his labors. It is profitable to study him at any angle. He was a great scholar, easily first in the apostolic group. He was the most masterful spirit in the realm of evangelism, going from city to city, with a tongue like a flame of fire. He was the finest defender of the faith, meeting any foe on any part of the ground. He was a matchless superintendent of missions, and the greatest master of constructive Christian work of his day. His was the greatest, most successful, completest life lived since Christ ceased to walk among men on this earth. And what completes its greatness is its superiority to all outward circumstances. To him the small distinctions of avocation, nationality, station, etc., amounted to nothing.

I come to a view of him which we may well consider in these days. Let us look at Paul, the tent maker. Following the wise custom of the Jews, young Saul learned a trade. He was a tent maker. This was a wise custom of that far-off time which all parents of today should follow with their children, boys and girls. Nothing can take the place of work in the formation of character. Not to know how to work is a dreadful weakness in any life.. One of the most famous generals of the Civil War said to me after the war closed: "I am so helpless. I would give anything to be a good blacksmith." Paul went about on his great mission, not only with a wholesome respect for work, but more with a sustaining sense of independence. He could never become helpless while he had health. I shall never cease to thank my parents, especially my mother, that I was made to work, even when it seemed useless, from the standpoint of anxiety about making a living. I could make a living blacking shoes, for I was trained to it. We need to keep close to the old paths in these fast days. Woe to idlers!

The time came when Paul's tent making stood him and his great cause well in hand. He made tents, not as a business, but as a temporary expediency to defray expenses and to enable him to carry on his work in a given place.

Today I received a letter from a brother preacher saying he is pastor of 3 churches and farming to make a living.

Woe to Idlers.

He added that he was often tempted to leave the field, but just could not. Blessed be God for men conscience bound, who can not leave important posts for ease or on any nice points of propriety.

The tent making incident in Paul's life throws a flood of light on the general question of preaching and the preacher's living. Very briefly let us study some lessons drawn from it.

1. A preacher is called to preach. That is his business. Everything else is incidental. In a sense, he is paid for preaching, but from the standpoint of his call to preach, he is paid that he may preach. If he makes tents, or farms, or clerks in a store, or teaches school, he is only making expenses, that he may go on with his real business of preaching the gospel.

2. Times come when preachers ought to make expenses by some sort of work while he preaches. The right to a support is clear in reason, and in scripture; but the preacher, anxious above all things to further the cause, may waive this right. Paul did it and showed his greatness in doing it. The man who stands always on his rights is a size or two under the man who will, for a great cause, forego his rights. Paul was great enough to make tents and preach. Let us thank God that we have men with us today great enough to plow and preach. Such men are God's heroes in the earth. Such men have laid the foundations of the cause from State to State in this western world—of whom the world is not worthy. If I am not mistaken, we are pressing the matter of pastoral support too far in some cases. All hail to the men who still walk in the illustrious foot-prints, as times demand, of the world's first man and greatest preacher, Paul, the tent maker.

3. What a flood of light does this incident throw on Paul's earnestness. He was no dilettante preacher, full of nice and delicate dignities to be coddled and cared for first of all. He had that stalwart dignity that came of living up to a great moral purpose. He was no carpet knight, but the

dust-covered hero from a great battle field, upon which had been fought out the destiny of immortal beings. His dignity was the simple but sublime dignity of usefulness, than which there is nothing greater in human character. From all this, I conclude that every preacher should stick to his business of preaching, even if he must make tents, saw wood, black shoes, dig ditches, drive a dray, teach school, practice law or sweep the streets for expenses. God has marvelously blessed men of Paul's spirit, and He will yet.

There is as much real dignity in serving God in one place as another. The honor lies not in the place, but in the service. Two brothers in the same church lived side by side. They discussed the destitution in a rather remote neighborhood. One was a preacher. Both were farmers. The preacher by agreement went and held a meeting in which many were converted. The other remained and laid by the corn for both. Who doubts that in the last day their reward will be equal? They will share the glory as they did the labor.

TWO POINTS OF VIEW—SELF AND SERVICE.

NEARLY everything depends upon getting the right point of view in looking at a landscape, a picture, a city, or a subject. If one, from some tower in a great city, looks across the streets, it will seem one interminable mass of disorder. If his tower happens to be at the crossing of two great streets, he can look in four directions and see that what otherwise seemed disorder, is magnificent order.

The real trouble most people have in studying the two standing questions for debate, predestination and free will, is getting the right standpoint. I never talked as much as an

By Dr. J. B. Gambrell, D. D.

half hour with an Armenian on the subject of predestination, that he didn't insist on considering it wholly from the standpoint of free will, or rather, from the human standpoint. Predestination from the finite, human standpoint, is foolishness. But let the man go over to the right standpoint, consider predestination from the point of view occupied an infinite God, who knows all things and works all things after the counsel of his own will, and anything but predestination is foolishness. From the Divine standpoint, salvation on any other idea than the election of grace, is ridiculous. If men are saved, somebody saves them. Everybody agrees that God saves. If He saves, he either does it on the grab-bag principle, or else He saves on purpose. If He saves on purpose, He had the purpose before He saved. Then the question: "When did He form the purpose?" The apostle answered: "Before the foundation of the world." God could not be an infinite God and not do that way. Free agency must be considered solely from the standpoint of humanity, and election from the standpoint of divinity.

There is a scene depicted in the gospels, tender, beautiful, instructive, which illustrates the difference between the standpoint of selfishness and the standpoint of service. Our Lord is in a circle of friends. Around Him are His disciples. There comes into that company a tender-hearted modest woman, and, without words, breaks an alabaster box of ointment, "very precious," and anoints our Lord in the presence of the company. Immediately, one of the men present raises the question as to the waste of this ointment, and suggests that it might have been sold and the money used to much better advantage in caring for the poor.

Here are two characters: one looking at everything from the standpoint of service, and the other from the standpoint of selfishness. Let us take a few lessons from Mary, the server, in this scene.

She had not as good opportunities as Judas, the objector, to know the deep things of the kingdom of God. She had not heard as much, had not seen as much, but she saw and heard with a different spirit, and looked at everything from a different standpoint. She had evidently seized upon the great central truth of the gospel, the divinity of Jesus Christ. Judas had not. She had further apprehended the truth that Christ was to die and be buried, for she anointed Him unto His burial. This was a truth that even the foremost of his apostles had scarcely grasped. The whole attitude and bearing of Mary, here and elsewhere, shows her tender and loving devotion. Love has a keen eye for duty, and for chances, while selfishness can stumble over the finest opportunities in the world and never see them. The spirit of service can see a long distance into spiritual things. Mary saw the crucifixion and the burial. Others did not see it.

The spirit of service was not quite so good in figures as the spirit of selfishness, but, without close calculation, it went further. When Mary anointed the Lord she anointed the poor of the earth. She anointed all humanity. Whatever magnifies and glorifies Christ and lifts Him up among men, benefits humanity in all conditions. There is a strain of opposition to missionary operations and ample provisions for church services everywhere, on the ground that we had better use the money some other way. Whatever upholds the gospel and its fulness and sweetness among the people most effectually reaches the very bottom round of society, and lifts up, sanctifies and helps. The act of Mary went to the very extremities of the race. Even further than she saw, doubtless.

There is another peculiarity of the spirit of service. While it cannot see the end of service, nor compass the good that may be done in the long run, it has an accurate eye for the right path, and whatever it does, it does in the direction of the remotest possible good. No humble soul knows just how much good it is doing. The young farmer in Iowa, who stood up in the country conference and begged that a young preacher might be given a chance, and when told and argued with that the young preacher was ignorant, still pleaded for him, and said: "Let's send him to school. I will give ten dollars toward sending him to school a year," didn't know much, but he had the real spirit of service. He did not know what he was doing for the world when he was helping to educate John E. Clough, the great missionary to the Telugus; but his earnest pleading carried the point in the church, and John E. Clough carried the gospel to the Telugus, and he has baptized multiplied thousands of them.

Mary did not know all she was doing. She did not know that from the resurrection of Christ onward to this hour, humble hearts would be catching inspiration from her noble conduct, and that her alabaster box of very precious ointment would fill all the world with the fragrance of her sanctified service.

Look again how things went from the standpoint of service. Once a person has thoroughly committed himself to serve, he arranges everything in life from that standpoint I have just this half hour read of how one of the richest young women in New York has joined the Salvation Army and is giving her social influence, her intelligence, her wealth, to the rescue work of that organization. She has come to look at service as the great thing, and all these others as incidental, to be used in service. So Mary saw it. She did not sit down to figure on the price of the ointment. She did not sit down to consider how much of other things might be bought, if she would sell it. There was but one consideration. That was the best use of it, and love told her that the best use of it was to anoint her Lord and Saviour. This is ever the spirit of service, and this is the way everything looks from the standpoint of service. There is not very much arithmetic in it, but there is more power, more graciousness, more blessedness.

A final remark on this side of the question is, that service glorifies everything. How many millions of times have women broken alabaster boxes! How many millions of times have women expended many times the price of that ointment! And yet there has been no lasting perfume, no enduring glory. It lacked the sweetness of service. All real service, out of unselfish hearts, is glorified and glorifying.

Now we will turn over to look at the ugly side of this picture and the lessons teem. Here is the first, and a very striking one. Out of the twelve men who first companied with our Lord, and who had His honor and His cause particularly in hand, one of them was an arrant knave. Judas never was anything but bad. He was a devil, and the main devil that was in him was the devil of selfishness. As Mary looked at everything from the standpoint of service, he looked at everything from the standpoint of selfishness. He stood connected with the twelve who stood immediately around the Lord. He saw the miracles, he heard the heavenly teaching. No doubt he was more or less moved from his teaching. No doubt he was more or less moved, but he was never moved from his selfishness. He was treasurer for the apostolic company, and carried the bag. This was exactly to his hand. What a lesson is here of the mixing of the good and the bad in religion. Sometimes people are dazed and amazed that bad men should be developed in religious circles. It is exactly the place where we should expect to find the worst of men, as well as the best. There never was anything good, never anything that could get a grip on humanity that evil men did not seek to get hold of it and control it in their own interests.

By Dr. J. B. Gambrell, D.D.

It was right up to the notion of Judas to run the whole ministry and work of Jesus Christ in the interest of his own finances, and Judas is the progenitor of a large family of spiritual children. That is what some people want with churches; that is what some preachers want with the ministry; that is what some others want with position. When Judas hanged himself he did not end his family by a big lot, and, according to the law of progression, some of them have gone to the point that they won't even have the public decency to hang themselves.

Look again at the methods of selfishness. It went to the heart of Judas that Mary poured out the ointment and anointed her Lord. "Why this waste?" Selfishness is given constantly to economical cramps and convulsions. You can notice the workings of it always along the lines of the severest economy, often on the point where economy turns into absolute waste. It wants to skimp and trim in all matters of service. The pastor is to be put upon the barest living. The whole service of Christ is to be laid out on the scantiest pattern, while there is abundance for everything else. It takes the right kind of eye to see through the varnish and veneer of this cry against waste and service, and to discern the real selfishness that underlies the whole thing. We know exactly what ailed Judas, and the whole narrative is set before us in the gospel to teach us that the spirit of selfishness is what it is.

Now look at the audaciousness of selfishness. "Why this waste?" Whose waste? Wasn't it Mary's ointment? Did it cost Judas anything? Was it any of his business? What concern had he with this gracious woman's love offering to her Lord? An unseemly spectacle is it, hard gritty, mathematical calculations over against the tender pulsations of a woman's love. But hasn't it been this way all the time? Who are the people today who are crying out waste? Are they the people who are giving? It is now forty years

I have been noticing things in religious circles, and, practically without exception, the cry of waste in the kingdom of God has come from those who are sitting in judgment on other people's giving. Mary wasn't wasting anything that Judas ever gave, and yet, Judas felt called on to regulate matters. He is the father of a pestiferous tribe in Israel, who pop up on all corners to regulate other people's doing.

We will take another lesson. Notice in this narrative how Mary struck another track. Here was a supreme occasion, a great hour, an opportunity to be used or lost once for all. Mary saw it. Mary glorified her Lord and herself by serving the hour, and that with all her heart. Judas did not see the hour; nor the time. He saw the money. He was good in figures, good in arithmetic. He wanted to stop the thing. Not to say that Mary shouldn't give—no, no—but to propose another object. Just then he had a spasm of concern for the poor. Nobody ever knew of him having it before, nor after, but that spell took him right on the spot, and he said: "It might have been sold for three hundred pence and given to the poor."

It's ever thus. Get after selfishness about missions, and immediately there is a great concern about the Orphans Home. When there is to be a great round-up for the Orphans Home then it is something else. Reader, did you ever chase a small pig along an old-fashioned worm fence, and try to catch him? Now you have him in this corner, and when you are about to put your hand on him he slips the crack and is over on the other side. You get over there and hem him after a time, and just before you get hold of him he is through another crack and back. You can not catch him. That pig is a picture of the selfishness that rules in the heart of many a man, from Judas down. You can never exactly find the right place, nor the right thing. Take your collection for what you will and there is something else that is in need. "By their fruits ye know them." Gracious Mary and selfish Judas represent two great types in the kingdom of God.

TRUMPETING HARDSHELLISM.

THE Hardshell Baptist paper, Baptist Trumpet, has had plenty to write about since we called the attention of the denomination to the revival of this peculiar and deadly cult. When the Trumpet says that there is a great deal of Hardshellism in missionary churches, we feel compelled to admit the truth of the statement. There is no danger that Hardshells outside Missionary churches will increase. The pure bloods do not propagate. The hybrids do.

The Trumpet has a great variety of choice expletives, which it applies vigorously to this writer, after the style of two generations ago. They do not need nor deserve special mention.

It is charged that we used to be a predestinarian, which is correct. Our objection to the Hardshells is that they are unsound on predestination. They are hard on one side. They are only half predestinarians. They believe in the predestination of the end, but not of the means. They deny half the Scriptures on predestination and convert the other Scriptures into nonsense. Let us illustrate: A man determines to have a well at a certain place, that is, he predestinates, or predetermines to have it. But he stops there and makes no plan by which the well is to be dug. That is Hardshellism.

Let us turn the other side. Another man wanders about and begins to dig; he does not know what, a well, a post hole, or simply a hole. He has not made up his mind what he will do, but he is digging. That is an Arminian, and he is as foolish as a Hardshell, but no more so. Another man makes up his mind to have a well and he chooses all the means necessary to carrying out his purpose. His predetermination takes in both the end and the means. This represents God's predestination. It is wise in all its goings, selecting and making efficient all the means leading to the end. "If a man is going to be saved he will be saved anyway," is not true. He will be saved, but God's way, not anyway. And God's way is by the preaching of the gospel, which he has given command shall be preached to every creature. Through the preaching of the gospel he will take out of all nations a people for himself.

This leads us to notice that the brother remarks that if "Dr. Gambrell" were called on to prove his statements he would whine. No, he would not. He would prove them if he thought it useful to do so. He will take three of them as samples, selecting those most complained of, and prove them without being called on. We charged that Hardshellism dismembers the Scriptures and sweeps half the Bible out at the back door, which means that they discard in practice a part of the Bible. Is this true or not? Let us take the commission. They hold to baptism stoutly. They take baptism right out of the middle of that great command. Before it comes "go preach," "teach," "all nations," "every creature," and after baptism, "teaching them to observe all things whatsoever I have commanded you." What is this but committing violence on the word of God? Is not a refusal to go and a refusal to teach the "all things commanded," downright rebellion against the King Eternal? It is this thing that obedient souls cannot fellowship.. We offer this as a specimen of the Hardshell method of tearing the Scriptures to pieces and throwing them away. The same thing runs through their whole cult.

We said they used one Scripture against another as a boy

Hardshellism Dismembers the Scriptures and Sweeps Half the Bible out at the Back Door.

uses one nail to drive another out. This hurts the feelings of the Trumpet brother. It is a severe charge, but if it is true, the remedy is not to call names, but to reform. Is it true? Take the whole Scripture teaching concerning effort for the saving of men, teaching in precept and in example which is abundant, and with Hardshells it is displaced by an insistence on predestination and related doctrines. This is the Hardshell method constantly employed. The Trumpet furnishes plenty of illustrations of what has just been said.

Then take the Scripture doctrine of giving, which is so clearly and strongly taught, and it is driven out by an unholy use of the Scriptures which inveigh against the love of money. For seventy years men who keep their money, who have never given a cent to bless the heathen with the gospel, who go in the face of the Scripture, that the laborer is worthy of his hire, berate those who give and sacrifice for loving money, as if, on the face of it, those who keep their money are not greater money lovers than those who give it. It is as certain as the judgment, that Hardshells do play one Scripture against another to justify their do-nothingism.

Another grievance is that this writer said Hardshellism cultivates ignorance and abhors light. This is true or false. The truth or falsity of the charge must be tested by our Lord's rule. "By their fruits ye shall know them." We appeal to history. During the seventy years of Hardshell existence have they not fought the missionaries on every move to enlighten the world? They have opposed missions and Christian schools of all sorts with a vehemence worthy of any cause. Where in all these years have the Hardshells built a school or founded a mission? If they are in favor of enlightenment, where are the fruits? We are not entitled to stand on professions, but must stand or fall by our deeds. If seventy years of history do not slander Hardshellism it is a deadly enemy to progress and enlightenment.

By Dr. J. B. Gambrell, D. D.

In all we have written on this subject we have had nothing but the kindest feelings for the Hardshells, as they delight to call themselves. Many of them have been our personal friends. We glory in the divine sovereignty in predestination and in the election of grace. But we speak of the cult, and it is, as sure as we live, an enemy to the progress of the gospel. As such, our soul abhors it. None of this is written with the thought that the out and out Hardshells will be helped. For the most part they are petrified. We write to save our own people from the doom that awaits all people who withhold their energies from the spread of the gospel. Anti-mission churches will die as certainly as the Commission is true. And they ought to die. They cumber the ground. The efforts to fill our churches with the unholy spirit of strife and selfishness is in the interest of Hardshellism. It is the old spirit and the old method and will bear the same kind of fruit. It will dry up all benevolence, starve pastors and drive prosperity from the churches. We should shun it as we would the black plague.

The most tremendous efforts ought to be made now to purge our churches of the leaven of Hardshellism. Papers and pastors ought to thunder against it incessantly. It ought to be stripped of all its deceitful disguises, and shown in all its littleness, in all its mischievousness and rebellion against the reign of grace in the world. No tame words will serve. Its alliances are with ignorance, selfishness, evil surmising, fuss mongers, and whatever is of the world, the flesh and the devil. In its deceitful meshes are devout souls, and it should be our care to deliver them from this snare of the evil one. It is our present, pressing duty. The fight should be taken up and waged to a finish.

THE WORKINGS OF HARDSHELLISM.

IT HAS already been said that Hardshellism is, as to progress, a negation. Its first name was "anti-effort." It is do-nothingism. Whether under one name or another, in the Hardshell ranks or in the Missionary ranks, it has the same spirit and works by the same methods, and leads to the same results. It flourishes best in dark places, remote from schools, and always feeds on ignorance and prejudice. True enlightenment is a sovereign remedy for the evil.

Take this denomination over the whole country and it has almost disappeared. In a section of country where the two wings were so evenly divided that it was thought necessary to compromise in many churches, there are now 25,000 missionaries and a few years ago seventy-two Hardshells, gathered in twelve churches, having nine ministers, and four out of the nine preachers were living separated from their wives. They were contrary to all men, and women, too.

This is hardly an astonishing statement. The spirit of objection, strife and division which they had cultivated as against the missionaries, could not help reacting disastrously on themselves. It is always so with us. He who shoots must suffer the recoil of the gun, and all sin is a gun that kicks back harder than it shoots forward. The persistent opposition to, and criticism of others, sets up a habit of fault-finding which goes to every part of a person's being and into every department of his life.

Moreover, when this habit becomes predominant and fixed, it is the big fish that eats up all the small fry of better traits of character. In so doing, the perverting and hardening effects of this evil habit go on to the utter destruction of the judgment and the elimination of sweetness from the soul. Evil surmises take the place of that charity that "thinketh no evil." The perverted mind sees back of everything done by the workers some sinister design.

By Dr. J. B. Gambrell, D. D.

The heart corrupted by its own do-nothing policy becomes, like a stagnant pond, the breeding place of slimy, creeping, sinuous thoughts and imaginations.

It is a cardinal principle in humanity to seek to justify itself. This is a widely recognized truth. A brother who does not wish to pay a debt is likely to fall out with his creditor. He seeks to find a good reason for not paying, not in himself, but in the other man. To this well-known principle of human nature we are to attribute the workings of hardshellism in and out of Missionary churches. It works the same way and to the same effect, no matter where it works or on what pretense.

A gentleman had trained a large dog to pull a light garden plow. Whenever any one came about, the dog would set up a terrific barking as if he would tear the intruder to pieces. The gentleman, who had observed the ways of the dog carefully, explained that there was no danger in the dog; that he only barked so as to have an excuse for not plowing. That was undoubtedly a Hardshell dog, tho possibly he was in a Missionary family or church.

When Dr. Broadus said the "workers never grumble and the grumblers never work," he was close to the exact truth. Working and grumbling do not harmonize. They are two opposite forces. Religious work promotes soul health, as physical work promotes bodily health. The most ear-splitting calamity-howlers are the men who have quit honest toil and taken to crying hard times, blaming it all on somebody else.

Concerning the truth of these observations, we ask our readers to make observations around about them. Who are the men and women in your church who are finding fault with the pastor, the deacons, the Sunday School workers, etc? Who is it that believes too much money is spent on the church? If we are not off in our reckonings the do-nothing element is the complaining element. Make a note of the workings of hardshellism in your church, and when you are satisfied with your observations at home extend them to your association. Note the brethren who make the most noise and clamor against large and liberal things, and

Men who Have Quit Honest Toil and Taken to Crying Hard Times.

see if large and liberal things are costing them anything. In our observation we have found, without exception, that back of every outcry against real progress was the hardshellish spirit of do-nothingism.

In an association a brother fought a mission measure from year to year. In a speech before his association he vowed he would never give a cent to that cause. A brother rose and asked him how long it had been since he had given to anything. It turned out that it had been years, just how many he could not tell. It was another case of stopping the plow to bark. And his case is by no means singular. Extend your observations as far out as you will and it will appear in the light of the facts, that religious idleness promotes obstruction, strife, discord, suspicion, meddlesomeness, backbiting, and every evil imagination. Do-nothingness, by a law of its own nature, perverts the soul, makes it acrid, unhappy and full of fault-finding. It dries up all nobleness of spirit and puts its victim on the spiritual down grade.

We have growing Christians, churches and associations stricken with this spiritual plague and dried up. It is as disastrous to a church as distemper is among sheep, or mange among dogs. Every vital force is paralyzed and all progress is stayed. Let even liberal souls come under the spell and all liberality is dried up. As in all other human experiences, there is action and reaction. Do-nothingism promotes fault-finding, and fault-finding promotes do-nothingism. This truth may well put us on our guard. Many a pastor has joined in to find fault with his brethren in the wider field and wound up by being starved out in his own field.

A PLEA FOR SIMPLICITY.

A BAPTIST is the product of the New Testament. Spurgeon said of them, "They are sprung direct out of the loins of Jesus Christ." Jesus Christ was the world's greatest citizen, the mold and perfection of the highest manhood. He was simplicity itself, in life, in manner, in teaching. He was the commoner of all ages. The common people loved Him gladly because they understood Him and because He loved them, helped them and gave them hope. But while Jesus was the unmatched commoner, he was, also, the very pink of true refinement, the beau ideal of a gentleman. And to the most exquisite refinement, He added the highest courage. I believe that no sane mind can contemplate Jesus Christ, as revealed in the gospels and even imagine this matchless man, young as He was, indulging any of the fads and eccentricities of dress, sometimes seen in His ministers. A clergyman's coat! Horrors, no. He was too great in his admirable symmetry of character and sincerity to resort to any of the small tricks of the grotesque weaklings to win notice. The peculiar garb, the fancy touches of theology, the catchy names peculiar to some religionists, were far removed from this matchless man whose simple goodness and greatness were his all-sufficient adornment. All special garbs are an offense to the refined Christian taste, whether the dress be the Quaker drab, or the priestly coat, or the old-fashioned Methodist cutaway, or what not.

My plea is that Baptists follow the simple manner of the Master. There is ethics in dress, and that we are most surely taught in the scriptures. Paul was on the true line, following in the steps of the Master. Christian women ought, as a matter of good religious taste, to avoid extravagancies in dress. An over-dressed woman in church is an offense against true refinement. A fussily dressed woman, blazing with diamonds, is an offense against good taste anywhere. True Christian culture will grow such crudities off; joining the church will not do it; but Christianity struck through will. Christian culture is the perfection of culture, the transforming of a human life into the image of the divine Christ.

I plead for simplicity in the pulpit. The gaudy worldliness, so much in evidence in some pulpits and so doted on by some feeble saints, is monstrous from the standpoint of the simple, pungent teaching of the great Teacher, and His apostles. It is like a street and dress parade at the judgment. No man ever affected such a style, nor tolerated it, when he got in earnest. Earnestness is always simple, direct, unaffected; and if there is but one earnest man in the world, the preacher ought to be that man. Much of the eloquence, so-called, of the pulpit today is nothing short of monstrous. It belongs in spirit and kind more to the theater than to the pulpit. This appeal may be greatly strengthened by considering its belittling effect on the whole subject of religion. Has it come to this that preachers must fish with such worldly bait to catch men for God? It is a reflection on the power of the Gospel and the work of the Spirit to assume that we must resort to such tricks as are commonly reputed to win men. Gowns, rituals, catchy subjects, etc., will not help Baptists. Our strength lies in preaching the plain gospel in simplicity, with hearts deeply embued with the spirit of Jesus, and not at all in frills and feathers, fads and folderol, starch and stilts. If there are some who can't be won without such things, they are not worth the cost of the catch. Every little catch-minnow device in a church is a detraction from the dignity of Christian worship and a departure from the simplicity of Christ. It continues to be true, that the preachers whose ministry is drawing the multitudes are the men who preach the old doctrine, with plainness and the power sent down from heaven. Let Baptists stick to their business, which is to follow Christ and not to ape Papists or any of the second crop of apists.

All Special Garbs are an Offense to the Refined Christian Taste.

I plead for simplicity of the meeting-houses. We are upon a great time for building meeting-houses, and what

By Dr. J. B. Gambrell, D. D.

a mess is made of it in many places. Spires away up higher than any other church in town, knobs, corners, stained-glass windows, vaulted ceilings to ruin the acoustics, with notions and fancies galore. Is it all worth while? No, it is not. It is much of it worse than waste; it is an offense to good taste, and a hindrance. Do we want good houses? We do. But we do not want flashy houses, and we do not want to spend great sums of money for what we do not want. In the light of the New Testament and conserving the tone and spirit of Christ, houses for Christian worship should be in simple taste, built for service, rather than for show. There ought to be a new dispensation of church building among Baptists. We have a few meeting-houses recently built in Texas, which are models of good sense, simplicity and good taste. They have in their outward appearance the true dignity of solidity and due proportion inside; they are every way suited to be the home of a church; auditorium where people can hear, with numerous working rooms. Everything neat, in its place, nothing fanciful, flashy or fantastical. Each of these has the organ placed in a way to suggest congregational singing.

It is argued, with seeming force, that Baptists must keep in style or their rich people will leave them. What shall I say to it? There are rich people and rich people, rich fools and rich wise. The rich fools must be held, if at all, by the power of God's living truth in their hearts, and to feed them on religious trumpery is to minister directly to the wrong side of their nature. The very moment we commence with the vanities of the world to hold people, we switch from the main gospel track, and get on a track leading into some other place, where they can beat us two or three to one. Some rich, uncultivated people, who are not certain whether they are respectable, will leave the Baptists. Unless they can get better, they ought to go for our good, and they will never get better by being fed with husks. The rich wise and cultured will be delighted with simplicity in our churches. They see enough of vanity, shallowness and show all the week. When they go to church, their souls long for the pure, simple gospel.

I hold that the Baptists above all other people ought to be set for the simplicity that is in Christ Jesus. Alas, for us if we go to putting on airs.

CONCERNING COLLEGE DEGREES.

HON. JOHN ALLEN, of Mississippi, in his last speech in Congress, appealing for an appropriation to establish a fishery station in Mississippi, facetiously remarked that there were millions of suckers in the world now and millions more just waiting to be hatched. Very few things go further to demonstrate the approximate accuracy of Mr. Allen's statement than the ease with which people are taken by college degrees. So large a place does the degree fill in the public mind, or at least in the minds of suckers, that I deem it worth while to make some observations on the degree business.

Be it known to all men by these presents, that the legal right to confer college degrees of divers sorts can be had of the Legislature of any State pretty much for the asking. A charter can be obtained giving to any set of men the authority to grant degrees under the seal of the corporation. A school in a State east of Texas, located in the country, having no building except a plain wooden structure; a school which seriously advertised itself to teach Caesar, Virgil and Latin; this rural Southern University was authorized to grant degrees all the way from B. S. to Ph. D., LL. D., and the degrees were granted with a lavish hand.

It is in the matter of college degrees, as touching the State, very much as it is in religion. Any kind of a society

by Dr. J. B. Gambrell, D. D.

may be chartered under the laws of the State in the name of a church. There are churches and churches, colleges and colleges, universities and universities, degrees and degrees, and suckers world without end.

In educational circles, where the genuine is sought rather than the pretense, there has come to be a standard somewhat definitely fixed for college degrees; but in every descending step from the high plane of the true college there are schools giving degrees with no corresponding scholarship. Yale, Harvard, Chicago, Brown and Baylor have approximately the same standard for B. A.; but schools whose work would hardly introduce a student to the Freshman class of a real college can give degrees, and do give degrees.

I come now to discuss the most important features of the degree business. Degrees are used by Cheap John institutes as a decoy. The fine boy or girl in the country, with no knowledge of educational matters, but with splendid possibilities, is told that by going to a certain school the degree of B. A. or something else, can be obtained in a comparatively short time. In the mind of the unthinking, B. A. stands for something in education. The sucker thinks if he can get the B. A. in school for two years, and it would take him four or six years in another, that he had better go where he can get it in two years. In his ignorance, he supposes that B. A. stands for an education, and it does, more or less; in a great many cases a great deal less. Schools that cannot do honest college work, and their proprietors know they cannot do it, give regular college degrees as an inducement to patronage. They water the stock and sell watered stock instead of genuine. I raise the question whether this is dealing honestly with the unsuspecting? To deceive the unwary in education is next to deceiving people in religion.

In order to get at the degree business properly, it is always proper to ask "From what school?" A degree is like a promisory note. The value of it depends upon what is back of it. A ten-dollar note signed by one man is worth more than a thousand-dollar note signed by some other man.

Degrees are Used by Cheap John Institutions as a Decoy.

I raise the question now whether there ought to be a general discussion of this whole matter to save honest people from being gulled, and whether there ought not to be a classification of the schools, that people might understand what they are getting when they get a degree. I understand the difficulty of any hard and fast lines, but in some way or another, for the dignity of education and the genuineness of it, too, there ought to be such a common understanding of matters as would break up the sucker fishing industry in the realm of education. To be very plain about it, I believe that colleges ought to be required to maintain a certain standard of work and that schools below that standard should not be classed as colleges. If the State is to take a hand in chartering institutions, why not charter them in such a way as to really further the cause of sound education and put it out of the power of just anybody to degrade degrees which are symbols of certain things educational, and thereby impose on the untaught and unsuspecting. One thing is certain. There ought to be downright honesty in dealing with all educational questions, and humbuggery in education is next to the worst humbuggery in the world.

NATIONALIZATION OF THE SOUTHERN SPIRIT.

THE South, like the nation, has grown by stages or epochs. There was first the colonization period, followed by the period of colonial development, leading up to and into the revolutionary period. Then came the period of constitutional adjustments and trials. During this long period, the nation was led by the South. But during this period the economic conditions of the whole country changed, slowly, under the operations of economic laws, shifted from the North to the South. No longer interested in the institution financially, the Northern conscience had an abnormal development. The South, deeply interested, could not see the inevitable, and the desirable, and hence did not provide for a peaceable solution of a grave question.

The war came and left the South bleeding, exhausted and friendless. Then came reconstruction, with nothing noble and inspiring in it, but everything ignoble and depressing. Following this period, was a long period of convalescence, with numerous backsets. We are now at the end of this period, and the South stands today like a robust giant, full of rich blood, ready for all eventualities.

With the beginning of the slavery agitation, the South began to take up a sectional attitude toward the nation. The spirit of the South took on a sectional tone. Two antebellum speeches have in them the germ and the potency of all that has happened since. I refer to the speech of Senator Hayne, of South Carolina, said to be answered by Senator Webster of Massachusetts. The first was a masterful discussion of the autonomy of the government, lean and sectional in spirit. The second was not an answer, but a reply. It clothed the skeleton and constitutional frame work with flesh and blood and gave it national spirit.

It was an evil day for the South, when it suffered itself to be led into a sectional attitude. It meant defeat in the council of the nation and finally on the battle field. It was a rash surrender of every advantage to those rated as our enemies, now happily, as I see it, our friends. I am not saying the South was not right from a constitutional point of view, but only that the South erred in policy. As one who gave four years to war to make good that error in tactics, I may be allowed thus to write. The sectional attitude of the South has been held in large measure, for 40 years. In a feeble way, I have sought to contribute one man's mite to thoroughly nationalize the Southern spirit for nearly that whole period.

By Dr. J. B. Gambrell, D. D.

I believe the hour has come for the South to get out of the corner, and let our influence and power flow even out into the currents of national life. The race question is now national, with the heavy end of it still resting on the South. But the North has all it wants of it; quite enough to bring them to sanity. Besides, our foreign possessions have forced a recognition of the fact that incompetency can not be trusted with government, the grave men of the Banther contention. President-elect Taft has had good schooling abroad, and will go into the White House with a diploma from the university of experience. He has already gone on record in a way to assure the whole South.

The South is on the eve of the greatest development the world has known. It will happen according to the Scripture. We will see good according to the days wherein we have seen evil. We are now receiving the first payment, under the law of compensation. A broad non-sectional spirit will immensely help us in the era of development into which we have already entered.

Sectional politics cannot help us or the nation. Since the war, the South's first concern has been to save her civilization from a deluge of ignorance and venality. Having saved ourselves, we must help to save others. The Southern alignment in politics is morally bad. The Northern Democracy is largely composed of the saloon, gambling riff-raff class; the class we would not wish to see in the saddle in the South. They can not win in the North, and ought not to win. I would not vote the Democratic ticket in the North, if I lived there, for about the same reasons I would vote the Republican ticket in the South—for the sake of good government. With the spirit of the South thoroughly nationalized, we might lead a great anti-liquor movement, and do for the nation in delivering it from the thraldom of the saloon what the North did in the matter of slavery, only without bloodshed. Aligned as she is, the South can never be a great national force in politics or morals. The South has a wide open door, out of a corner out into a wide field of usefulness and power, with everything to gain and nothing to lose by walking out and leaving the dead past to bury its dead.

From a Baptist standpoint, the call is loud to come out into a wider field of activity and influence. There are 26,000,000 people in the South, and, in round numbers 4,000,000 of them are actual communicants in the churches of the baptized. There are in round numbers 50,000,000 in the North and approximately a million Baptists. These figures suggest both an opportunity and a duty. The religious life of the nation will affect the national life. Government is founded, taught and enlightened by religion. The largest contribution Baptists can make in morals and morals rest in conscience, to the national life and safety is to teach the precepts of the New Testament and diffuse the spirit of the New Testament throughout the masses of our citizenship. This is the antitoxin for the Romist leaven every where seeking to innoculate the body politic.

But the Baptist program must always proceed from a single starting point: the individual conscience enlightened by the word of God. So our first business is to win men to the truth and then to teach them to apply the truth along the whole cause of life. It is a simple program, with a simple book for a guide. The Baptist message was made for the masses. It will not fail, preached with the tone of the New Testament. Amid the jangling and multitudinous voices of the North where fads and fancies have fed on the souls of the people, Christ's message will win, if it be not diluted or warped or compromised, or entangled with other things.

The point I am coming to is, that the great Baptist strength of the South ought to be turned toward the spiritual contest of the nation. There must come a readjustment of forces, having in view a better handling of them, for the war we are in, so that the Baptists of the South may bear a worthy part in redeeming the nation.

By nationalizing the Southern spirit the South may enter into a new era of national growth. She may lead in a sane and permanent settlement of the race question, both in America and in our colonial possessions, a thing now in process. For forty years the nation has floundered about in the dark and has only learned how not to setttle it.

The South may lead with a solid front, in the pending settlement of the liquor question, and take a leading part in emancipating the nation from its greatest curse and peril. The temperance reform is needing a strong base to press on to national success. The South may easily become such a base, if it will cut itself loose from its bad political alliances in the North, and speedily strangle the monster, in our own territory. A solid Prohibition South, with other impending policies suited to the impending industrial development, which will enrich our people beyond a dream; with new national adjustments, and a new outlook on the world, with the spirit of leadership restored to us, the South will take its proper place in the councils of the nation. It may be the head of a great intellectual and moral development instead of being the tail of a very sorry dog as it is now, stuck on to the Northern riff-raff, called Democracy, which is largely rumocracy.

Baptistically, with proper readjustments to our Northern brethren, we may lead America in a new movement for the bringing in of the reign of Jesus according to his word. But we must abandon the sectional spirit and come out of a corner to do any of it.

THE WORK OF PREACHERS.

RECENTLY a lawyer in a tirade of abuse, in which he declared that women and preachers could neither perceive nor tell the truth, also said preachers are parasites in society, living on the honest toil of other people while making no return for what they get. The applause given the sentiment by some preachers present and by others indicates that the sentiment has something in some part of the public mind to support it. I have long seen inklings of the fact that there are preachers who feel that the ministry is a class exempted from the honest toils of humanity. These feel no moral obligations to earn a living. They are sponges and dead-beats. To say this, is in no way to concede the truth of the allegation aforesaid, any more than to affirm that there are lawyers who are court-house bullies and all-round toughs is tantamount to vulgarizing the whole legal profession.

Passing from the low exceptions in the ministry to the general high level of the highest calling on earth, and remarking as we pass that preachers need not complain at being classed with women in any classification of virtues, I come to deal with the work of preachers. They must stand or fall by their Master's rule: "By their works ye shall know them." The man who reads history cannot remain ignorant of the fact that with the coming of Jesus Christ into the world there came the greatest regenerating force among men humanity has felt. His teaching went to the secret sources of all human conduct. When Jesus left the world, He gave His teaching into the hands of His chosen ministry. They expanded Judaism, stripped it of its swaddling clothes, gave it a new heart-beat, opened to the world its true meaning, and taught the sanctity of all human life and the universal brotherhood of man. Ministers bearing

By Dr. J. B. Gambrell, D. D.

the message of their Master, renewed the hopes of the race. They lifted humanity above the beastialities of heathenism and reconstructed the thought and life of the people who heard them. When the vast Roman empire fell by its own corruption, ministers garnered the seeds of the Christian civilization which now is, and sowed them amid persecutions, poverty and martyrdoms beside all waters.

Ministers, directly and indirectly, have founded every college, seminary and university in Christendom. Oxford, Cambridge, Edinburgh, Glasgow, Berlin, Heidelberg, Harvard, Yale, Princeton, Brown, all of them and all the rest, State universities not excepted. Ministers have not only founded these, but they have stood by them and guarded them through the centuries. Ministers have been the foremost force through the ages in popularizing learning. They do now give and always have given a greater per cent of their scanty income to schools and education than any other men on earth. They have stood for the church and the school house side by side, and these are the light houses that dispel the enveloping darkness of all times. These, the church first, are the civilizing forces operating constantly to build a better social order.

Preachers have made and enriched the literature of civilization. They have written a vast volume of the world's best books. They have held the light for the writing of what else is good. But for the work of preachers enlightening the masses in England there would have been no Shakespeare, no Lord Bacon, no written English jurisprudence. Over the mother isle today would reign the uncultured barbarism of our heathen ancestors. Our own great country would be unknown on the map of the world. No statue of liberty enlightening the world would have been dreamed of. There would be no liberty. England and America would be no other than heathen nations. Christianity is the heart and life of modern civilization, and preachers are the heaven ordained light-bearers of Christianity.

Preachers, more than all others, have built the American commonwealth with the truth they are commissioned to preach. The Bible is humanity's book. Its Divine Author is humanity's best friend. The Gospel is a message of freedom to the race; freedom from destructive vices first, and freedom from outward oppression next. It is no accident that where there is the free preaching of the Gospel the people enjoy liberty. A great political philosopher said: "All people are as free as they deserve to be." The Gospel builds character and secures freedom by making people ready for it. Preachers, with the scantiest living, plain, unpretentious men, have traversed mountains, valleys and plains, laying the foundations of civilization, and have builded the present social state, themselves little knowing the value of their service to the world. They thought most of heaven, but enriched both worlds. Preachers have enriched the commerce of the world. They have gone to all lands and taught people how to live. Barbarians are neither good producers nor good buyers. The higher Christian life is the longer life. Its power to produce is enlarged. Its needs are multiplied. Christianity is the commercial force in the world, because Christianity leads the race toward all possibilities. Many a preacher, moreover, has enriched a neighborhood by a hundred fold more than he was paid for his services. He has broken up saloons, led men to sobriety, and taught them to use their money in right ways. Thus whole communities have risen from poverty and squalor to affluence and refinement, and the preacher did it with his heavenly message, told may be in poor English.

Preachers have, by their teaching, contributed more than physicians to the health of humanity. Better than healing is prevention. Christianity tends powerfully to the longevity of the race, because it works in the individual the conditions of health. Whatever properly regulates the life makes for health.

Preachers have stood for every great moral and social reform. They have heroically fought back the destructive tides of evil which submerge human hopes in despair. They, as a class, stand for sobriety against the saloon, for honesty against gambling, for home against the brothel, for marriage against concubinage; they stand for law against licentiousness. The church and the preacher are the bulwarks of society against all combinations of evil.

Preachers have been the founders and unfailing supporters of all forms of benevolence. They have followed the drunkard, the libertine, the gambler to his last hour with calls to a better life, and when he sank into the grave, the victim of his own vices, they said the best words they could at the grave, and then took his orphans to some friendly asylum and cared for them till they could care for themselves. All this preachers have done, without money and without price, purely for the love they feel and preach.

As a great class preachers have done all these things and more, all the time knowing they could never hope for more than a common living. They have enriched the world, content themselves to remain poor. There is not another class among men who have done half so much for the world and received so little of this world's goods in return. Their reward is on high. They do not expect it here; they do not seek it. But to call them parasites is a graceless falsehood.

CONCERNING RELIGIOUS NOTIONS.

IF THE religious notions of people could be given tangible form, they would make a rare collection of bric-a-brac. There would be all sorts of odds and ends, closely resembling the contents of a boy's pocket after he has had free range for several days. Yet many people cling to their peculiar notions with even more tenacity than the small boy holds on to his store of bent and broken nails, old screws, bits of crockery and glass, holes, with just enough of something to go around the holes; strings, tin things, dog teeth, and what not.

Religious notions stand for many in the place of religion itself. They have no religion and do not want any, but they are devoted to their notions. They seem to have a notion that notions about religion are all any one needs. They stock up on notions and let the devil take their souls. These little conceits become fads. People will discuss their religious fads till all the sands of life run out and they go unregenerate into eternity. All fads, whether religious or not, are small vanities. There are fads in ladies' bonnets, in neck-ties, in watch-charms, in shoes, in books, in pronunciation. All of them are as the mistletoe to the solid wood. They come and go with times and seasons. There is in dress and in literature a kind of fashion of fads. But belonging to the same light order of things is the eccentric fad. You can see this in the way some do themselves up for company. I have in mind now a preacher with natural oddities of facial formation. He cuts his beard in a way to bring out these peculiarities to the greatest possible degree. The effect is ludicrous. Another preacher accents his general build by wearing a coat nearly to his heels. Another, with bald head, wears an enormous mustache coming out and over his mouth like a buggy top. These are eccentric fads.

By Dr. J. B. Gambrell, D. D.

Even great men may indulge eccentric fads. A great speaker wore a large ring on the little finger of his left hand, and gesturing, so held his finger and hand that everybody was bound to notice the ring. This was unconscious, no doubt, but the ring was his fad.

Fads of fashion, fads of eccentricity may be very innocent. They may even be of some service by making people laugh, but religious fads hardly ever fail to hurt. They are especially damaging to weak minds and to the strong self-willed. They are the notions upon which so many plant themselves. Little? Yes, but many a minnow has been caught on a pin-hook, and even large fish are now and then caught in the same way. The dextrous handling of a line with a pin-hook on it has landed many a trout on dry land. It will make sure work of nearly any fish if he will hold on to it. Fads are the devil's hooks for foolish souls.

The man with peculiar notions is common. He abounds most where deep religious convictions and feelings least abound. These religious fads grow thickest in the dry bark, furthest from the life-blood of genuine piety. Two causes will account for nearly all of them. Ignorance of spiritual things is the mother of religious notions, but conceit has a large share in the business. These two easily combine into obstinacy, and then we have a bad case. Often a sinner chases a little notion right into the jaws of death. Many are hopelessly conceited. It is striking, picturesque and remarkable to be odd. The silly fool thinks his notion marks him a man of broad mind, and he has not enough mind to know that he has no mind to mention on the subject of religion. Young people at the big-head age are especially afflicted with notions about religion. Questions which men like Lamar, Gladstone, Webster, Wayland and other like thinkers pondered long and solemnly and settled all one way, **the man of notions settles before he gets his shoes on in the** morning, and comes out with a lot of notions flying as loose as his uncombed hair.

Where trivial minds have notions, God has thoughts. God's thought concerning religion, as it touches our souls and lives for this world and the world to come, are recorded in that marvel of all literature, the Bible. God has thoughts of us; of our state, of our needs; thoughts of our frailties, our dangers—all about us. These thoughts are to a hair line. They are as deep as our nature, and as far-reaching as the soul's eternal destiny. They compass us on all sides. They are strong, terrible and tender. They reach to the highest heaven and to the lowest hell. God made us. He knows all about our complex and mysterious being. In His Word He talks to us about Himself, about ourselves, about the worlds, about sin, about salvation. The Bible is a book of God's great thoughts, compared with which human notions are not so much as the motes that fly in the air. To accept God's thoughts is to think like Him. They will make us wise, humble, careful, happy and great. They will make the noblest character, the most useful men and women.

The man with a peculiar notion is apt to be neither great nor useful. We have seen him in many places. While 1 was holding a meeting in Springfield, Ill., two men with notions showed up. One had a notion that he ought to go out as an unbaptized preacher, just to demonstrate that baptism does not save. His notion was that the church ought to receive him and ordain him for that purpose. He was ready to argue it by the hour, and insisted that I should hear him. He had some peculiar notions, which he was sure would interest me. "Not a bit," was the reply. "Your notions are not worth your shoe-strings. Your shoe-strings do keep your shoes on, but your notions separate you from God, from His church and from His service. They are utterly worthless, and indicate a vanity too light to discuss. If you

By Dr. J. B. Gambrell, D. D.

were right with God, you would throw your peculiar notions to the winds and accept God's law." We parted. It is usually a great mistake to dignify people's religious notions or fads by serious discussion. In treating a field overgrown with weeds, it is not worth while to take time to pull up a weed at a time. Give it a thorough, deep plowing, and you kill all the weeds, while you are preparing the soil for a crop.

This big-headed notionful age needs more than trimming in—it needs deep subsoiling with the plowshare of God's eternal truth. Whoever saw a broken and a contrite heart pestered with notions? There was a very light crop of notions in Israel when the law was given on Sinai, and the people did exceedingly fear and tremble. One of God's great thoughts of sin and eternity will make an end to all dallying with notions. Do not dignify religious fads by seriously arguing with the man with a notion.

A student came up to a crowd of students, and striking an attitude, said: "Boys, I am an agnostic." "No, you are not," said a sensible boy, "Herbert, you are just a plain fool, and don't know it. That's is all that ails you." Ignoramous is the Latin for fool, and agnostic is the Greek for it. The boy was right. The remedy was quickly applied, and the cure was complete.

On a train a disciple of Ingersoll was detailing his notions, and a man near by said:

"You don't believe that," whereupon the fool avowed that he did. Then the other said:

"Well, if I did, I would keep it to myself, for it don't sound smart."

This ended it amid a roar of laughter from the passengers. All these answers were good and are given as a short method with notions.

Dr. Willingham, in a fine address on missions, in the First Church, Dallas, gave some telling blows on some people's notions about missions. There are just two views. One is God's and one is the devil's. God's law is, "go preach to every creature." The devil's notion is "don't do it." The man who is not out and out for preaching the gospel to every creature is with the devil on that subject, and that is the short of it. Reader, where are you? With God or the devil?

Beware of religious notions. They are worth nothing, and may do you endless harm. Have convictions rooted in God's Word. In the wind-up only truth will abide. If you want fads in anything let it be in something as light as the fad. In religion seek the verities. Rest only in the Word which shall endure forever. Let no vanity beguile your soul as to eternal things. An hour with the Bible in honest search for God's way, is worth cycles of time running after human notions. It is said, if you give a monkey a rock to hold and he falls into the water, he will go to the bottom holding to the rock, and will drown without ever thinking to turn it loose. I do not know whether this is true of monkeys or not, but I do know that many men will go to ruin before they will turn loose a little notion not worth a toothpick.

THE CASE OF THE MISSIONARIES.

THE present disturbances in the far East have revived the infidel and barbarous objections to missions, which have been forthcoming on all like occasions since the inauguration of modern missionary enterprises. Certain writers, or more correctly speaking, writers of uncertain grade, are lamenting that civilization must now take up the missionaries' burden. These "barbarians in broad-cloth" have many ways of expressing their inward feelings concerning missionaries, but whatever the form of expression, the spirit is the same, and that spirit is alien to

By Dr. J. B. Gambrell, D. D.

Christianity and to modern civilization. These writers have become the apostles of liberty, but the liberty they extol is the liberty of heathenism, darkness and barbarism. It was such liberty as our forefathers enjoyed when they lived in huts and lodges and went half clothed.

The case of the missionaries rests on the fundamental principles of civilization. It is a law of nature, as well as of Christianity, that no people can keep what they do not give away. Receiving and giving are the two conditions of health and growth, and no people can violate either condition and flourish. The great principle of the Scriptures is "As you have received so minister." The very existence of Christianity depends on the fulfillment of these conditions. The people who have been missionary abroad have grown at home. It comes to it, therefore, that, if America is to be Christian, America must be missionary. Nothing is more certainly taught in the word of God, and nothing more completely harmonizes with the law of nature, than that blessings unused are taken away. The teaching of the parable of the talents carries this lesson. The man with one talent, who wrapped it in a napkin, was a hard-shell. He violated the great law of increase, and, therefore, the Master took the talent from him and gave it to the man who had used his talents.

In considering the case of the missionaries, therefore, we are to consider whether America is to be Christian or heathen. If we withhold the light from the nations of the earth, that light will be taken from us, and the gentlemen who are now distressed at the burden of the missionaries or their descendants, will have the delight of living as free as the Filipinos or the Chinese. This is the first count in the consideration of the case. The next is that the people who are now concerned and wish to withdraw all missionaries on account of the troubles in the East, are not Christian at all. They walk by the light of the Christian, enjoy the order, the peace, the prosperity, the general enlightenment of the Christian, but are themselves anti-Christian. No man who is willing to leave the nations of the earth in heathenish darkness, in the face of the commands of Jesus Christ, has any just claim to Christianity. The all-pervasive and reigning spirit of Christianity is the spirit of altruism.

Because this country is largely dominated by Christian feeling and thought, we have our matchless schools, our newspapers, our great railroad systems, our large commercial life—in short, our social order. The fountain of this stream itself has been much corrupted in its onward flow. It is impossible that a country like this should live to itself. To do so would be to reverse all the processes of thought and spirit, which have brought us to the very zenith of human accomplishment. Because we could not live to ourselves, the war with Spain was begun. Because of the high spirit of our people, twenty millions of dollars were given for the Philippine Islands, when we might have taken them for nothing. Because of the humane feeling cultivated in us by Christianity, our ships bore the Spanish soldiers back to their homes from Cuba. Because of this very thing we have the spirit of all civilization, and we cannot recklessly lay down our obligations in the East. The question goes deeper than party politics and formal declarations. The whole matter rests in the deep consciousness of a great people, along whose pathway the light of truth is shining.

When William Carey began his missionary enterprise in India, he had a noisy set in England to deal with. He was the butt of ridicule in the British Parliament. The East India Company refused him a foothold within its territory, and argued that it would not do to interfere with the long established religious feelings of the natives. But Carey lived to see a complete change of feeling. He became by all odds the most important man in India to the British Government, and later in life, he was, perhaps, the most honored

By Dr. J. B. Gambrell, D. D.

man in the British Empire. He prepared the literature which opened the way for commerce and for political improvement. The missionary movement in India has long since overthrown the most inhuman of the heathen practices of that country. There is growing up a new civilization from the seed planted by Carey. That civilization calls for clothes, farming implements, and houses, and it has enriched the commerce of the world by more money than there is gold in the world today.

Missionaries have been the pioneers of civilization in every part of the world. The plain men who have gone with the stream of immigration west in this country for two centuries, have done more to build the American States than any other class of men in the world. They have everywhere laid the foundations of social order. They have everywhere taught the sacredness of human life. They have everywhere insisted on the sanctity of the home. They have everywhere been the enemies of drunkenness, gambling, rioting and every species of disorder. They have made the work of the statesman possible. Without the work of the missionaries of America, there would be no liberty, as we now know it.

This government is not called on to teach religion. Indeed, by the very nature of things it is forbidden to teach religion, but the free exercise of religion is a fundamental principle of our government. This government is called on to protect its citizens in every part of the world, according to the terms of the treaties with the several nations of the earth. A government that will not do this, deserves no support at home nor respect abroad. The missionary has the same right to be in China about his business as has the merchant. The troubles in that country have not come through missionaries. They have come by the enormous outside pressure and by the innate opposition of the Chinese mind to all human progress.

I think it may be taken for certain, that China cannot, in the nature of things, be a hermit nation. The time is out for that. The man who believes that can be is too far back to be talked to. The reconstruction of China is as inevitable in the great sweep of Providence as is the movement of the heavenly bodies. If Christianity is good for America, for England and other nations, it is good for China. At any rate the world has reached a stage through the enlightenment of Christianity itself, when the right to think is regarded as inherent. The Chinese can not be an exception to the course of events throughout the world. This being true it must be admitted that the case of the missionary in China is the case of the missionary everywhere else. He is a good man in America and he is a good man in India. He is a good man in the Philippines, and he is a good man in China. He has no sword to enforce his teaching. His success depends upon enlightenment. He has a patent from heaven to shed light. He has blessed every spot he has ever touched on this earth. He will bless, regenerate and elevate China. In the last analysis there is no choice between the missionaries and heathenism. It is to be regretted that we have American journalists who prefer heathenism.

"POOR, YET MAKING MANY RICH."

IF THE reader will turn to Second Corinthians, 6th chapter, 4th to 10th verses, he will see a picture of the life of many a preacher. Only it does not fall to the lot of any of us in these latter days to be imprisoned. But it would be easier than some other things.

Last year, in an humble home in the country in Mississippi, died a man who literally lived a life of self-denial, and yet who enriched the whole country. He was Elder Isaac

BY DR. J. B. GAMBRELL, D. D.

Smith, my friend and brother, and co-laborer of other years. He was my pastor, and I was his pastor. I taught his children. He was a strong supporter of the school, which had a good deal to do with changing things round about.

Bro. Smith was a man of moderate ability and moderate education. He never preached a great sermon in his life. His gifts lay more in the way of exhortation and in song. He was mighty in prayer and gracious in living. I suppose during his whole lifetime in the ministry he never received $500 a year for preaching. He owned a little farm, and what with doing work on that and preaching to the churches, by close management, especially by the help of a frugal wife, he raised his children in credit, and managed to give largely his time to enriching others.

The section of country where he ministered is a broken country. In the early settlement of it wickedness abounded. Nearly all the people were poor, and many of them kept themselves and families distressingly poor by drinking. There was in this country, and six miles from my father's home, a little town called Ellistown. Here we received our mail, and had blacksmithing done, and here our family physician lived. It was the center of a community of several thousand people. Just east of the little town is an elevation in the road, and from that one can look down the flat, wide street, through the place; for, after all, Ellistown was not much more than a broad place in the road. My first recollection of it is of a little group of houses with three saloons, two stores, a doctor's shop, a blacksmith shop, a cabinet-maker's shop. The fences on either side are so connected with the houses that one could not pass without going through between the stores and whiskey saloons.

It almost passes in belief in these days the things that occurred in Ellistown, and I have no doubt, in hundreds of other places in early times. There were regular feuds—the lower neighborhood against the upper neighborhood. Then there were family feuds, and these feuds were kept up from year to year, very much as they are in the mountains of Kentucky now. The battles were fought out at Ellistown. When it was a neighborhood feud, the members of the different family feuds would merge and fight it out on the neighborhood line. When it was a family feud they would fight it out among themselves. No pistols nor knives were used at that time. It was regarded as the extreme of disgrace for a person to use a "weepin."

On occasions the people gathered. You could see them darting in on their little horses, or climbing over the fences, if they came afoot, and coming cautiously out in the open, looking in every direction to see who was there. It rarely or never occurred that there was fighting without first steaming up for it. When no movement was made and time dragged heavily on, some man would bet a treat for everybody that some other man could throw somebody down, or could outrun him, or outjump him; or the bet was on the toss of a coin, heads or tails. Anything to bet on. Whiskey was about thirty cents a gallon. Of course, in every case, somebody lost the bet, and everybody got the drink. I have seen them line up a hundred strong, like a military company, upper neighborhood and lower neighborhood men side by side; and a man would take a bucket of whiskey with a gourd, go down the line, and let every man drink as much as he wanted. This would be repeated a time or two, and then the quarreling and fighting would begin. More than once, as a small boy, I have stopped on the little elevation just east of the town, and seen a group of men fighting all over the street. And as the postoffice was at the other end of it, I sat there on my horse in fear until there should be a slack in the fighting.

Of course all sorts of ugly things were done in the fights. Men's noses, ears and fingers were bitten off and eyes knocked out. If the fighting was unusually lively all

BY DR. J. B. GAMBRELL, D. D.

hands would stop at night and co-operate in building a ring of fires so as to have light, and then go in and fight it out.

One of the last times I was in Ellistown, before going away to school, and afterwards to the war, I saw what has never faded from my mind. It made a profound impression on me at the time, but the pathos of it has grown with the years. A very large, strong man, not over thirty-five, was drunk, yelling like an Indian and going up and down the road, bantering everybody for a fight. It was in January. The ground was frozen, and following after him was a girl about twelve years old, thinly clad and walking barefoot on the frozen ground. I remember well her pathetic plea to her father to come home. Her mother had sent for him, and there was no wood. When he went home I do not know.

A good many years passed, the war was over, and, a grown man and a preacher, I went back to Ellistown to help in a meeting. A mighty miracle had been wrought. There was a meeting house right down in the little village. As I sat with the pastor in the pulpit, I saw the man who had staggered up and down the street with his little girl following him, drive up with a two-horse wagon. His family, quite a large one, got out, all well dressed and happy, and he a noble looking specimen of manhood. He came into the church and sat down on the front seat. As the crowd gathered, one of the former saloon-keepers, with a bit of his ear gone and his face scarred all over with innumerable fights, came to the front and sat down. All around were sitting the men that I recognized as belonging to the upper and lower neighborhoods and to different families. They were members of the church, clothed and sitting at the feet of Jesus in their right minds.

I noticed, also, as I went through the country then and afterwards, a great transformation. The homes which were the abodes of squalor and the habitations of cruelty had taken on a new look. They had been improved in innumerable ways. Farms were enlarged, fences were better. The stock that the people used, instead of the little, scrubby ponies, ill fed and ill kept, were sleek, well kept and serviceable. The whole country had changed. In due time the saloons had disappeared. Prohibition prevailed, and with the course of years, schools were everywhere. The people became enthusiastic for education, temperance and everything that is good, and all things had become new.

Now, how did this happen? Elder Isaac Smith was sent a missionary to Ellistown. At his first appearing these rude men gave him to understand that he was not wanted. When he attempted to preach they threw rocks at the house, and, as he good-naturedly said, "You know when I could not preach I could sing." He would stop in the middle of his sermon, and, with his rich, mellow voice, sing a song, and then, when the stoning ceased, he would take up his subject and go on. The ever-recurring miracle of grace took place. Men who would bow to nothing human, under the power of the story of the cross bowed to Christ. They were made new creatures. The love of God was shed abroad in their hearts, and that love diffused itself in richness throughout their homes, and everything was benefited. Religion had come to the front. Wickedness, of course, went to the rear. The regenerated husband at once began a new life. He looked after the interests of his family, enlarged his farm, and took care of his stock. True religion will benefit everything. It will make better mules, better dogs, better cats, better fences, better houses, better everything.

To a large extent the squalor and misery disappeared from that country, and the saloons have gone long ago. Elder Isaac Smith did not continue at Ellistown many years. Others succeeded him. He preached around in other places in that country, notably at one church for thirty or forty years, building it up from the foundation. Of course throughout all that belt of country there were men of like mind and spirit, and they worked together to a common end. But no man stood better for every interest of humanity than Elder Isaac Smith. Whatsoever things were pure, whatsoever things were of good report readily had his endorsement and his help. Every church had a friend in him. Every school had him for a friend. Every movement in the direction of temperance had a friend in Isaac Smith.

Now, let us stop and consider. Taking twenty miles square in that country, and it is perfectly certain that $50,000 given away every year for the betterment of the homes and the lives of the people would not have resulted in anything like as much comfort and happiness as that which resulted from the plain preaching of the gospel by that humble minister. Money could have bought shoes for the girl that walked on the frozen ground; it could have piled up wood at home for the shivering family; it could have supplied clothes and food; and what money could have done for her it could have done for scores and hundreds of other families. But it would not have brought happiness to the home. There cannot be any happiness where there is brute wickedness, and if $50,000 had been spent any year on that country in the interest of the suffering women and children there would have been the very same need of $50,000 next year, only, perhaps, a greater need; for the burden of support would have been taken off of the husbands and fathers, and they would have gone deeper into dissipation. Reformation of the country came through the preaching of Jesus. Nothing can be done for people who will not do right for themselves. It was the truest philosophy to elevate the country by lifting the men in the country. There are no bad countries where there are good people, and there are no good countries where there are bad people. A dissipated population could not be enriched. A religious, industrious, self-respecting people will never be utterly poor. I say with all confidence that the work that Elder Smith did for the people throughout that belt of country is worth to them in money not less than $50,000 a year, and it is worth to them in happiness what no tongue can tell. He made many rich, though, I suppose, never in his life was he worth as much as $1,500 in money. And yet he never complained, never sought riches, and always counted it his supreme honor and happiness to be a blessing to others.

That is one picture—the picture of one man's life, and it is the picture of the lives of thousands of plain gospel preachers, whose record is on high. Not much is known of their work. Indeed, as a rule, they do not know much about it themselves. Perhaps most preachers think very little of the ultimate results of their work. They keep their minds on the thing that is next to them, and working, planting and cultivating, they do not look to the ultimate harvest in worldly returns.

It is easy from this concrete example to understand the real civilization of the world. Civilization does not consist in clothes. It does not consist in money. It consists in spirit. And people are civilized just in proportion as they approximate the perfect standard of life set forth in the gospel. Jesus Christ was the only perfect civilian that the world has ever known. All the rest vacillate between civilization and barbarity.

Contemplating the work of one faithful minister of Christ and then turning for a moment to think of a paid attorney in a Texas courthouse, who, in the presence of a great rabble, could characterize preachers as incapable of telling the truth and as parasites on society, a feeling of immeasurable disgust takes possession of the mind.

Fifty years Isaac Smith talked, preached, sang, prayed and lived the gospel among a plain people. His work redeemed many homes from blight and ruin. Out of those homes have already come bright and shining lights to bless the world. Full of years and goodness, last year he lay down in his log house, and he heard a voice from above saying, "Come up higher." His brave spirit went away from the tabernacle of clay to rest with God forever. Men like Isaac Smith are the real heroes and the real benefactors of the human race.

THE SAFETY OF THE BAPTIST METHODS OF WORK.

TWO ARTICLES have preceded this, one bearing particularly on the corrective force of free government, and the other on the working value of the government. In the first it was attempted to show that while there would be disturbances among all free people, the disturbances themselves would throw off the causes of them with an unerring certainty, just as water, by its commotion, purifies itself. In the second article an attempt was made to show that because the free idea appeals directly to the renewed heart, without going round about, and without the interposition of human authority between the divine Lord and the redeemed soul, it has the greatest religious force. And also, because, by its very simplicity, there is less friction and an easier method of detaching those who cannot be induced to work in peace.

There remains one other phase of the question to be discussed. Are the present methods of work among Baptists safe? A little while ago, in a Baptist meeting, a brother conceded the great force of the present organization of the Baptist working forces of the state, but deprecated as dangerous the "centralization of power" in the hands of the few. This was said particularly with reference to the schools and the present system of correlation. This writer, there and then, submitted the substance of what is going to be presently submitted in this article. The same brother has recently stated that the defense was so weak that it could not be answered. There seemed to be some difficulty about answering it, but we apprehend that the palpable truth of it was the difficulty in the brother's way.

Before presenting the thought I desire to be indulged to make a few remarks. It has been more than forty years since I began to be an attentive reader of Baptist papers. During that whole period there have been only short intervals in which no man rose up to cry out against "centralization" and the "danger to the churches." The men who have made this outcry for these forty-five years past have all been involved in some sort of a fight on the denomination, and have always lost in the fight, as they always will and always should. One thing has characterized the malcontent element for the whole period in question. They have constantly and tremendously turned up to advocate the independence of the churches—a thing there has not been a Baptist during the whole period to deny. The old London Association was formed more than three hundred years back, and from then onward to this day the independence of the churches has been as much a recognized doctrine among Baptists as the doctrine of immersion, and there has not been, during that whole period, a man to deny it, so far as history goes. Taking the Baptists as they stand today, and a man could not, with a search-light, find one who does not believe in the absolute independence of the churches. This is kept in the forefront in all of our denominational organizations, and it not now, and never has been, a matter of disagreement. The nearest that we come to a disagreement is, that some think the independence of one church laps clear over on another. The plain Baptist notion is, that the independence and sovereignty of a church is limit-

BY DR. J. B. GAMBRELL, D. D.

ed to itself, and cannot be carried beyond its own membership.

Following this is the universally accepted doctrine that associations and conventions are advisory bodies simply. The old form of letters to associations was: "We send our beloved brother, So-and-So, whom we deem worthy to sit with you in council." There is not an instance on record in which an association or convention ever attempted to regulate the affairs of a church, though they have always regulated their own affairs.

Now, with these postulates, let us consider the safety of our method of conducting denominational affairs by councils, without authority over churches, the churches always remaining free to co-operate or not co-operate in any proposed measures, while the associations or conventions are free to act in their sphere. That is, beyond question, the Baptist idea. In 1880 there was a trouble, and that trouble deeply affected the general work of the Baptist General Association. There was a called session of that body. Dr. Burleson made the opening address. Here is what he said in part: "Our constitution fully authorizes us to settle this question, but only so far as membership in this body is concerned. Our decision can only refer to membership with us, and does not, and cannot fix any man's standing in his church." That is precisely the view that Baptists have always taken. There is no difference of opinion among Baptists who deserve to be known by that name as to: First, that a convention or association can settle matters with reference to its own membership; and, second, that it cannot settle matters of membership in churches.

Let us turn now to look at the general effect of our system. Suppose the Baptist General Convention, under bad leadership, goes wrong. That is a possibility; but suppose the whole matter is discussed openly before the churches and the masses of the people interested, and these discussions are continued long enough for the masses of the people to get the facts and form a judgment. Then, what will happen? It will happen that a consensus of opinion will be expressed through messengers in the General Convention. Let it be assumed, for instance, that the present attitude of the Convention, with reference to the schools of the state, is vitally wrong, or with reference to the mission work, or anything else. Then the enquiry is raised, how does it happen that the Convention is wrong? It must be, of course, because a majority of the messengers composing the Convention are wrong. If that is true, then how does it come that a majority of the messengers composing the Convention are wrong? Well, it's because the churches sending them are worng. If a majority of the churches sending them are wrong, then how does it happen that these churches are wrong? It must be because a majority of the people in the churches are wrong. Well, suppose a majority of the people composing the churches are wrong. After a thorough discussion, continuing long enough to elicit the truth, if a majority are wrong, then the bottom has dropped out and the whole idea of a democratic form of government is a mistake.

The present method of doing things is just as safe as the people themselves are safe. It is just as good as the people are. And the man who mistrusts such methods of eliciting the judgment of his brethren really mistrusts the churches and mistrusts the people who compose the churches, and if he believes this a dangerous method, then he must believe that we cannot depend on ourselves. That is the very foundation stone of the argument of hierarchs, for the authority of one man hedged about more or less. The man who believes it unsafe to appeal to the denomination at large, by open discussion of the truth, and then take their judgment, as the manner is among Baptists, is a man who, in his heart, suspects the Baptist position, and is, as to the government of Baptists, an unbeliever.

BY DR. J. B. GAMBRELL, D. D.

Let's turn this question around and look at it another way. Is it really safer to believe that the great majority of the people, with opportunities for knowing the truth, persistently go wrong; or is it more reasonable to believe that a croaking, fault-finding faction, full of suspicion and evil surmising concerning the soundness of the very foundation principles of the Baptist denomination, is wrong? I have no difficulty in thinking that these disappointed factions are wrong. That they have been wrong during a period of more than forty years is certain, as things have worked out and been demonstrated. That the method of broad, honest, thorough discussion of issues, and a wide-open policy with reference to facts, is of the Lord, I as much believe as I believe that God made the light. But such discussion as this is to be differentiated distinctly from the policies of invective, vituperation, slander, personal attacks on men, false statements about facts and figures, men and measures, which have obtained from time to time, from the apostolic age down to the present. Men, whose contentions are after this latter order, do not discuss, they do not criticise. They are of those who increase confusion by vain babblings. Discussion, with the facts known, will bring God's people to the right position with as much certainty as a loadstone attracts a needle, because God's people have an affinity for the truth.

In this view of the case all the truth wants is an open field, and a fair hearing. It wants to be seen in the cool, white light of reason, and it will win. Men who go afield with prejudices and with a malicious spirit, can indeed confuse matters for a time, but there is one end for all of them, and that is utter defeat.

I come back to say, before closing, that the man who mistrusts the great mass of people composing the churches of Jesus Christ, and feels unwilling to leave the churches to select their messengers, to compose a council to settle matters of common concern, deep down in his heart mistrusts the whole Baptist position, and is a good helper for every hierarch who comes round to berate God's free government and open methods for His free people. It is possible for some people to reach the point of believing in nothing. This is commonly the case with violent minorities.

If the foregoing views be correct, ill-tempered disturbers of the peace of Zion have no chance with a sound-minded people. And all experience among Baptists testifies to the truth of this position. As often as a great Christian democracy is aroused to express itself, it sweeps from the field the whole spawn of false issues. Truth goes up, and mere agitators go down.

THE FORM AND THE POWER.

ALL LIFE takes on some kind of form. To all animal life the Creator Himself gave form. All social and spiritual life takes on forms, usually according to the environments. Religious life has always expressed itself in religious forms. It was so in Old Testament times, even from the beginning. At first it seems that the form was very simple; later, as the true worshippers multiplied and the family grew into the nation, forms were multiplied and became more complex. They were not only in their time expressions of religious thought, but they were teachers of religious thought and feeling, and these two things pertain to all religious forms.

There are not two religions taught in the Bible, one belonging to the Old Testament, and the other to the New. Some one has well said, "The Old Testament is the New Testament concealed; the New Testament is the Old Testament revealed." In essence they are the same. There has never been two living ways, but only one. Christ was as much the Savior in the Old Testament day as in the new.

By Dr. J. B. Gambrell, D. D.

He was always to the lost world the lamb slain before the foundation of the world. The people of the Old Testament time looked forward to Christ; we look back. God saved the Old Testament saints on a credit, on the promise of the Son to put away their sins in the fullness of time; He saves New Testament saints by making in advance provision for their redemption. The old and the new meet in Christ.

But the forms of the two administrations are different. Under the old there were many forms suited to the times, and to the conditions of the human mind. The types and shadows of the sacred writings, in one way or another, had respect to Christ. The offering of them in faith carried the sinner to the great High Priest.

With the revelation of the fullness of the gospel in the New Testament, the complex system was done away with, and there was left but two forms, or rites—baptism and the Lord's Supper. The trend from the old to the new was toward simplicity. Today, the prescribed order of service is exceedingly simple. To put the thought in current phrase, there is less of the shell, and relatively speaking, more of the meat.

The history of religion reveals some striking characteristics. It has been difficult for the human family to stand by the simple order of God's house. There has been a constant divergence in two directions. It is well to consider these two distinct trends.

First, there has been a constant tendency to multiply forms beyond what is written. There is but one day ordained and established to be kept holy, and that is the Lord's day. All along, however, good people have insisted on keeping other days—Good Friday, Easter, and the like. This they can do if they choose, not holding it as a doctrine, but as a practical help to themselves. Paul says they may keep days, if they keep them to the Lord, but in another place Paul marks the tendency of it to those who keep days, "I am afraid of you." The multiplication of days and forms is a dangerous thing; it is a movement in the wrong direction, though not in every case sinful.

As a matter of fact, as piety has declined, a great many people have felt a sense of lack, and sought to make up by multiplying "forms of godliness." Yielding to this tendency, we have a great many bodies exceedingly sensitive as to forms, but lost to the power. If a minister were to preach without his "sacred vestment," the people would be shocked. That he habitually preaches without power creates no impression whatever. This was the state of the case with the Jews. Punctilious to the last degree about all rites of Judaism, those prescribed by God and those set up by men, they nevertheless were dead to all that the forms rightly meant. It was a nation intolerant, even to the smallest points of outward forms, but lifeless to the simple principles of piety. This is one of the ways that true religion dies. There is an insect which incases itself in a shell, closes up and dies, making its own coffin. So many a church has done.

Writing this article for a Baptist paper to do good to its readers, I may put a question strong. Have not many of us come to think more of baptism and the supper, and the form of the church, than we do of the life and meaning and power of these heaven-ordained institutions? We have come to think of baptism, our personal baptism, as something to be desired, and yet it must be said in all charity, that we do not think of it as Paul put it in the sixth chapter of Romans, making it a ground of appeal for high and holy living.

A man to be baptized must, indeed, be dead to sin and alive to God; and having been baptized, he must ever regard himself as standing in a different relation to God's people and God's cause in the world.

We do well to stand by the form of the church, the form of the Lord's Supper, and the form of baptism. They are themselves all teachers, and the world will never go far wrong, spiritually, if the world be right with respect to these three things. But to stand more by the form than by the power is to utterly prostitute sacred things. It is very grievous that so many depart from the form of God's teaching, but it even more grievous that so many depart from the power. It is the departure from the power that brings on the grievous departures from everything else, and the general decay in religion. Baptists have a distinctive mission, to hold to the form of sacred things; they have a larger mission, to hold to and live out the profession of an endless life.

Let us turn now to the other side. In recent times, almost to an alarming extent, it has come about that many who profess great spiritual power discount all forms. We have lived to see intelligent persons who, in their zeal for spirituality, and with professions of extraordinary power, set aside the divinely instituted forms of religion. To many of these, baptism is of little or no account. The Lord's supper is left to the days of crude thought. Congregations, bearing the name of Christ, are formed to suit any one's taste. We have what is now known as the gospel of progress, and, indeed, we may well say that it is progress, but certainly into the wilderness. To discount the plain teaching of God's Word with respect to the order of religion, is not in the least a sign of spirituality, but rather of arrogance. We have fallen upon a time of dreaming, when the imaginations of heated minds are supposed to stand good against the revelation of God.

This dreaming spiritualism, taking now one form and then another, but always assuming an independence of the Word of God, is the Jack-o-lantern of the modern religious emotionalism, leading out into a dark and starless night. I do not trust much to the man who reads the signs of the times. The trouble is that most of them read too little, and see a few things too large. I have no great opinion of my own power to interpret times and seasons, but venture to say that it seems to me we have come to a time when Baptists, not only have a great opportunity, but weighty responsibilities. These crazes have affected the Baptist denomination less than any other. This accounts for the fact that the white Baptists of America last year gained more than 250,000 members; a number far greater than all the other denominations gained. Some of the denominations are reaping now what they have sown. If we, as a people, want to do well, let us stand by the forms and also the power, not one but both, and both joined together forever as God joined them. We are simple men. It is not for us to go on excursions to invent new things in religion. It is for us to make plain the mind of the Master, expressed in His divine Word concerning all things pertaining to salvation. Doing this, we will fulfill our missions, and may go to the Master and report that in our day, we kept the Word, and did not deny the faith.

A SLING AND A KING.

KING DAVID is one of the most interesting studies in all history. He touches strongly at more salient points in human nature than almost anyone of the Bible characters. He was a great man, measured by any rule, and he fulfilled a modern saying, "If a boy is to be great, he must show himself betimes."

David was a great general, and his personal courage was of the highest order. His courage, measured by the standards of human conduct, was audacious. He was a great leader of men. He was a great poet. He was a strong and wise governor. And, according to the time you take him, he was a great sinner or a great saint. The one word that expresses his character better than any other, is forceful.

By Dr. J. B. Gambrell, D. D.

We first get a glimpse of him as a lad, keeping his father's sheep. Evidently, his older brothers, and perhaps his father, had little idea of the rare qualities of the boy, but, as a shepherd, he showed the two qualities that will make any man admirable. He was trusted with his father's flock. There came a bear one day to take away one of the sheep. The average boy would have run. It was before the days of repeaters, Mauser rifles and the like. The weapons of warfare were primitive and harmless, compared with those in use today. David, however, did not run. He had been religiously raised. He felt that the bear was invading a trust, and that it was his business to guard the flock. So he went for the bear and killed it. A lion came on the same mission and fared no better. We are not told how David killed the bear and the lion. We would think that it was done with a sling, however.

The first time the young fellow figures conspicuously after his anointing, is when he goes down to see his brothers in the army. What a natural thing it was for him to go down to see his brothers, to find out about them and bring word home. When he got there he saw something that, as Shakespeare would put it, "raised his gorge." He saw a Philistine berating the armies of Israel, and the armies of Israel all in fear. King Saul himself was ready to submit to the indignity of the Philistine put on the armies of Israel. It was too much for David, and he went to the king to say that he would go down and kill the uncircumcised heathen. Just at this point, we get a great lesson in life. Here was a tremendous undertaking before him—one the contemplation of which made every man in the army shake. But his past exploits now buttressed his courage. He tells how, in the name of the Lord, and by God's help, he had killed the bear and the lion, and if he had done that to the bear and the lion, he could kill Goliath. The victories already won encouraged him.

We read of the deriding of his brothers. It is all very natural reading. It has always been so. The average man mistrusts a person who undertakes to do an extraordinary thing. In the long run, no doubt, it is the average man that saves the country, but the average man never saves it on the short run. His brothers thought it was a bit of uppishness. King Saul doubted it, but finally yielded. The truth of it is, David had a mission from God to kill Goliath, and when anybody has a mission from God, opposition don't stand much in the way. There is a way through it, or under it, or around it, or over it, always. In my day, I have seen young men undertake things beyond the ordinary, and all the wiseacres shook their heads, but the young fellow went along, and after a while, everybody said: "Well now, that was fine."

David's exploit in killing Goliath has been much dwelt on in sermons. His common sense showed itself in refusing to burden himself with Saul's armor, which was entirely too large, and in sticking to his sling. It is about the sling that I wish to make some observations, and the first is: It was a very simple thing. Nothing could be plainer than a sling. It was a very cheap thing. David had probably made it himself, and he knew the swing of it. He could not do very much with a sword, and as to an immense spear to match Goliath's, he could do nothing at all. The spear would have borne him down. There was great wisdom in sticking to the sling. He had tried that. He had, no doubt, stood on the hillsides while the sheep were grazing, and, after the manner of boys in all times, hour by hour, hurled rocks out of his sling, until he had learned to place them exactly where he wanted them.

Here was an unusual occasion—one the like of which would come to him no more in life; the like of which would come to no other youth in all history—a lad to fight a giant, and with such tremendous issues depending on the outcome. Did ever a boy face such an opportunity and such a responsibility? That would increase the desire for some extraordinary weapons with which to fight against an extraordinary enemy. But David's head was cool and level. He stuck to the sling.

The lesson we get is, we must all use, in our Christian warfare, exactly the kind of weapons that suit us. Many a preacher has become noted for doing great things among the common people, so much so, that he is wanted on an extraordinary occasion, such as preaching a convention sermon or a commencement sermon. He feels at once that the simple way of preaching in the country would not fit the college or the convention, and so he tries a new style, only to suffer mortification. If I might whisper a word into the ear of young preachers, touching this point, I would say: It's precisely the kind of preaching that moves the heart of the people in the country, and in the plainer districts, that the town people want to hear, only, perhaps, they don't want to hear it it quite so long as is common in the country. Let the preacher, on the greatest possible occasions, stick to his sling.

Here is another observation. Many an exhorter who, in his neighborhood and along with a good pastor, has been a great power for good, has been ruined because he quit his sling, and tried to preach. What has become of all the exhorters anyhow? It is a real misfortune for a man to be brought into the Christian ministry, who hasn't the Scriptural qualifications for the ministry. His life becomes abnormal. He fits nowhere; he is a discomfort to himself and to everybody else. And then, many a good deacon has been spoiled trying to make a preacher. One good deacon is worth a good many poor preachers. And so we might go on to talk about the men who are good for pastors and want to be editors; good for evangelists and want to be pastors, and good for one thing, and yet, want to be another. If every one would stick to his own sling, the Goliaths of sin could be laid out in long rows.

The real success of David was laid in his early experiences. I doubt not that his mother chided him severely for venturing to fight a lion and a bear, and yet, if he had run away and left the flock to the mercy of the lion and the bear, it is pretty certain he never would have been the great King David of Israel we read about. God saw the sterling qualities of fidelity and courage in him, and when He wanted a man to be faithful to Him, and to stand up for Him everywhere, He sent his prophet to anoint the lad. The real foundation of usefulness and success in life is laid in early life. In most cases before the boy is ten years old, he has his bent for good or bad. The throne of David rested on his fidelity to his father's sheep, and on his good sling well used in time of need. God saw that such a character would be good to take care of his people. The principle of divine movement in matters of this sort, is laid down in our Lord's teaching, Whoever is faithful over one talent, will receive other talents, and whoever is faithless in the matter of one talent, will have even that taken away from him.

Taking the whole life of this extraordinary man, from beginning to end, from the time he stood, fresh from his father's sheepfold, before the prophet to be anointed, on till the time he lay on his deathbed an old man, the one most striking thing about him was his courageous devotion to duty. That meant stalwart manliness. He did not always do right. More than once he did terribly wrong. But there was one thing he never did do; he never shirked. He never asked others to bear burdens he would not bear. When the death angel was decimating the ranks of his people for the sin of which he was guilty, he did not shirk the responsibility of it. When an offering was to be made to God, and his loyal subject offered his oxen and the implements of the threshing floor, David, with a stalwart manliness that I wish might become common among us, refused to offer to God what did not cost him anything. When that great house of worship was to be built, David did not content himself with planning for it and begging for it. He led the offerings with a great offering of his own, as every preacher ought to do, and every preacher will do, that leads his flock successfully in the work of the Lord. King David was impetuous. He had the imaginative, poetic temperament. I have often imagined he was red-headed. But, with all of his impetuosity, with all of his moods, he was ever a courageous, true man.

Here is another lesson. It is for all of us. God doesn't use cowards. He doesn't employ shirks and dead-beats in His service. He honors courage, fidelity, sacrifice, and He has never yet failed to honor the people that honor Him with heroic service. The method of divine Providence has not changed. It's the same today as it was a thousand years ago. The brave pastors, who are standing today for the best things, some of them with great odds against them, are the men whom God will honor. The pastors who are yielding to a spirit of criticism and selfishness, and trying to make up with the enemies of the Lord, are everywhere losing their grip. They will be cast-aways. The very men they seek to placate will feel a disgust for them.

A saloon man, living in a town where there had been the hottest prohibition campaign, and which had succeeded to the overthrow of his business, had a great sorrow to come into his home. His little child was taken away. In that campaign one preacher in the city had refused to open his mouth, except to say that he had no war to make on anybody's business. The heart-broken wife said to her husband: "I think we need to have prayer. We have come to an hour so dark that we need a light from another world." And he said: "I feel the same way." She said then: "Shall we send for Mr. ——," the preacher who had been neutral. "No," said the man; "send for Mr. ——. I don't want any man to come to my house to pray for me who could hold his peace against the iniquity of the bar-room." The most outspoken pastor in the city was sent for to come and pray for the man whose business he, more than anybody else, had overthrown. God and men honor courage and fidelity.

David was king by the grace of his sling. He trusted God when he killed the bear and the lion, but he did not stop with trusting. He went against Goliath in the name of the God of Israel, but as he went, he stopped to select five suitable stones for business. Faith and the sling did the rest, and on he went to the throne. We must all trust, but let us not forget the sling and the needful stones.

THE NATURE AND USES OF CONVENTIONS.

THE NEW TESTAMENT ecclesiastical unit is a local church, and there is no other. Each church is independent of every other, and to each is committed the oracles of God to be preserved, taught and executed. Each church is subject alone to its Head, the Lord Jesus Christ.

All ecclesiastical power or authority is vested in each separate church, which is an executive of the will of Christ. Church power is all delegated by Christ, and can not be redelegated. The expression "church sovereignty" is not strictly correct. Christ is the only sovereign, and His churches are His executives, acting under His law and guided by His representative on earth, the Holy Spirit. Even the word independent applied to churches, must be used within narrow limits. The churches are wholly dependent on their head and subject to His law, but independent of each other and of all other bodies whatsoever. To each separate church the whole commission is given, and it is given to no other kind of body. Nor can churches transfer it to another body.

By Dr. J. B. Gambrell, D. D.

These propositions have common consent among the advocates of the New Testament ecclesiology. But everywhere among the same people are other organizations variously called societies, associations or conventions. Into the nature, functions and purposes of these, we do well to look. With respect to general organizations, their nature and relation of the local bodies to them, there are two general theories extant. To one or the other all Christendom holds.

By one theory, the local bodies merge into the general body, become a part of it and are subject to it. Whatever of authority or power belongs in the local organization is transferred with varying degrees of completeness to the larger organization. This is the Romish theory. All hierarchical bodies hold it. So, also, in a more modified form, all Presbyterial bodies. Hence the expressions, "The Holy Catholic Church;" "The English Church;" "The Methodist Church South;" "North;" "The Southern Presbyterian Church," etc. In all these bodies the local congregations have been legally merged.

There is no such phraseology in the New Testament. We read of the "Churches of Galatia," "all the churches," "the church at Corinth," "Ephesus," "Philippi," etc., but never of one church taking in the local congregations of a province or of the world. On this apostacy from the New Testament ideal of a church, Rome and all hierarchical and Presbyterial denominations are built. The restoration of the true conception of a church would destroy them all in a day.

The second view is that held by the Congregationalists and Baptists. According to this, the church never merges into, nor becomes a part of a general body. It is, indeed, common to hear statements to the effect that a certain church belongs to a certain association or convention, the meaning being, that it is one of a group of churches which affiliate with and work through the body named. As to the body itself—that which meets from time to time for the consideration of questions of common interest—churches do not and can not belong to it. They could only do so by meeting all together, or by delegating and transferring their functions and powers, through chosen men, into general bodies. Under the first conception, the churches would merge into a great mass meeting and lose their autonomy. Under the second, as under the first, the churches would violate their divine charter and cease to be New Testament churches.

The true conception of a general body is, that it is for counsel, with no ecclesiastical functions, and, therefore, having no authority over the churches. No particular kind of organization is ordained for general gatherings, though the Scriptures warrant both counsel and co-operation between New Testament churches. General bodies are variously formed, according to the wishes and needs of those forming them. They severally exist under their own constitutions. Connection with them is purely voluntary. Some of them admit messengers from churches only. Some adopt the numerical basis. Others adopt the financial basis. Others still, a mixed basis. The whole matter of organization is with those framing the constitution.

It is of the utmost importance to keep it clear that these general bodies, however great or worthy, can add nothing to the churches. The least church in the land is complete by itself. If it co-operates, it is simply a church. If it does not co-operate, it is not any the less a church. A convention adds nothing to a church. Whatever privileges any church may enjoy in co-operation spring from the constitution of the convention, and not out of the constitution of the church. Privileges of membership may be, and constantly are, enlarged or contracted, according to the judgment of those forming these general bodies.

Arguments from the nature of churches in support of representation, according to numbers and from churches only, all arise from a misconception of the true idea of conventions. They are not and can not be representative bodies in the common acceptation of the term representative. The churches can not invest messengers with any of the rights, powers, authority, or responsibilities of the churches themselves.

The foregoing being true, why Baptist conventions? If the churches can not transfer to a general body any of their functions or burdens of responsibility; if every ecclesiastical quality must remain at home, even in the weakest of the churches, why be at pains and expense to hold conventions?

Conventions stand, like Sunday Schools, newspapers, printing houses and much else, in the order of means, and not in the realm of doctrine and divine order. For lack of a proper discrimination between what stands in the order of means and what stands in the order of doctrine, many minds have been confused. Singing and making melody in the heart to God is doctrine, never to be changed by church choirs or what not. Hymn books and organs are means to be used or not, as worshippers choose.

Church independence, like the freedom of the redeemed soul, is a great blessing, full of gracious possibilities. But it may be turned to a very poor account, if there be not sound discretion. It needs to be well considered. Independence is not isolation. Free men and free churches need not adopt a hermit life. Independence ought to and will stand for all that common sense, led by the Spirit, makes possible, if we be worthy of it. The New Testament doctrine of church and individual liberty opens the way for all co-operation gracious hearts and wise heads can think or plan. In the apostolic age blood-bought liberty turned, under the lead of the Spirit and by the persuasion of a common purpose, to co-operation. Antioch and Jerusalem co-operated in counsel and act to uphold sound doctrine. Many churches co-operated in spreading the Gospel, as Paul's letters show.

The purpose of a convention is to promote co-operation in matters of common concern. How is this accomplished? Let us consider the following: A convention should be, and usually is, composed of that element among us most interested in the things for which the body was organized. For this reason, a financial basis is wise and right. Those who see the farthest, feel the most and give as they feel, will make the best leadership in thought and plan. While the churches can not delegate anything, nor in any wise project their powers beyond their limits, still, if they choose, they can name brethren to attend a convention. These "messengers of the churches," male and female, representing the working and most interested part of the various church memberships, will bring with them, not the authority of the churches, but the feelings and wishes of the bodies sending them. Assembled in numbers from over a given field, convenient for co-operation, the general body will represent a consensus of opinion and feeling, and out of that consensus will come plans to submit to the churches for their adoption and use if they so wish. These messengers are the nexus through whom the wishes of the churches are conveyed to the convention, and the common feelings and wishes of the brotherhood, conveyed back to the several churches. The effect is unity in plans, great spiritual stimulation, and, as a result, practical co-operation and increased usefulness in doing the work committed to the several churches. And this is why we have conventions; to unify thought by disseminating information, to perfect plans, to promote active co-operation by opening channels through which the churches may unite their efforts in Gospel work. All this is done without the least authority from the churches to the convention, or from the convention to the churches. It proceeds on the great New Testament principle of voluntary

By Dr. J. B. Gambrell, D. D.

service. If any dream that this is a weak arrangement, the answer is easy. It is as strong as the piety and common sense of redeemed people, and nothing in religion can be stronger. Whatever is more than this is of men and is weakness. No service to God is good or acceptable that does not proceed on the voluntary principle, guided by an intelligent piety.

It is proper to note and emphasize the fact that conventions in reality do nothing which the churches are organized to do. They do not ordain men to preach, either directly or indirectly. All authority to preach comes from God and is recognized and sanctioned in ordination by the churches. Boards which are creatures of conventions, agree to pay men to preach at certain places on certain terms. But the boards do not actually do mission work. They are channels through which the churches do the work, just as the brethren, "messengers of the churches" we read of in Paul's second letter to the Corinthians, were the channels through which the churches fed the poor saints at Jerusalem. Boards are channels, not fountains. They are means, not forces. The churches use them to convey their contributions as men turn a thousand streams into one channel to carry their united volume of water to arid plains that they may be watered and become fruitful fields. To elicit, combine and direct the energies of willing workers for the carrying out of the will of Christ is the function of a convention, and this it does, not by authority, but by persuasion and the influence of intelligent piety.

The practical use of conventions is demonstrated in the conservation of forces. By a wise organization of forces, more people are reached, more money elicited, and by an intelligent direction, it accomplishes more good. A Single great organization, as the Southern Baptist Convention, pursuing several lines of work, will not only conserve the forces that are to co-operate to the accomplishment of one line of work, but by a sympathetic correlation of forces, help every line of work. For instance, the Home Mission Board, with all of its influence, mightily stimulates the spirit of missions and opens up fountains of missionary supply for the Foreign Mission Board. While it is doing this, the Foreign Mission Board exerts a powerful influence on the Home Mission work. The Sunday School Board, disseminating intelligence, becomes a great factor in denominational life by helping both of the Boards. Intelligence in Christian work, and organization for economy, and for the proper conservation of forces, through great denominational councils, becomes a denominational duty. The Scriptures abhor waste, and everywhere teach the lesson of economy. Sporadic, divergent and often antagonistic movements, always tend to waste. Unified, sympathetic movements, running, perhaps, on different lines but in harmony, always tend to economy and the highest efficiency.